GHOSTED

CREATED BY
JOSHUA WILLIAMSON

GHOSTED

JOSHUA WILLIAMSON
WRITER

GORAN SUDZUKA
ARTIST CHAPTER ONE

DAVIDE GIANFELICE
ARTIST CHAPTERS TWO - FIVE

MIROSLAV MRVA
COLORIST

RUS WOOTON
LETTERER

SEAN MACKIEWICZ
EDITOR

SERIES COVERS BY
DAN PANOSIAN

COLLECTION COVER BY
MATTEO SCALERA

IMAGE COMICS, INC.
Robert Kirkman – Chief Operating Officer
Erik Larsen – Chief Financial Officer
Todd McFarlane – President
Marc Silvestri – Chief Executive Officer
Jim Valentino – Vice-President

Eric Stephenson – Publisher
Ron Richards – Director of Business Development
Jennifer de Guzman – Director of Trade Book Sales
Kat Salazar – Director of PR & Marketing
Corey Murphy – Director of Retail Sales
Jeremy Sullivan – Director of Digital Sales
Emilio Bautista – Sales Assistant
Branwyn Bigglestone – Senior Accounts Manager
Emily Miller – Accounts Manager
Jessica Ambriz – Administrative Assistant
Tyler Shainline – Events Coordinator
David Brothers – Content Manager
Jonathan Chan – Production Manager
Drew Gill – Art Director
Meredith Wallace – Print Manager
Monica Garcia – Senior Production Artist
Addison Duke – Production Artist
Tricia Ramos – Production Assistant
IMAGECOMICS.COM

SKYBOUND

For SKYBOUND ENTERTAINMENT
Robert Kirkman - CEO
Sean Mackiewicz - Editorial Director
Shawn Kirkham - Director of Business Development
Brian Huntington - Online Editorial Director
June Alian - Publicity Director
Rachel Skidmore - Director of Media Development
Helen Leigh - Assistant Editor
Dan Petersen - Operations Manager
Sarah Effinger - Office Manager
Nick Palmer - Operations Coordinator
Lizzy Iverson - Administrative Assistant
Stephan Murillo - Administrative Assistant

International enquiries - foreign@skybound.com
Licensing inquiries - contact@skybound.com

WWW.SKYBOUND.COM

CHAPTER ONE

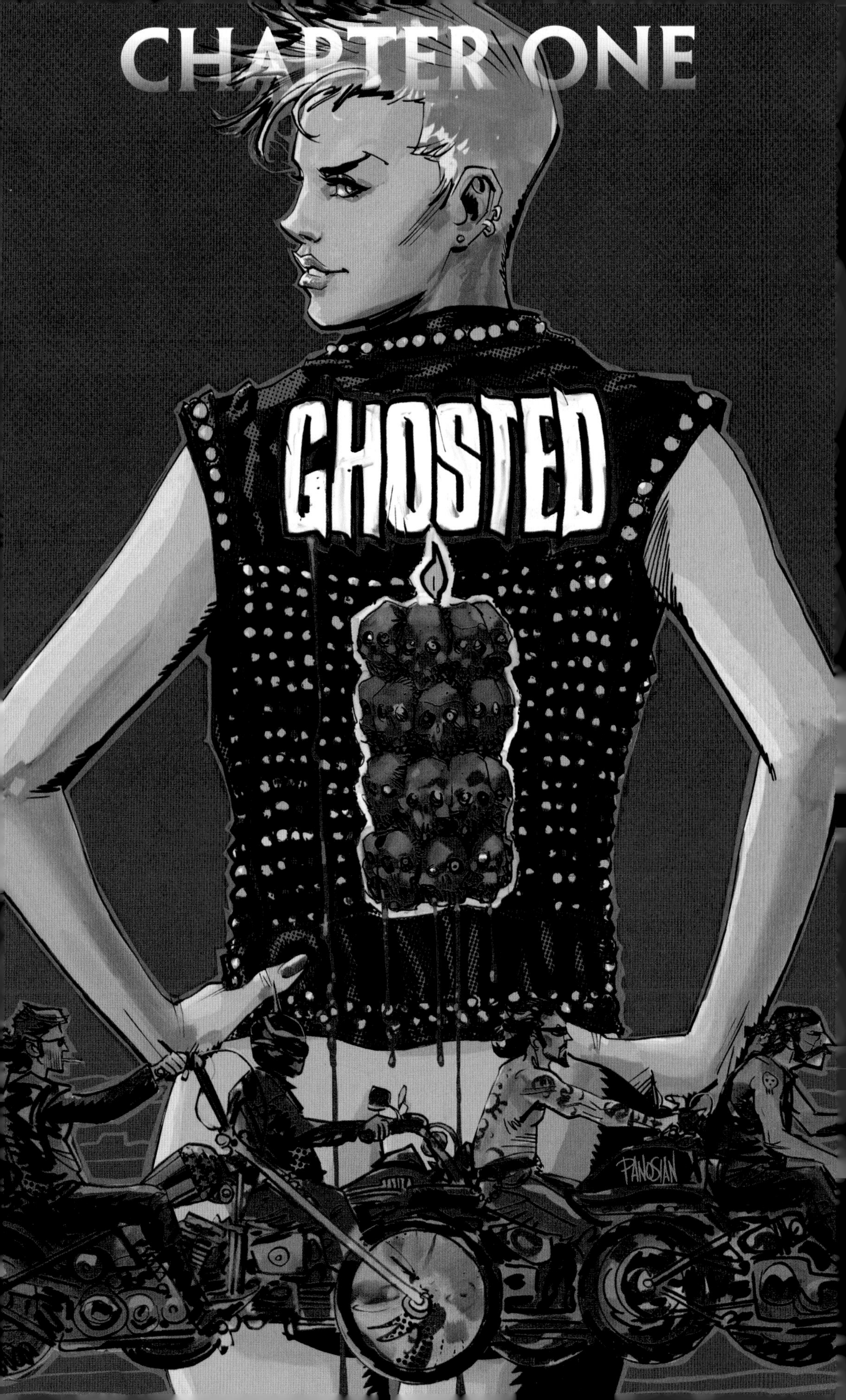
GHOSTED
PANOSIAN

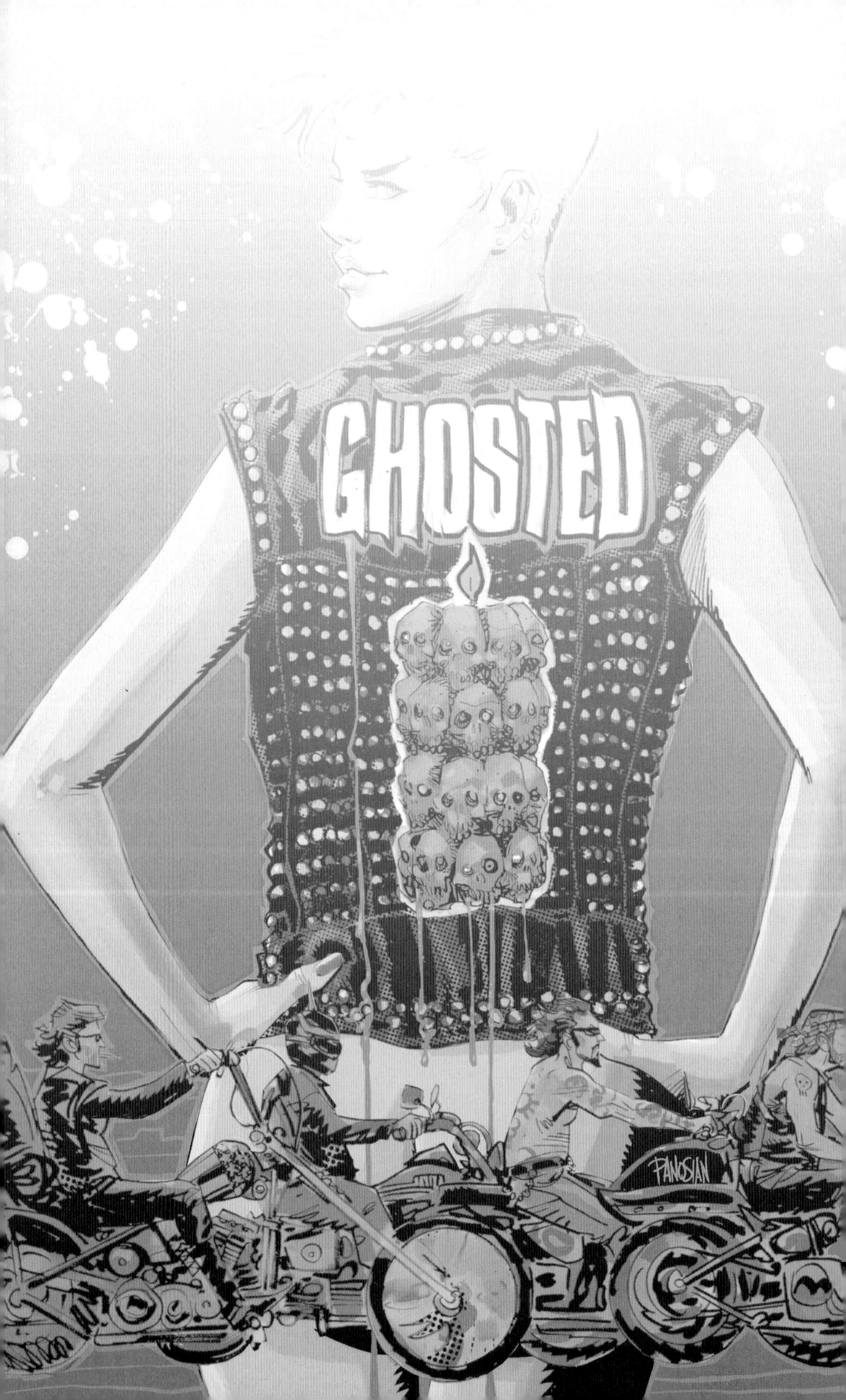
GHOSTED
PANOSIAN

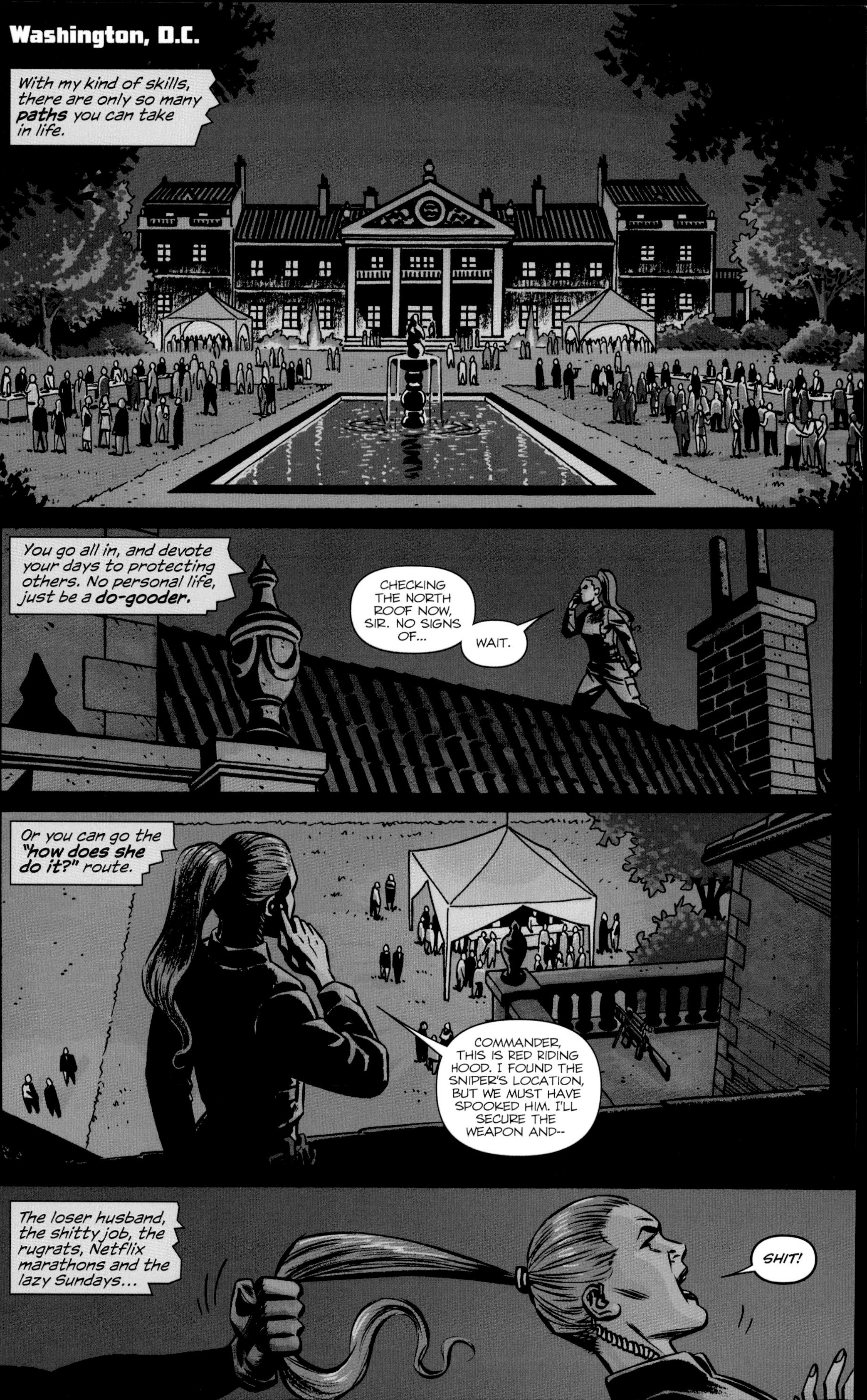
Washington, D.C.
With my kind of skills, there are only so many paths you can take in life.
You go all in, and devote your days to protecting others. No personal life, just be a do-gooder.
CHECKING THE NORTH ROOF NOW, SIR. NO SIGNS OF...
WAIT.
Or you can go the "how does she do it?" route.
COMMANDER, THIS IS RED RIDING HOOD. I FOUND THE SNIPER'S LOCATION, BUT WE MUST HAVE SPOOKED HIM. I'LL SECURE THE WEAPON AND--
The loser husband, the shitty job, the rugrats, Netflix marathons and the lazy Sundays...
SHIT!

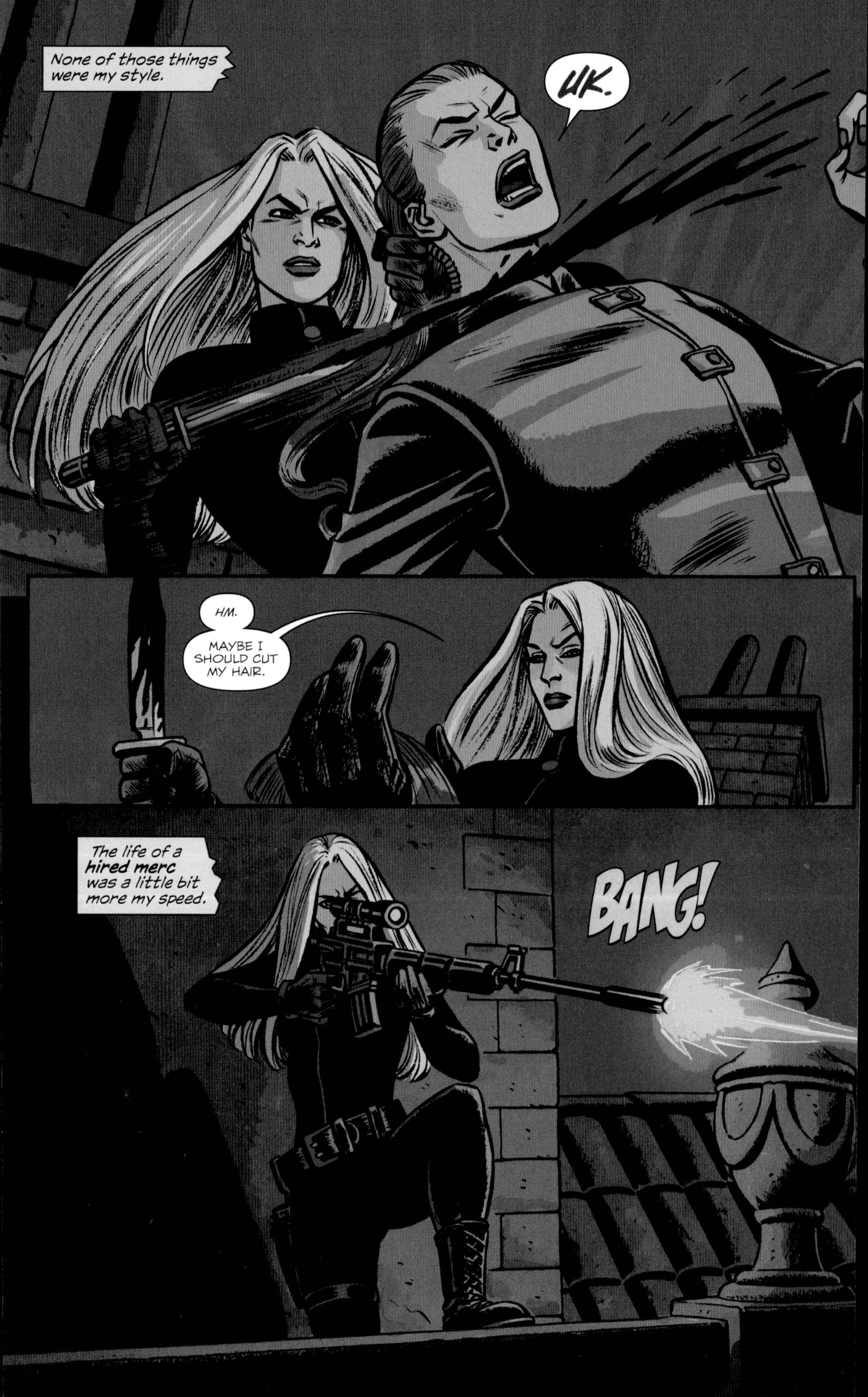
None of those things were my style.
UK.
HM.
MAYBE I SHOULD CUT MY HAIR.
The life of a **hired merc** was a little bit more my speed.
BANG!

Because you see... I knew early on that I was good at two things and **two things only**.

Killing, and fucking shit up.

JOB IS DONE. **PAY UP**.

Most of my **connections** came from kind faced gentlemen who only had my best intentions at heart.

ANDERSON, IS THAT ANY WAY TO SAY **HELLO**?

PLEASE, PLEASE SIT. LET ME BUY YOU A DRINK.

One of the major problems with dealing with the scum of the earth was that... well, they were the **scum of the earth**.

JUST SPIT IT OUT. YOU GOT MY MONEY?

YES, **AND** A NEW GIG.

SOME GOOD OLD BOYS DOWN SOUTH HAVE BEEN RUNNING GUNS UP FROM FLORIDA. CUTTING INTO THE CUBAN'S BUSINESS.

YOUR MISSION IS TO FIND OUT EXACTLY WHAT KIND OF HARDWARE THEY'RE MOVING, AND THEN **KILL** THE LEADERS.

YOU'LL NEED TO **FIT IN** IF YOU WANT TO GET CLOSE TO THEM.

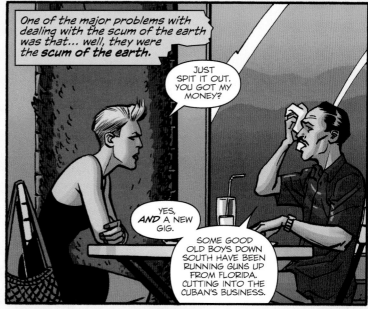

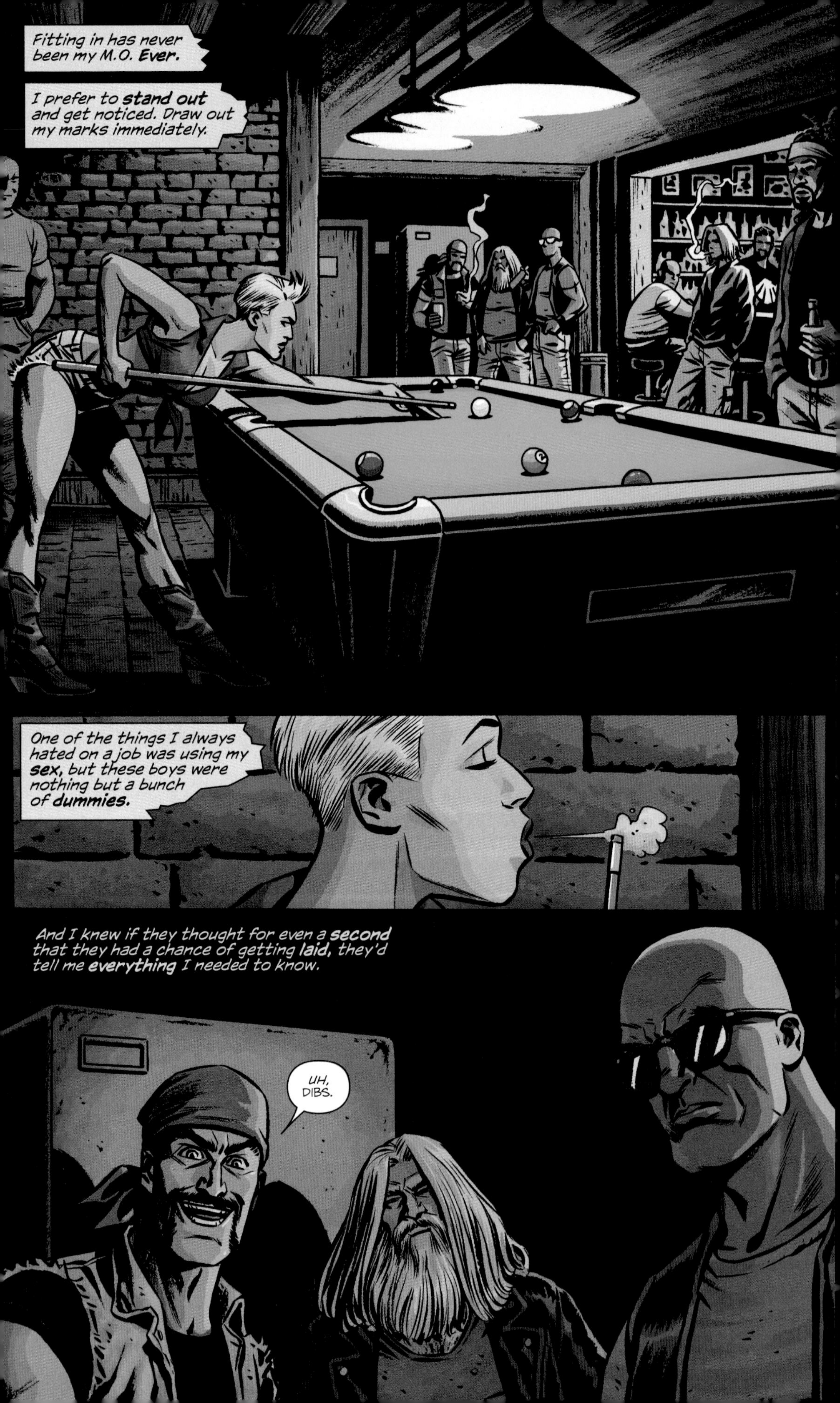
Fitting in has never been my M.O. Ever.
I prefer to stand out and get noticed. Draw out my marks immediately.
One of the things I always hated on a job was using my sex, but these boys were nothing but a bunch of dummies.
And I knew if they thought for even a second that they had a chance of getting laid, they'd tell me everything I needed to know.
UH, DIBS.

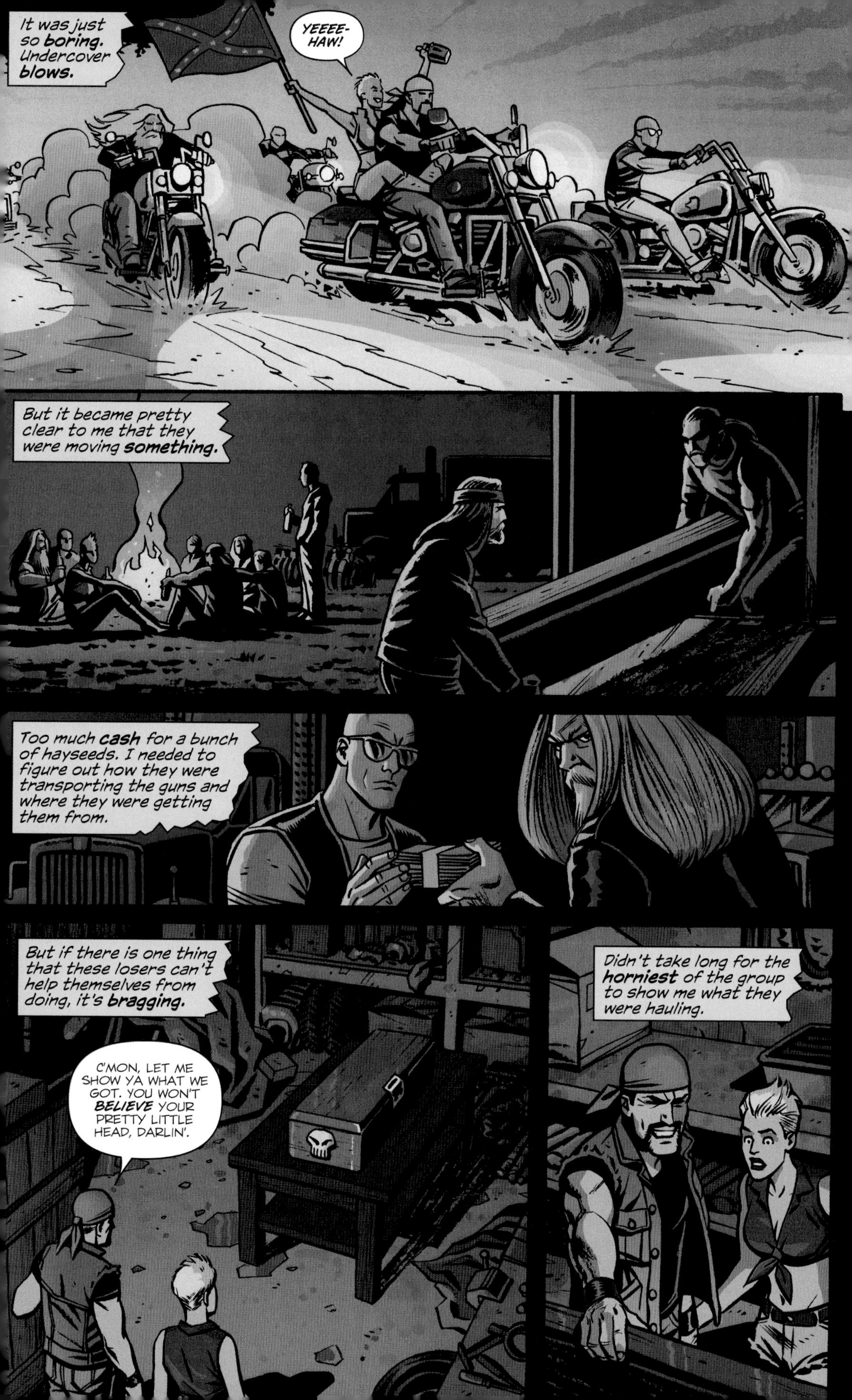
It was just so boring. Undercover blows.
YEEEE-HAW!
But it became pretty clear to me that they were moving something.
Too much cash for a bunch of hayseeds. I needed to figure out how they were transporting the guns and where they were getting them from.
But if there is one thing that these losers can't help themselves from doing, it's bragging.
C'MON, LET ME SHOW YA WHAT WE GOT. YOU WON'T BELIEVE YOUR PRETTY LITTLE HEAD, DARLIN'.
Didn't take long for the horniest of the group to show me what they were hauling.

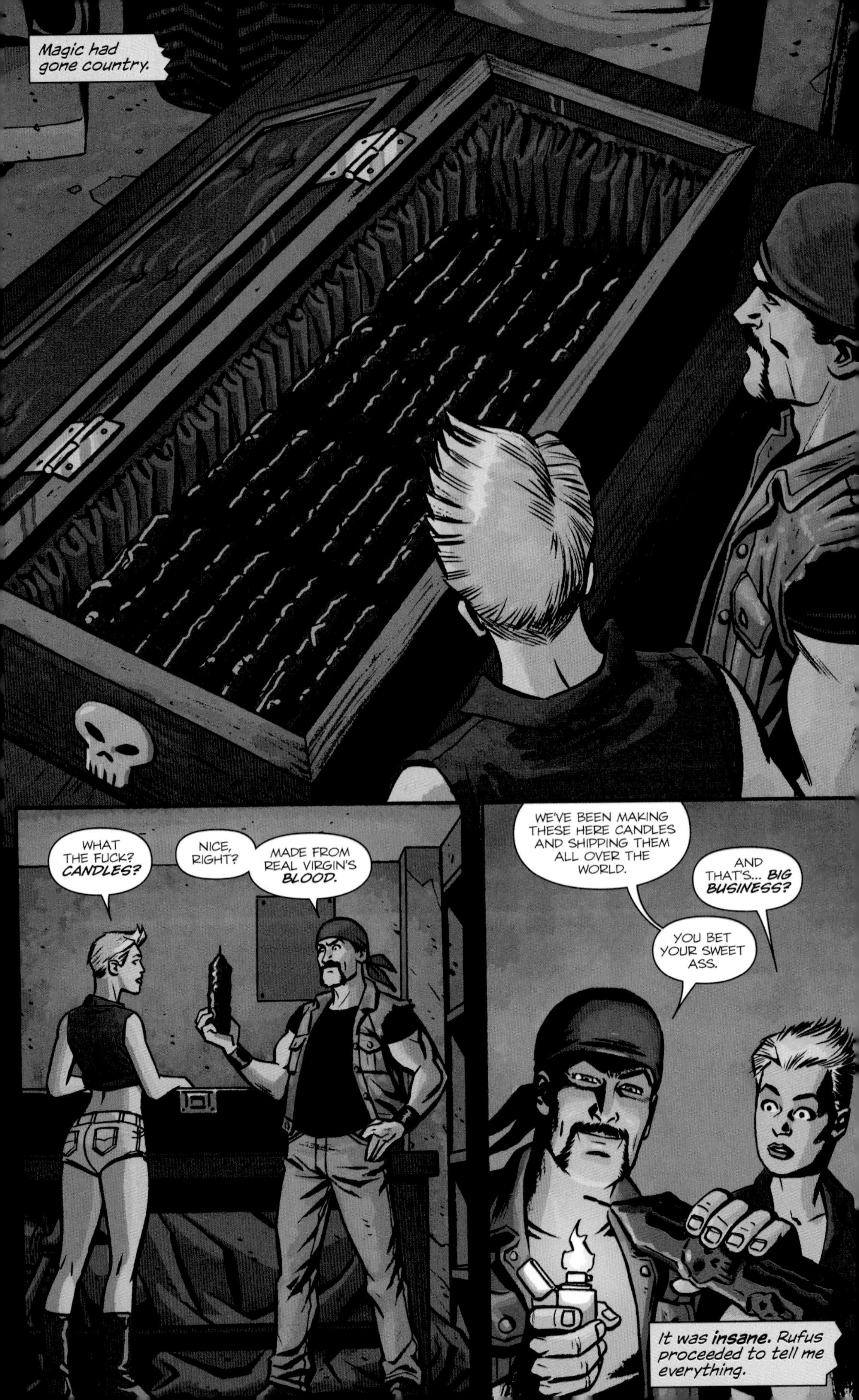

Magic had gone country.
WHAT THE FUCK? CANDLES?
NICE, RIGHT?
MADE FROM REAL VIRGIN'S BLOOD.
WE'VE BEEN MAKING THESE HERE CANDLES AND SHIPPING THEM ALL OVER THE WORLD.
AND THAT'S... BIG BUSINESS?
YOU BET YOUR SWEET ASS.
It was insane. Rufus proceeded to tell me everything.

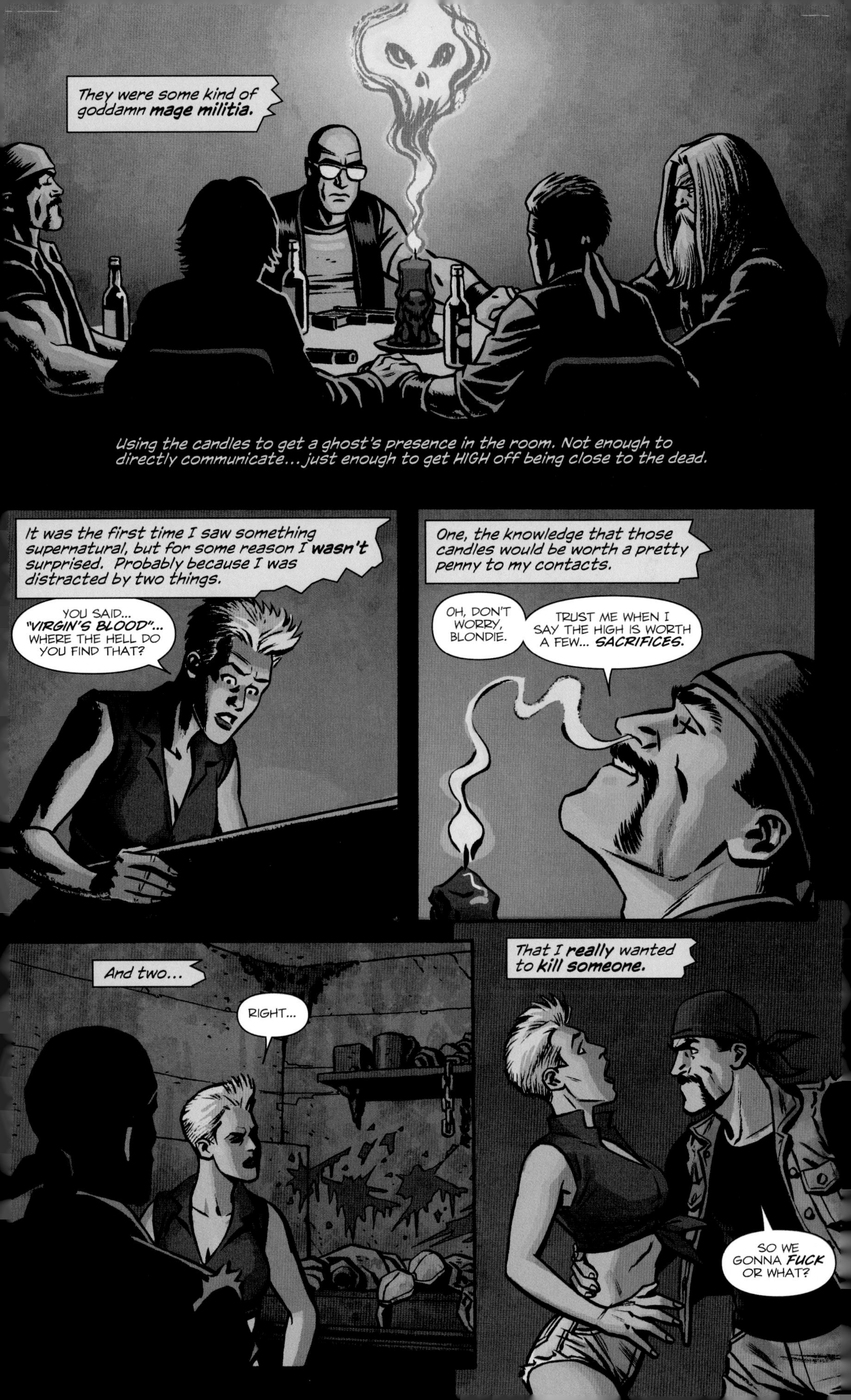
They were some kind of goddamn **mage militia.**
Using the candles to get a ghost's presence in the room. Not enough to directly communicate... just enough to get HIGH off being close to the dead.
It was the first time I saw something supernatural, but for some reason I **wasn't** surprised. Probably because I was distracted by two things.
YOU SAID... **"VIRGIN'S BLOOD"...** WHERE THE HELL DO YOU FIND THAT?
One, the knowledge that those candles would be worth a pretty penny to my contacts.
OH, DON'T WORRY, BLONDIE.
TRUST ME WHEN I SAY THE HIGH IS WORTH A FEW... **SACRIFICES.**
And two...
RIGHT...
That I **really** wanted to **kill someone.**
SO WE GONNA **FUCK** OR WHAT?

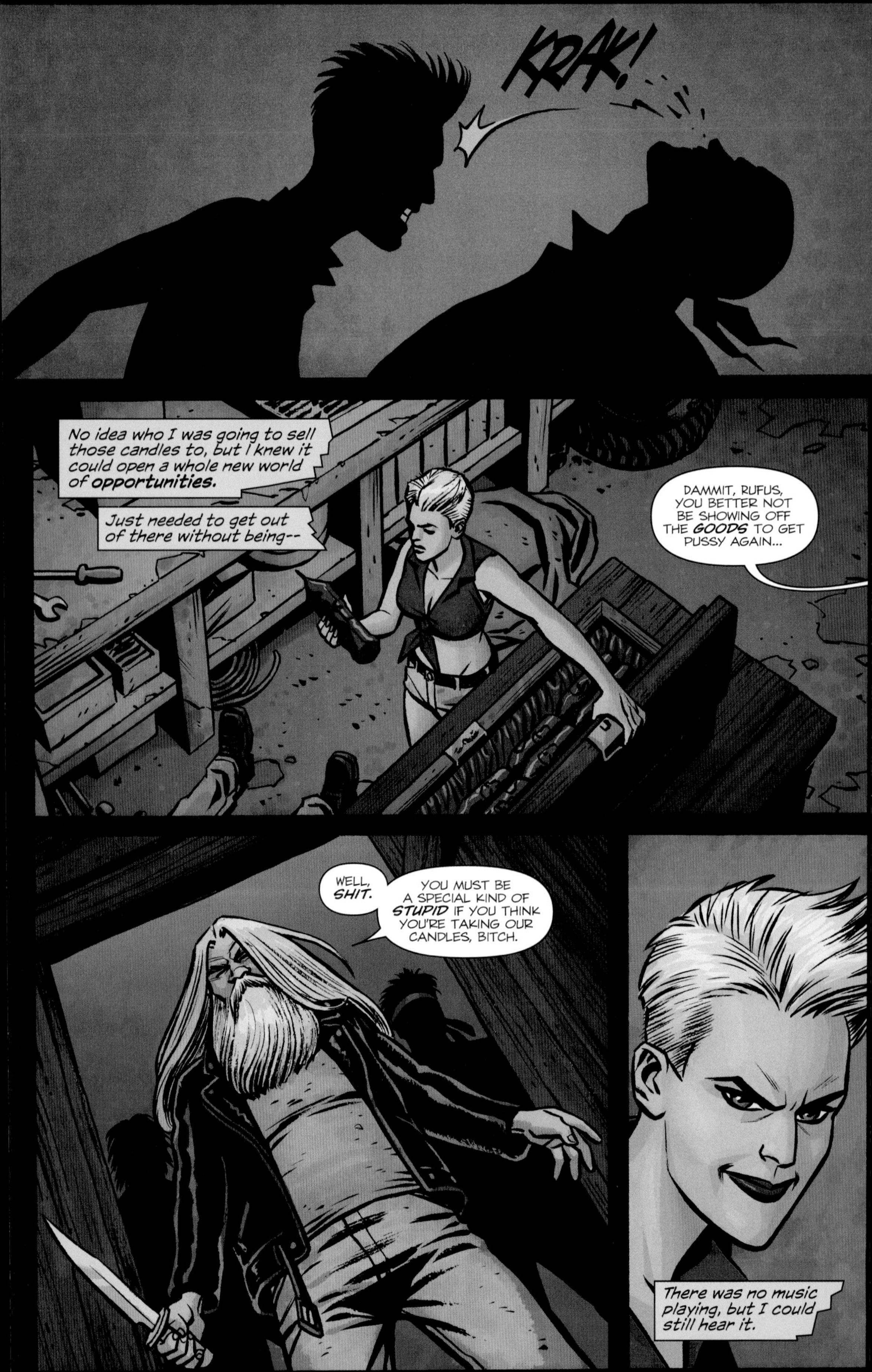
KRAK!
No idea who I was going to sell those candles to, but I knew it could open a whole new world of **opportunities.**
Just needed to get out of there without being--
DAMMIT, RUFUS, YOU BETTER NOT BE SHOWING OFF THE ***GOODS*** TO GET PUSSY AGAIN...
WELL, ***SHIT.***
YOU MUST BE A SPECIAL KIND OF ***STUPID*** IF YOU THINK YOU'RE TAKING OUR CANDLES, BITCH.
There was no music playing, but I could still hear it.

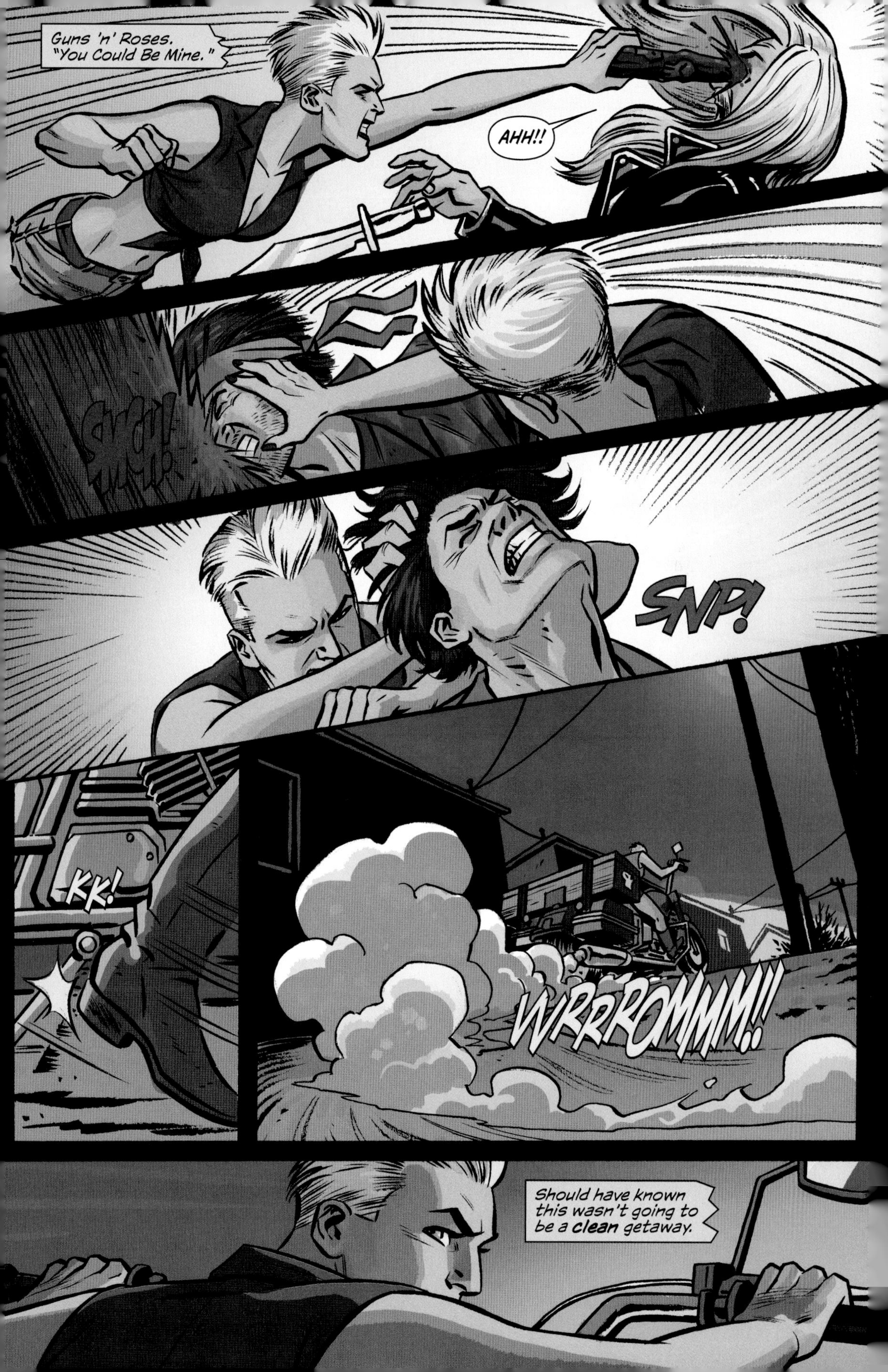
Guns 'n' Roses. "You Could Be Mine."
AHH!!
SNP!
KK!
WRRROMMM!!
Should have known this wasn't going to be a clean getaway.

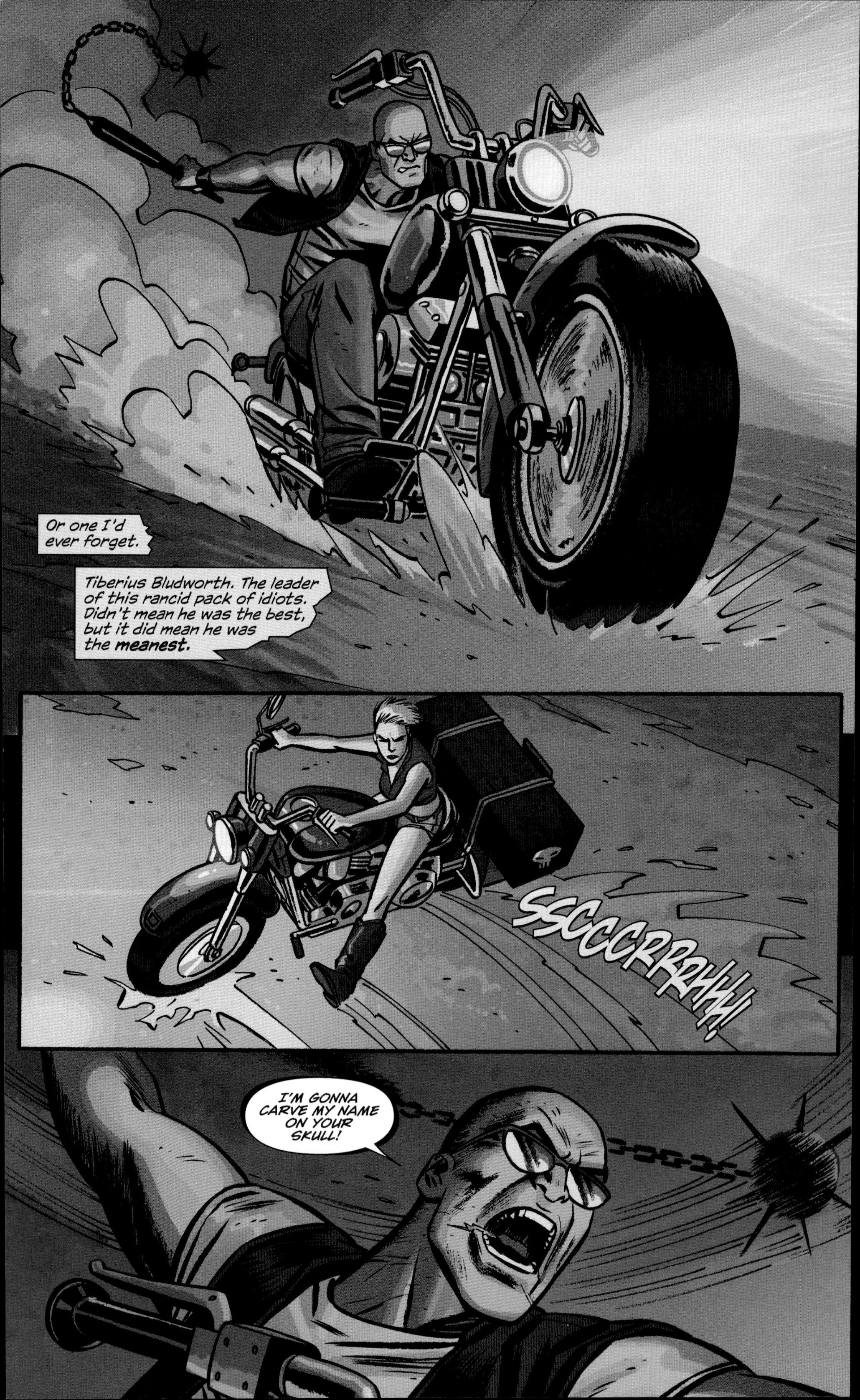
Or one I'd ever forget.
Tiberius Bludworth. The leader of this rancid pack of idiots. Didn't mean he was the best, but it did mean he was the **meanest.**
SSSCCCRRRHHH!
I'M GONNA CARVE MY NAME ON YOUR SKULL!

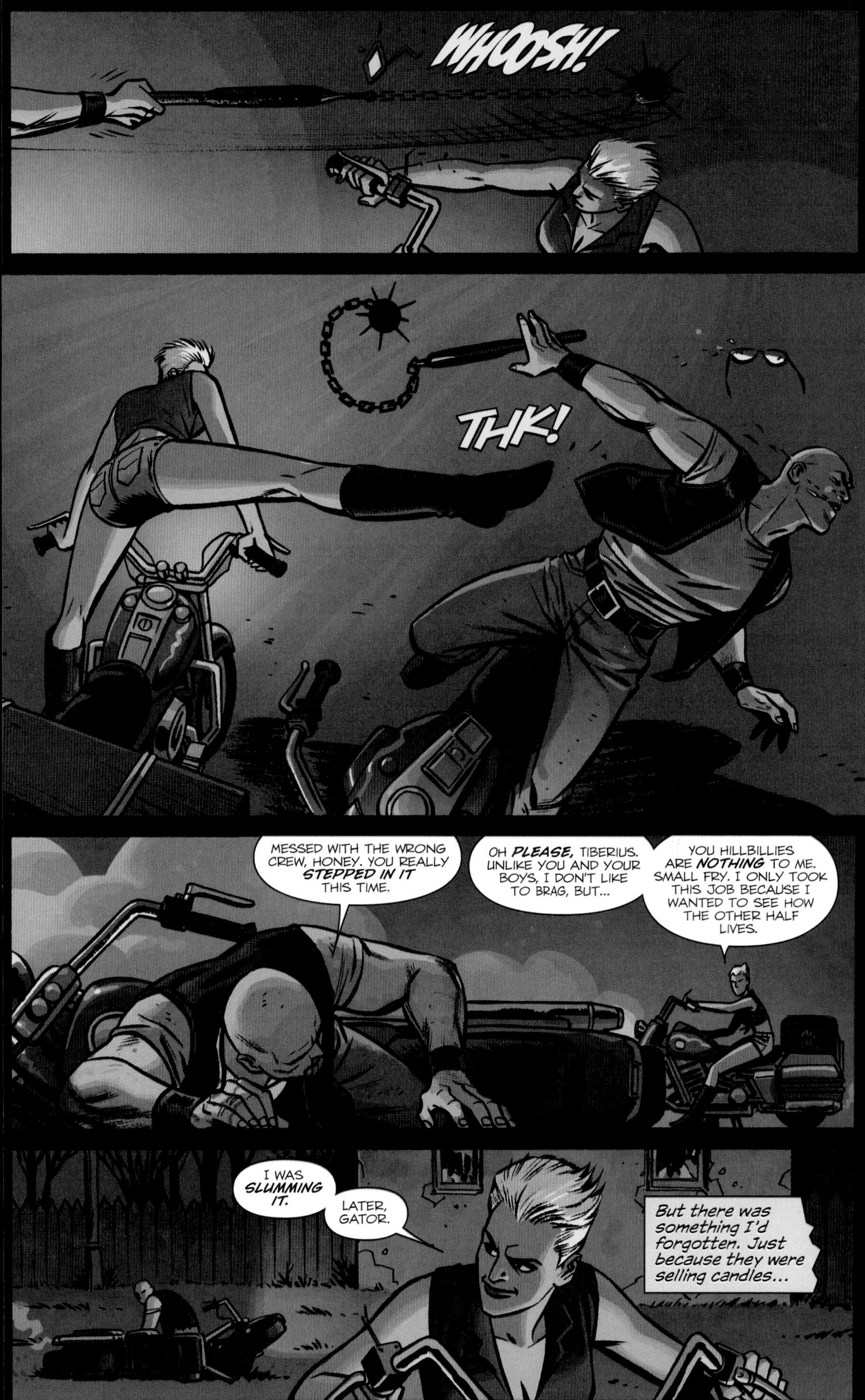
WHOOSH!
THK!
MESSED WITH THE WRONG CREW, HONEY. YOU REALLY STEPPED IN IT THIS TIME.
OH PLEASE, TIBERIUS. UNLIKE YOU AND YOUR BOYS, I DON'T LIKE TO BRAG, BUT...
YOU HILLBILLIES ARE NOTHING TO ME. SMALL FRY. I ONLY TOOK THIS JOB BECAUSE I WANTED TO SEE HOW THE OTHER HALF LIVES.
I WAS SLUMMING IT.
LATER, GATOR.
But there was something I'd forgotten. Just because they were selling candles...

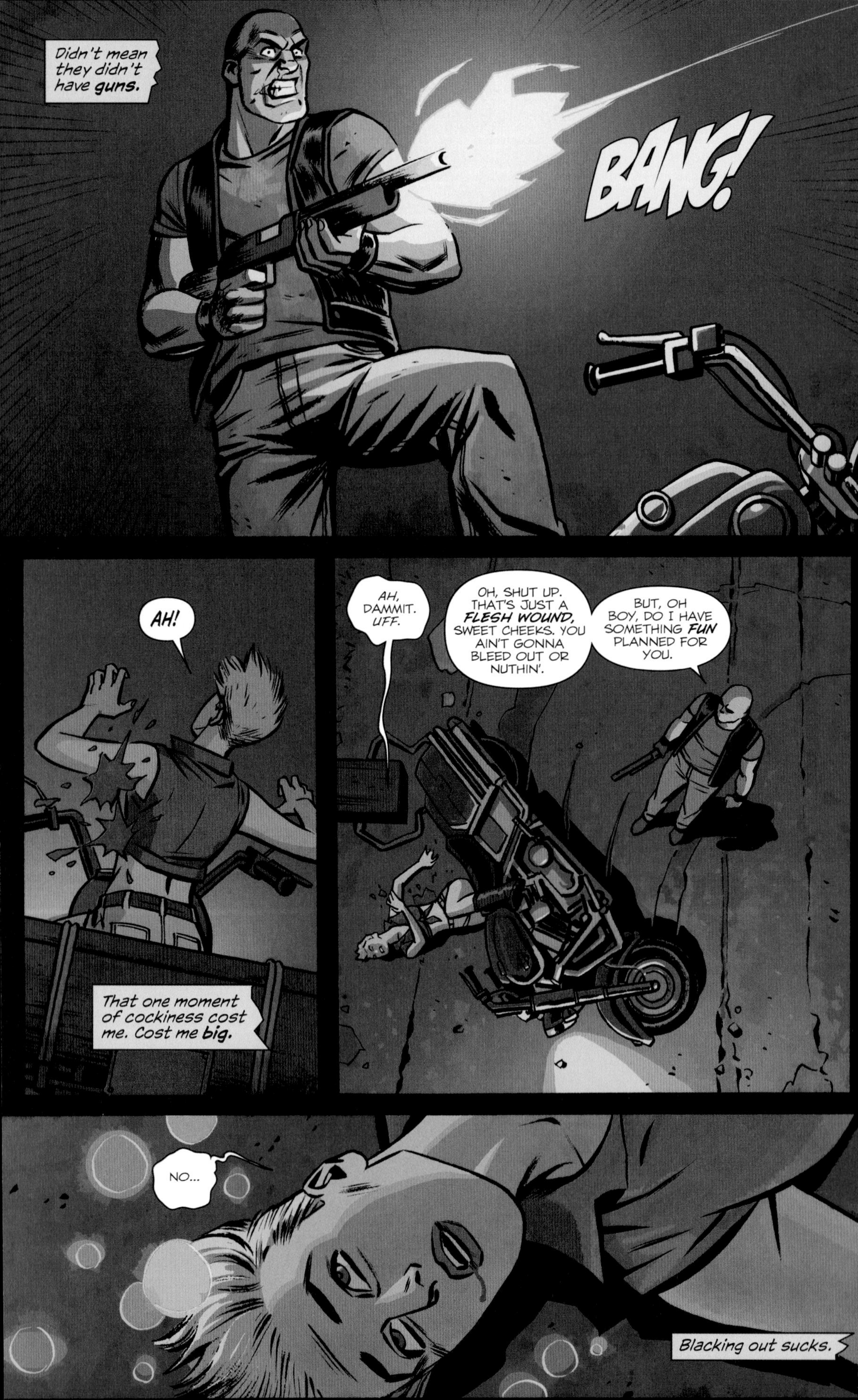
Didn't mean they didn't have **guns.**
BANG!
AH!
That one moment of cockiness cost me. Cost me **big.**
AH, DAMMIT. UFF.
OH, SHUT UP. THAT'S JUST A **FLESH WOUND,** SWEET CHEEKS. YOU AIN'T GONNA BLEED OUT OR NUTHIN'.
BUT, OH BOY, DO I HAVE SOMETHING **FUN** PLANNED FOR YOU.
NO...
Blacking out sucks.

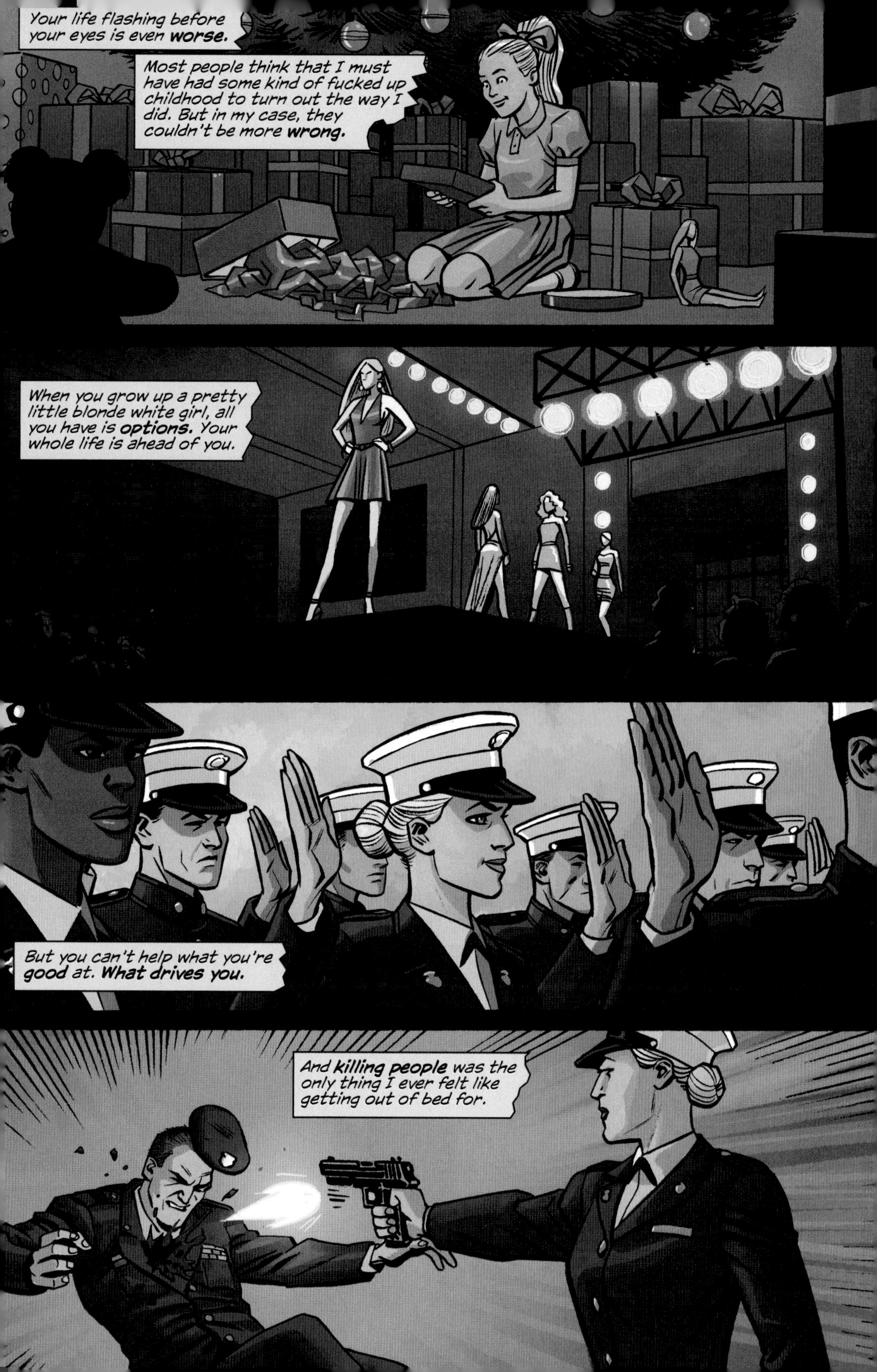
Your life flashing before your eyes is even **worse.**
Most people think that I must have had some kind of fucked up childhood to turn out the way I did. But in my case, they couldn't be more **wrong.**
When you grow up a pretty little blonde white girl, all you have is **options.** Your whole life is ahead of you.
But you can't help what you're **good** at. **What drives you.**
And **killing people** was the only thing I ever felt like getting out of bed for.

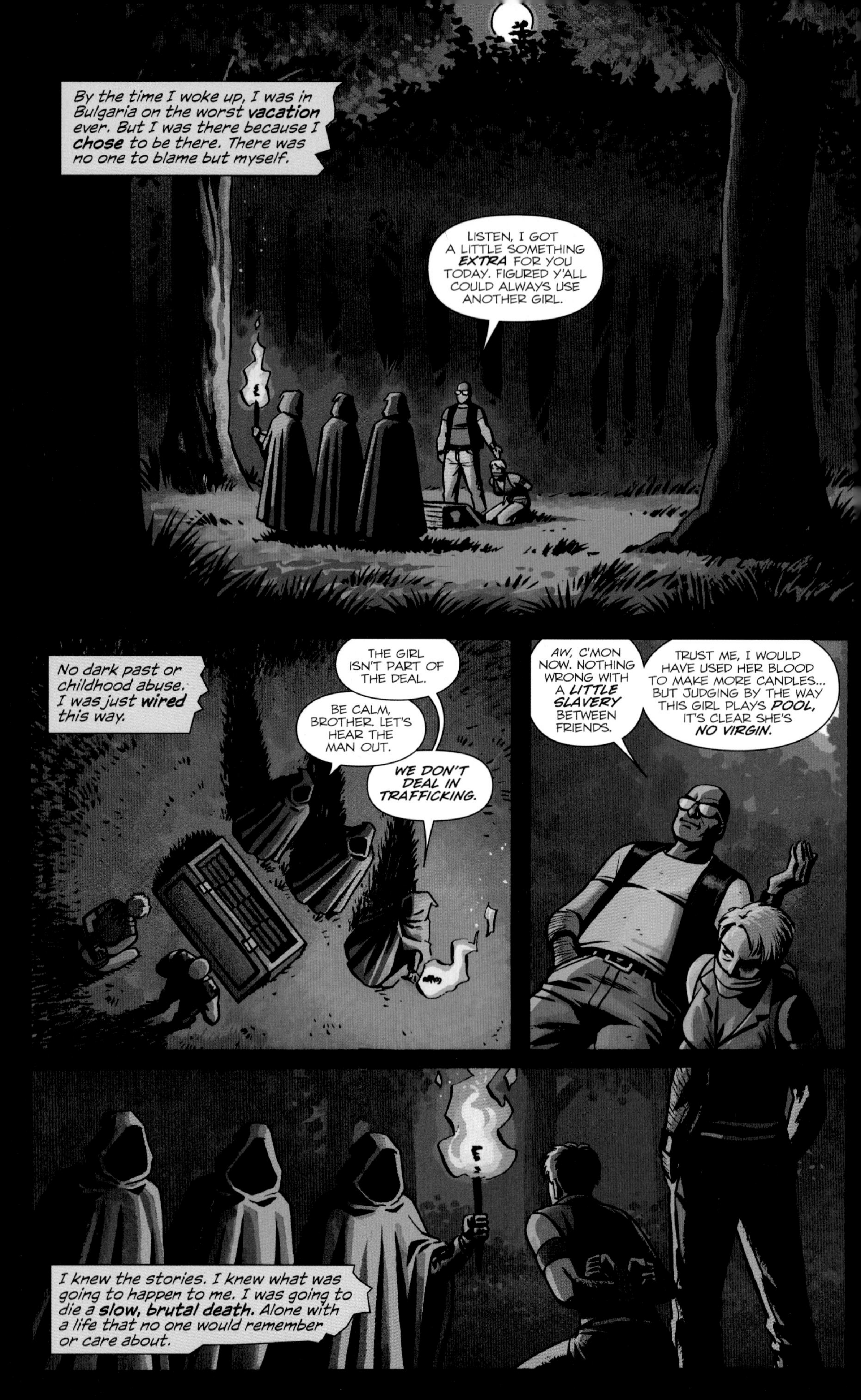
By the time I woke up, I was in Bulgaria on the worst vacation ever. But I was there because I chose to be there. There was no one to blame but myself.
LISTEN, I GOT A LITTLE SOMETHING EXTRA FOR YOU TODAY. FIGURED Y'ALL COULD ALWAYS USE ANOTHER GIRL.
No dark past or childhood abuse. I was just wired this way.
THE GIRL ISN'T PART OF THE DEAL.
BE CALM, BROTHER. LET'S HEAR THE MAN OUT.
WE DON'T DEAL IN TRAFFICKING.
AW, C'MON NOW. NOTHING WRONG WITH A LITTLE SLAVERY BETWEEN FRIENDS.
TRUST ME, I WOULD HAVE USED HER BLOOD TO MAKE MORE CANDLES... BUT JUDGING BY THE WAY THIS GIRL PLAYS POOL, IT'S CLEAR SHE'S NO VIRGIN.
I knew the stories. I knew what was going to happen to me. I was going to die a slow, brutal death. Alone with a life that no one would remember or care about.

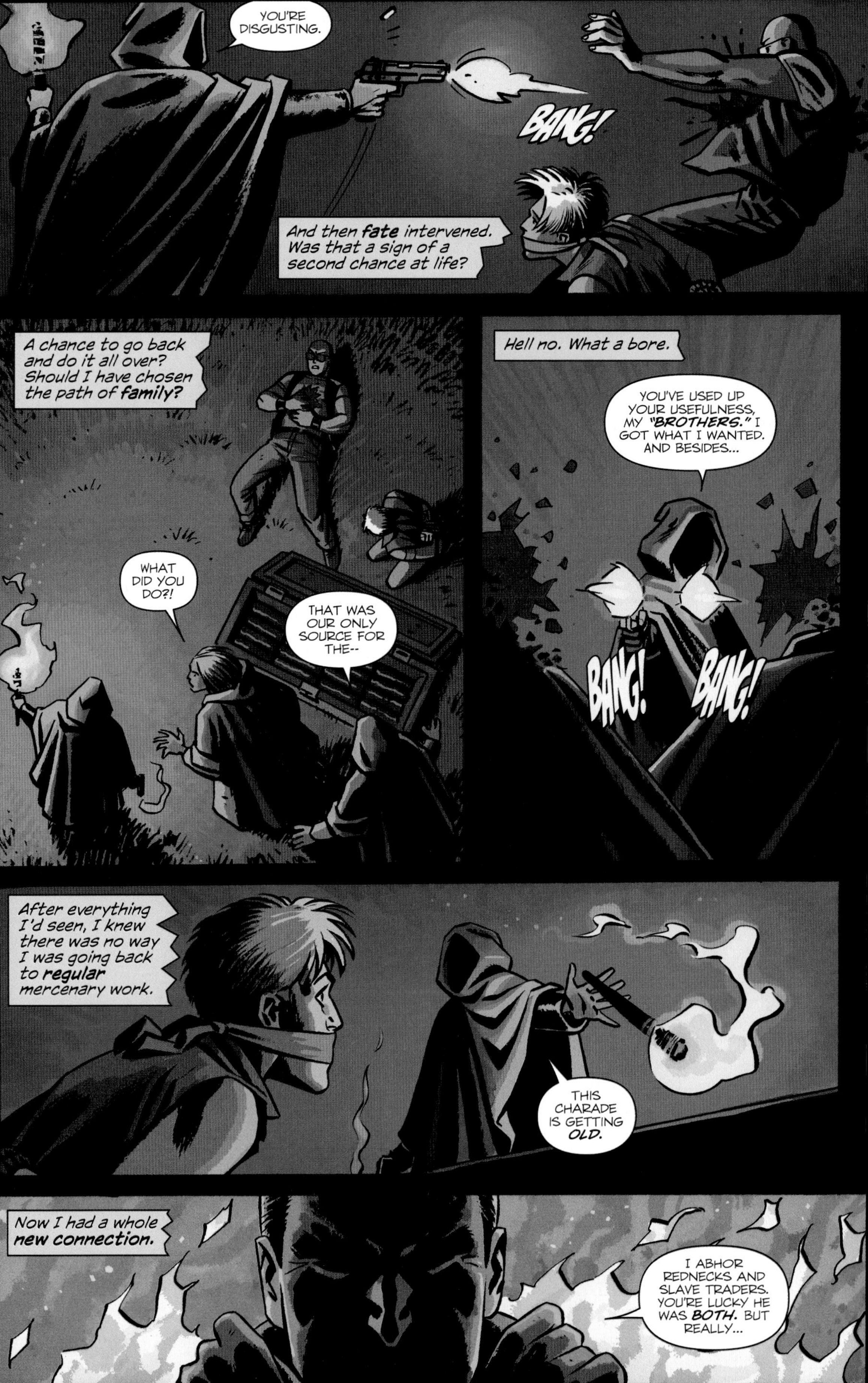
YOU'RE DISGUSTING.
BANG!
And then fate intervened. Was that a sign of a second chance at life?
A chance to go back and do it all over? Should I have chosen the path of family?
WHAT DID YOU DO?!
THAT WAS OUR ONLY SOURCE FOR THE--
Hell no. What a bore.
YOU'VE USED UP YOUR USEFULNESS, MY "BROTHERS." I GOT WHAT I WANTED. AND BESIDES...
BANG!
BANG!
After everything I'd seen, I knew there was no way I was going back to regular mercenary work.
THIS CHARADE IS GETTING OLD.
Now I had a whole new connection.
I ABHOR REDNECKS AND SLAVE TRADERS. YOU'RE LUCKY HE WAS BOTH. BUT REALLY...

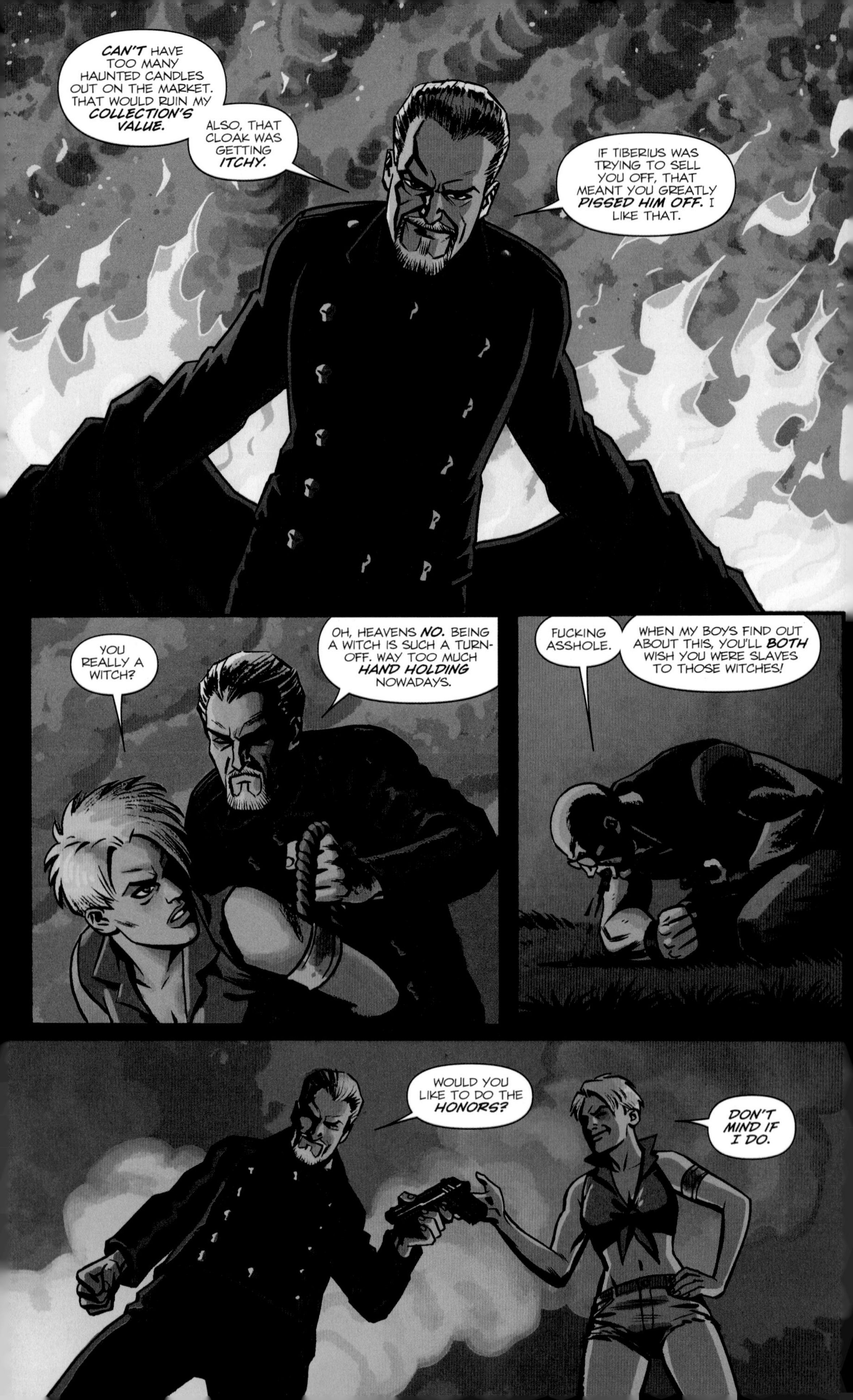
CAN'T HAVE TOO MANY HAUNTED CANDLES OUT ON THE MARKET. THAT WOULD RUIN MY COLLECTION'S VALUE.
ALSO, THAT CLOAK WAS GETTING ITCHY.
IF TIBERIUS WAS TRYING TO SELL YOU OFF, THAT MEANT YOU GREATLY PISSED HIM OFF. I LIKE THAT.
YOU REALLY A WITCH?
OH, HEAVENS NO. BEING A WITCH IS SUCH A TURN-OFF. WAY TOO MUCH HAND HOLDING NOWADAYS.
FUCKING ASSHOLE.
WHEN MY BOYS FIND OUT ABOUT THIS, YOU'LL BOTH WISH YOU WERE SLAVES TO THOSE WITCHES!
WOULD YOU LIKE TO DO THE HONORS?
DON'T MIND IF I DO.

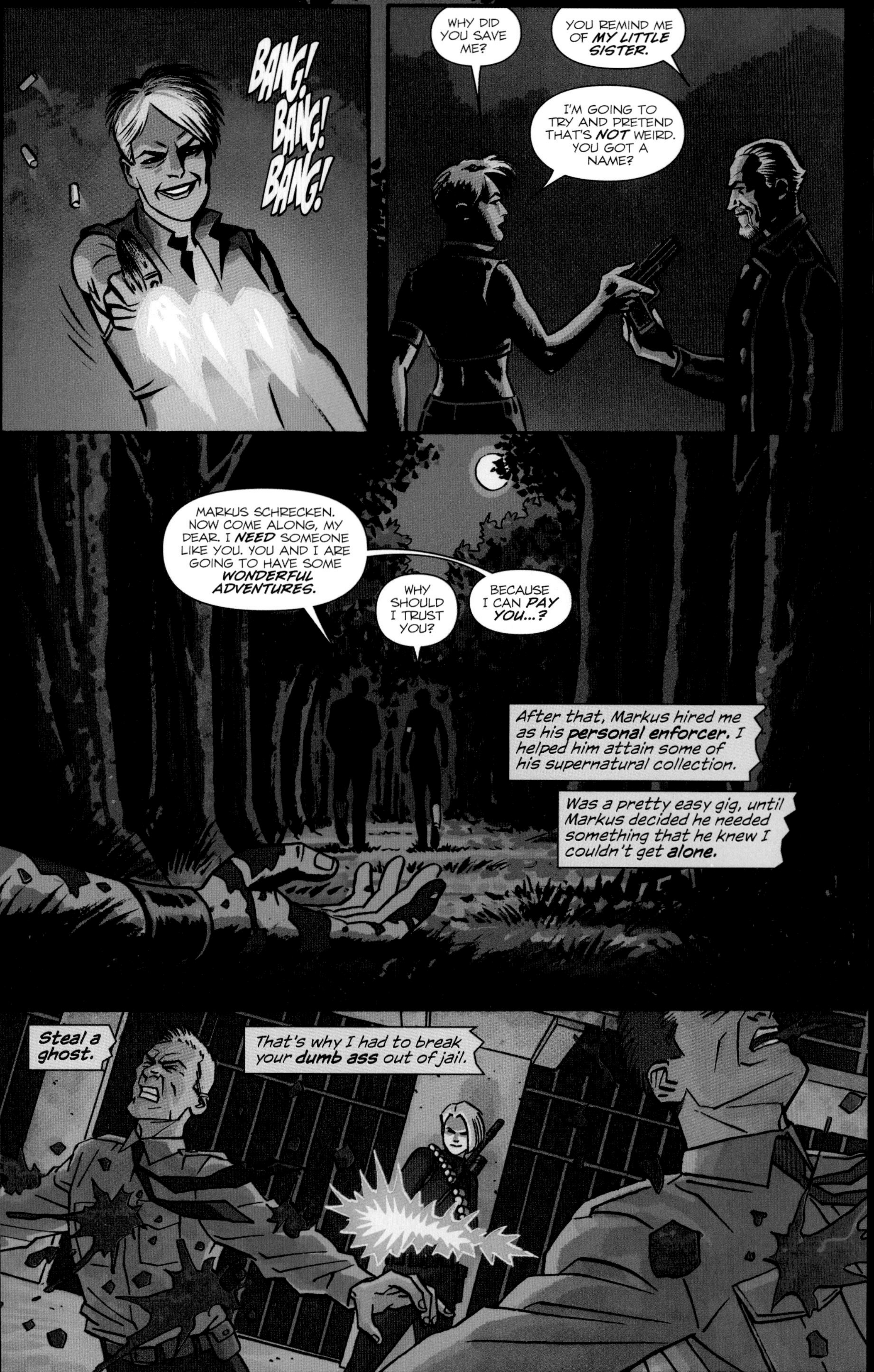
BANG! BANG! BANG!
WHY DID YOU SAVE ME?
YOU REMIND ME OF MY LITTLE SISTER.
I'M GOING TO TRY AND PRETEND THAT'S NOT WEIRD. YOU GOT A NAME?
MARKUS SCHRECKEN. NOW COME ALONG, MY DEAR. I NEED SOMEONE LIKE YOU. YOU AND I ARE GOING TO HAVE SOME WONDERFUL ADVENTURES.
WHY SHOULD I TRUST YOU?
BECAUSE I CAN PAY YOU...?
After that, Markus hired me as his personal enforcer. I helped him attain some of his supernatural collection.
Was a pretty easy gig, until Markus decided he needed something that he knew I couldn't get alone.
Steal a ghost.
That's why I had to break your dumb ass out of jail.

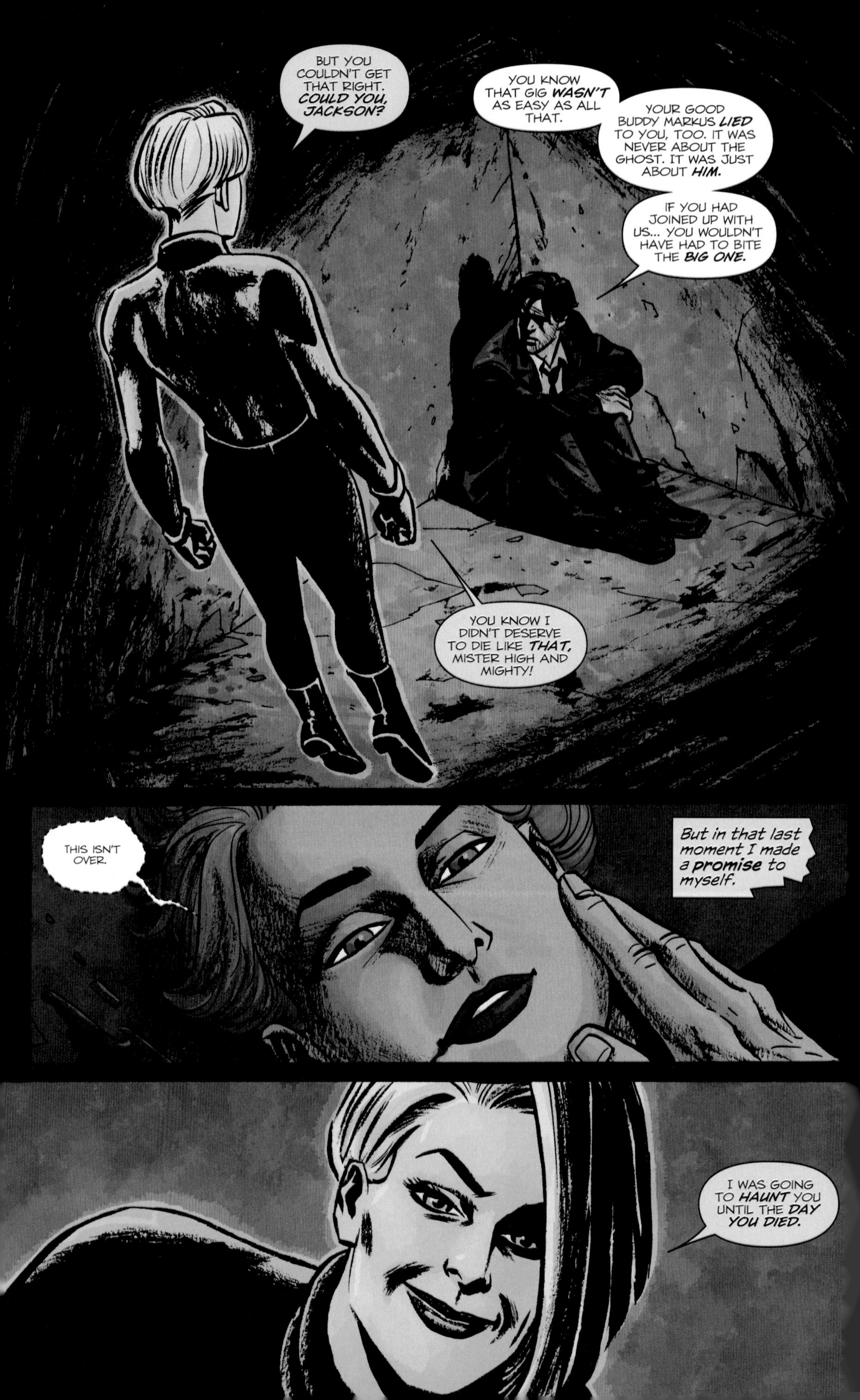
BUT YOU COULDN'T GET THAT RIGHT. **COULD YOU, JACKSON?**
YOU KNOW THAT GIG **WASN'T** AS EASY AS ALL THAT.
YOUR GOOD BUDDY MARKUS **LIED** TO YOU, TOO. IT WAS NEVER ABOUT THE GHOST. IT WAS JUST ABOUT **HIM.**
IF YOU HAD JOINED UP WITH US... YOU WOULDN'T HAVE HAD TO BITE THE **BIG ONE.**
YOU KNOW I DIDN'T DESERVE TO DIE LIKE **THAT,** MISTER HIGH AND MIGHTY!
THIS ISN'T OVER.
*But in that last moment I made a **promise** to myself.*
I WAS GOING TO **HAUNT** YOU UNTIL THE **DAY YOU DIED.**

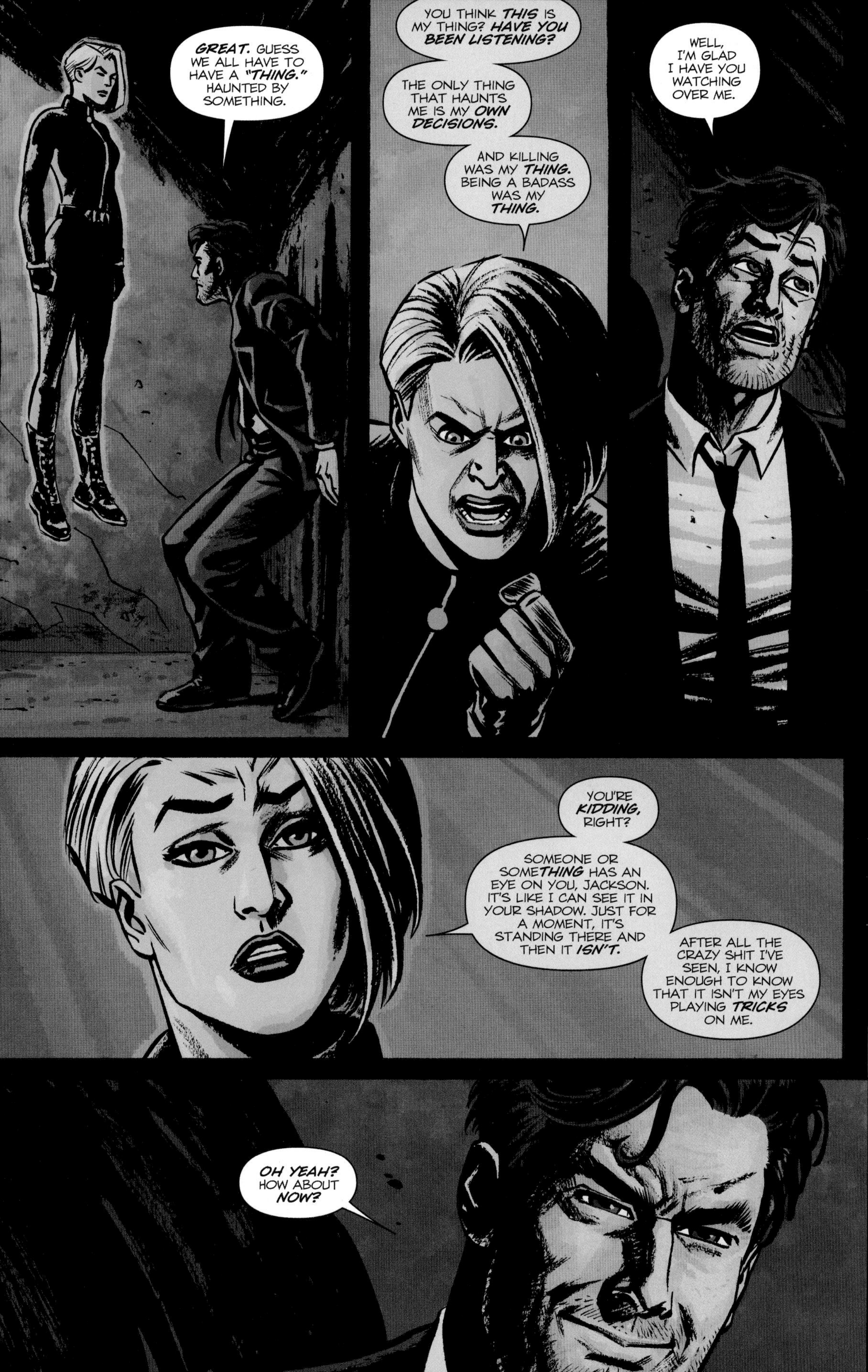
GREAT. GUESS WE ALL HAVE TO HAVE A "THING." HAUNTED BY SOMETHING.
YOU THINK THIS IS MY THING? HAVE YOU BEEN LISTENING?
THE ONLY THING THAT HAUNTS ME IS MY OWN DECISIONS.
AND KILLING WAS MY THING. BEING A BADASS WAS MY THING.
WELL, I'M GLAD I HAVE YOU WATCHING OVER ME.
YOU'RE KIDDING, RIGHT?
SOMEONE OR SOMETHING HAS AN EYE ON YOU, JACKSON. IT'S LIKE I CAN SEE IT IN YOUR SHADOW. JUST FOR A MOMENT, IT'S STANDING THERE AND THEN IT ISN'T.
AFTER ALL THE CRAZY SHIT I'VE SEEN, I KNOW ENOUGH TO KNOW THAT IT ISN'T MY EYES PLAYING TRICKS ON ME.
OH YEAH? HOW ABOUT NOW?

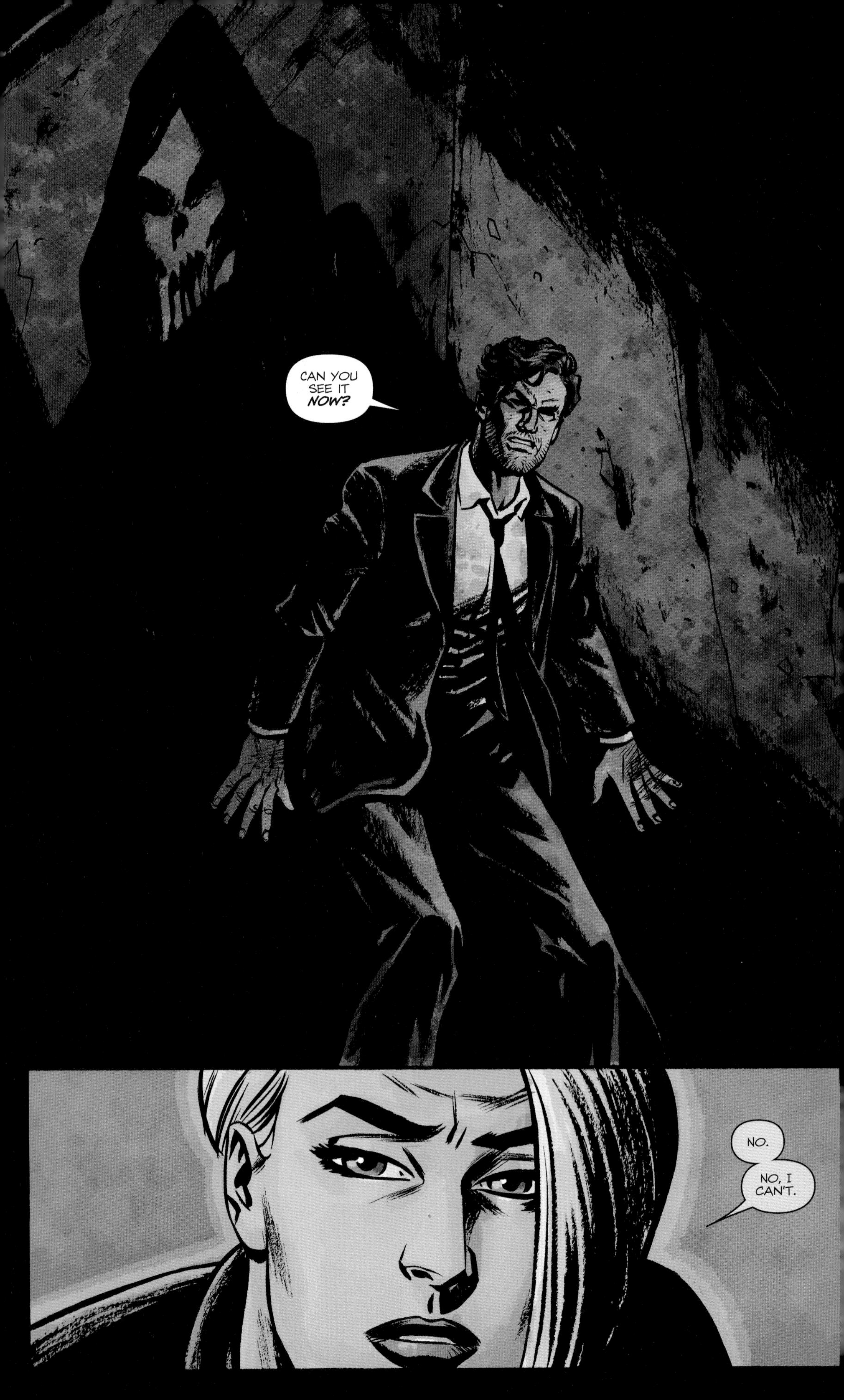
CAN YOU SEE IT NOW?
NO.
NO, I CAN'T.

CHAPTER TWO

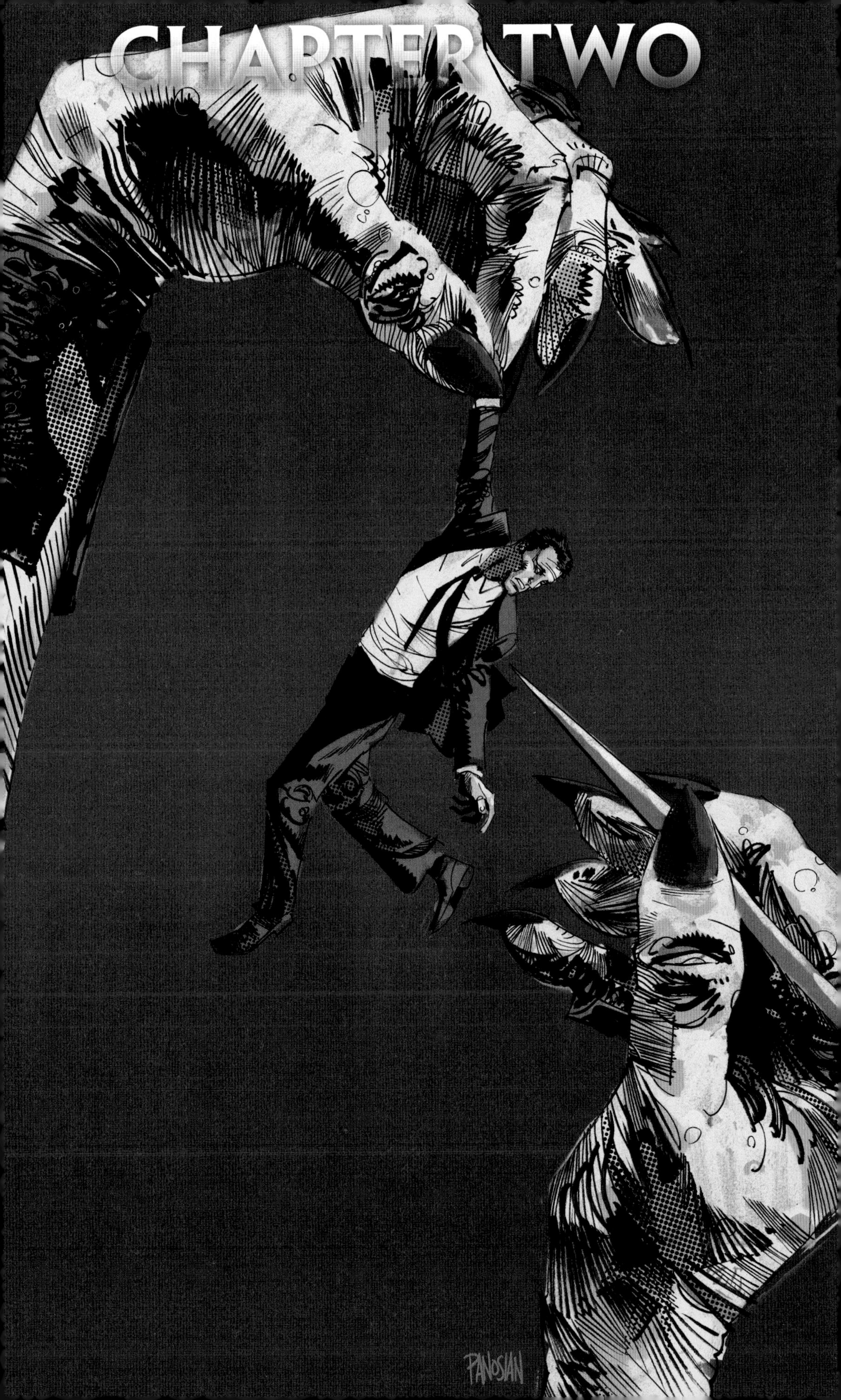
PANOSIAN

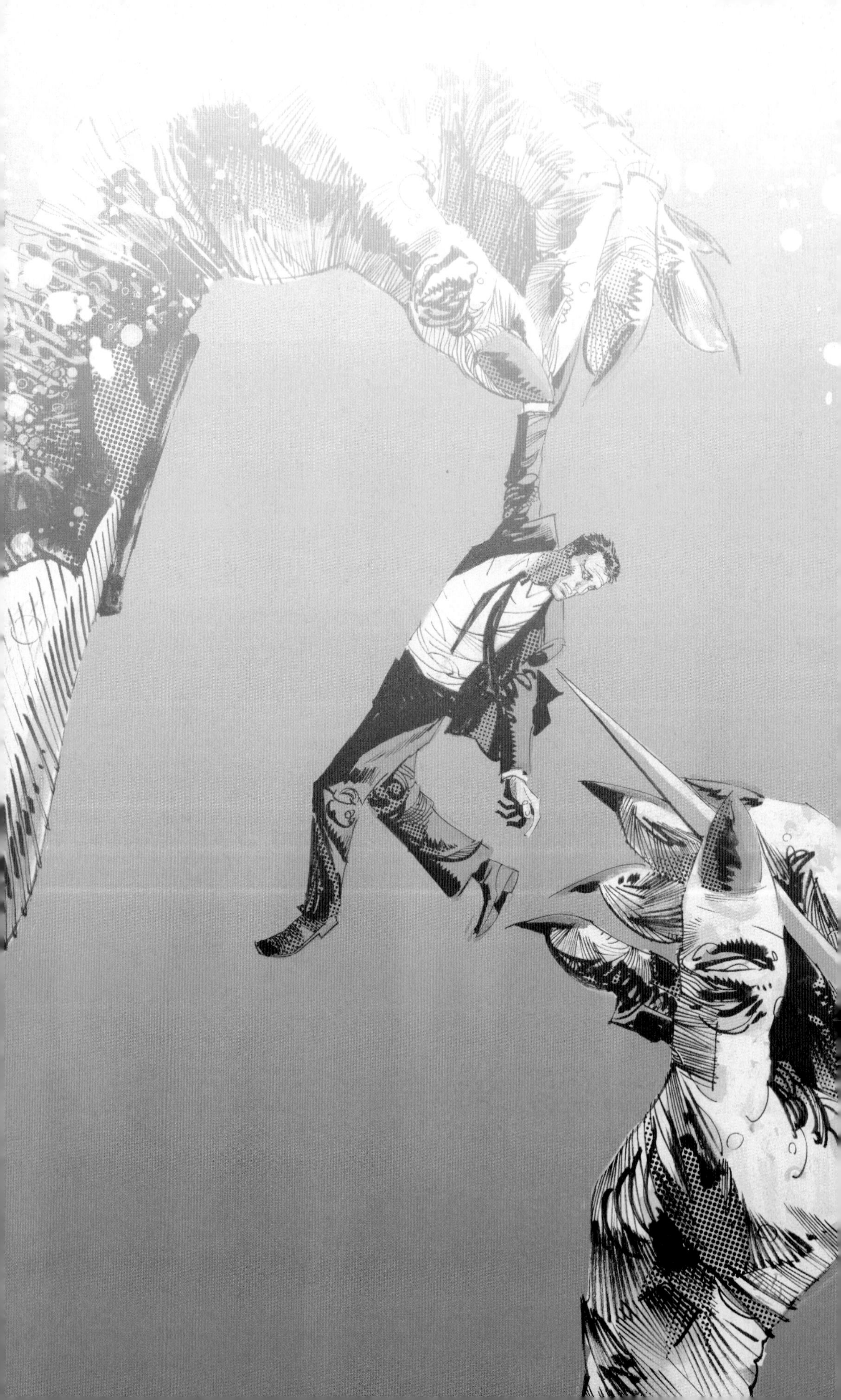

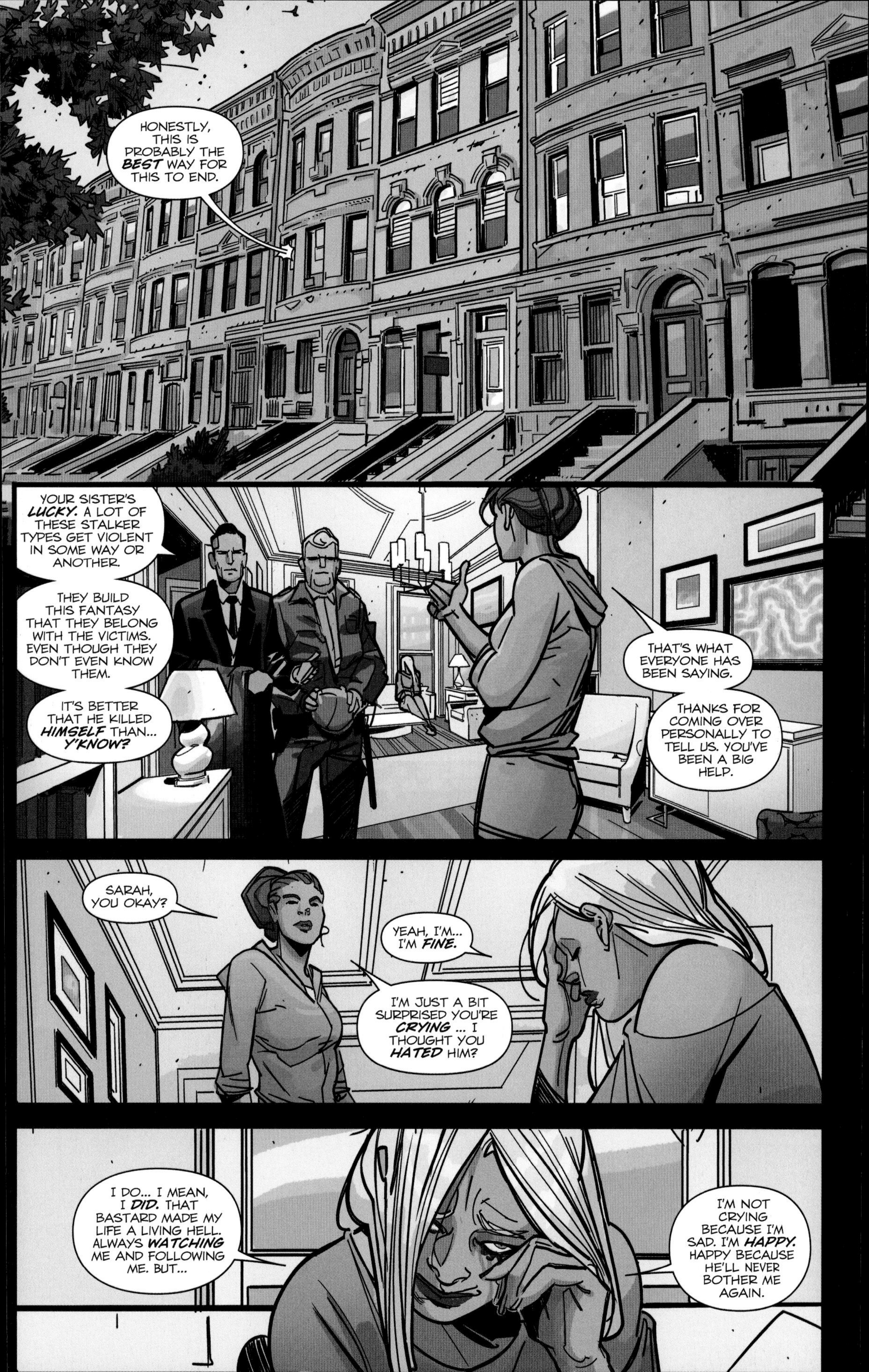
HONESTLY, THIS IS PROBABLY THE BEST WAY FOR THIS TO END.
YOUR SISTER'S LUCKY. A LOT OF THESE STALKER TYPES GET VIOLENT IN SOME WAY OR ANOTHER.
THEY BUILD THIS FANTASY THAT THEY BELONG WITH THE VICTIMS. EVEN THOUGH THEY DON'T EVEN KNOW THEM.
IT'S BETTER THAT HE KILLED HIMSELF THAN... Y'KNOW?
THAT'S WHAT EVERYONE HAS BEEN SAYING.
THANKS FOR COMING OVER PERSONALLY TO TELL US. YOU'VE BEEN A BIG HELP.
SARAH, YOU OKAY?
YEAH, I'M... I'M FINE.
I'M JUST A BIT SURPRISED YOU'RE CRYING ... I THOUGHT YOU HATED HIM?
I DO... I MEAN, I DID. THAT BASTARD MADE MY LIFE A LIVING HELL. ALWAYS WATCHING ME AND FOLLOWING ME. BUT...
I'M NOT CRYING BECAUSE I'M SAD. I'M HAPPY. HAPPY BECAUSE HE'LL NEVER BOTHER ME AGAIN.

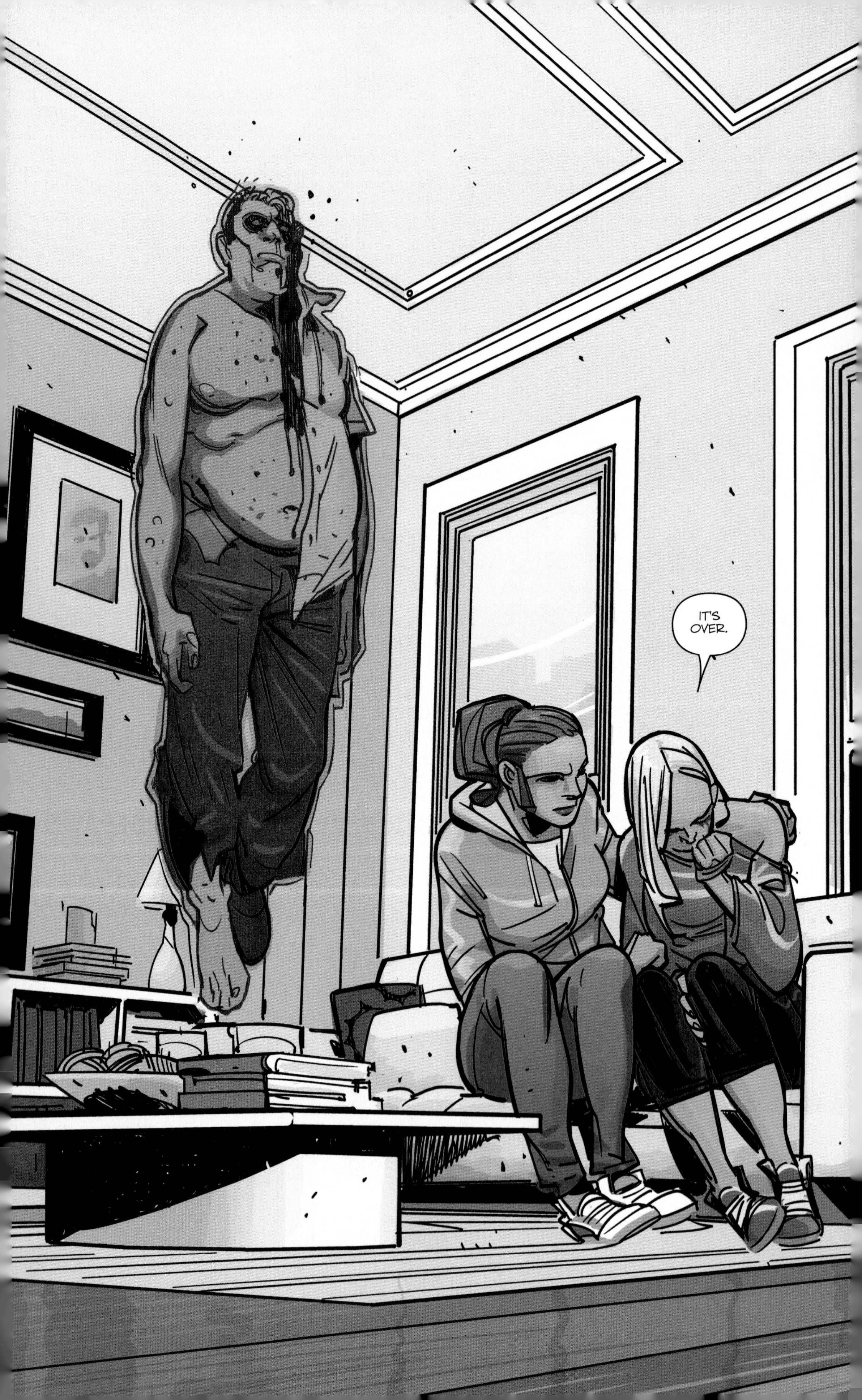
IT'S OVER.

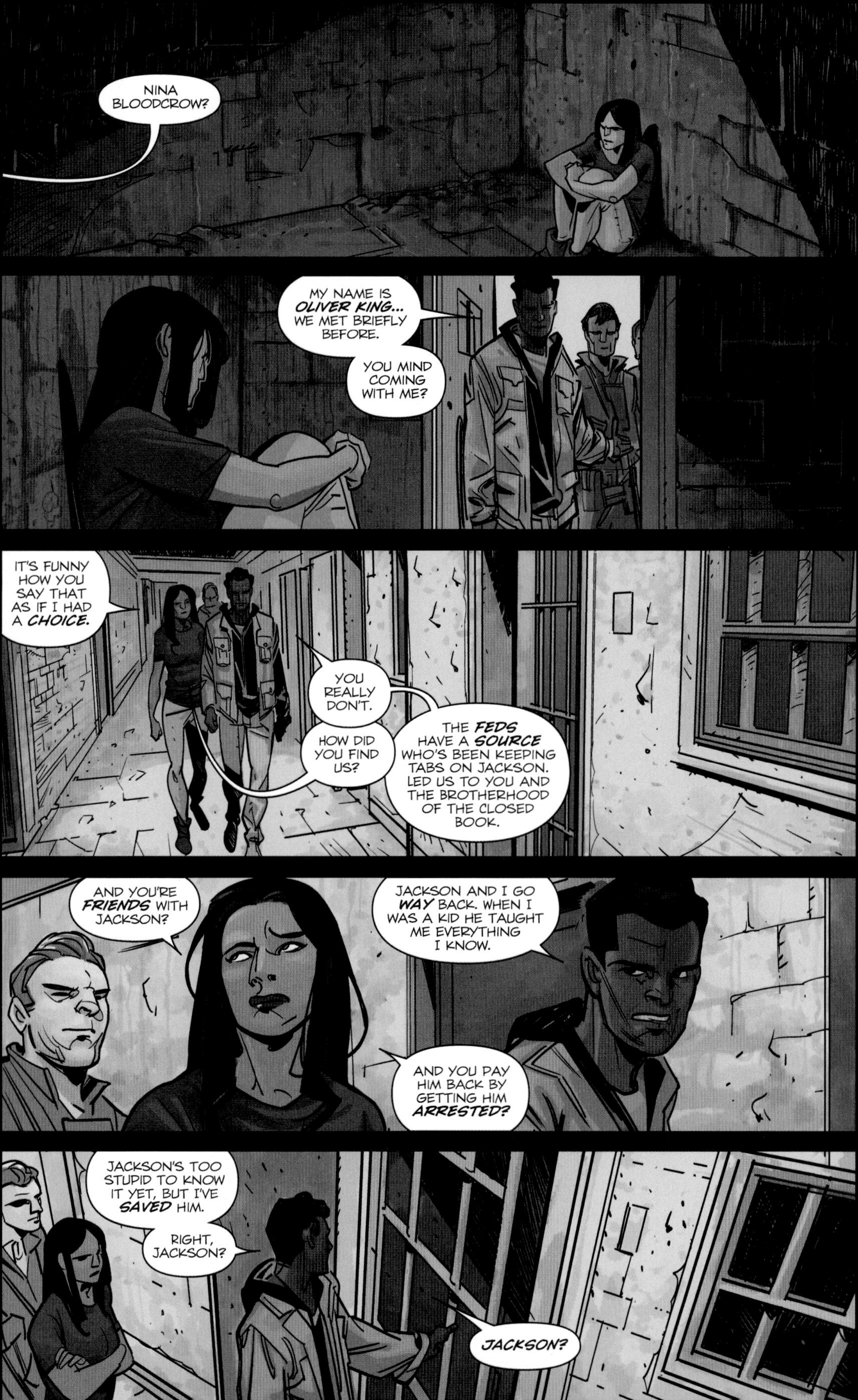
NINA BLOODCROW?
MY NAME IS OLIVER KING... WE MET BRIEFLY BEFORE.
YOU MIND COMING WITH ME?
IT'S FUNNY HOW YOU SAY THAT AS IF I HAD A CHOICE.
YOU REALLY DON'T.
HOW DID YOU FIND US?
THE FEDS HAVE A SOURCE WHO'S BEEN KEEPING TABS ON JACKSON. LED US TO YOU AND THE BROTHERHOOD OF THE CLOSED BOOK.
AND YOU'RE FRIENDS WITH JACKSON?
JACKSON AND I GO WAY BACK. WHEN I WAS A KID HE TAUGHT ME EVERYTHING I KNOW.
AND YOU PAY HIM BACK BY GETTING HIM ARRESTED?
JACKSON'S TOO STUPID TO KNOW IT YET, BUT I'VE SAVED HIM.
RIGHT, JACKSON?
JACKSON?

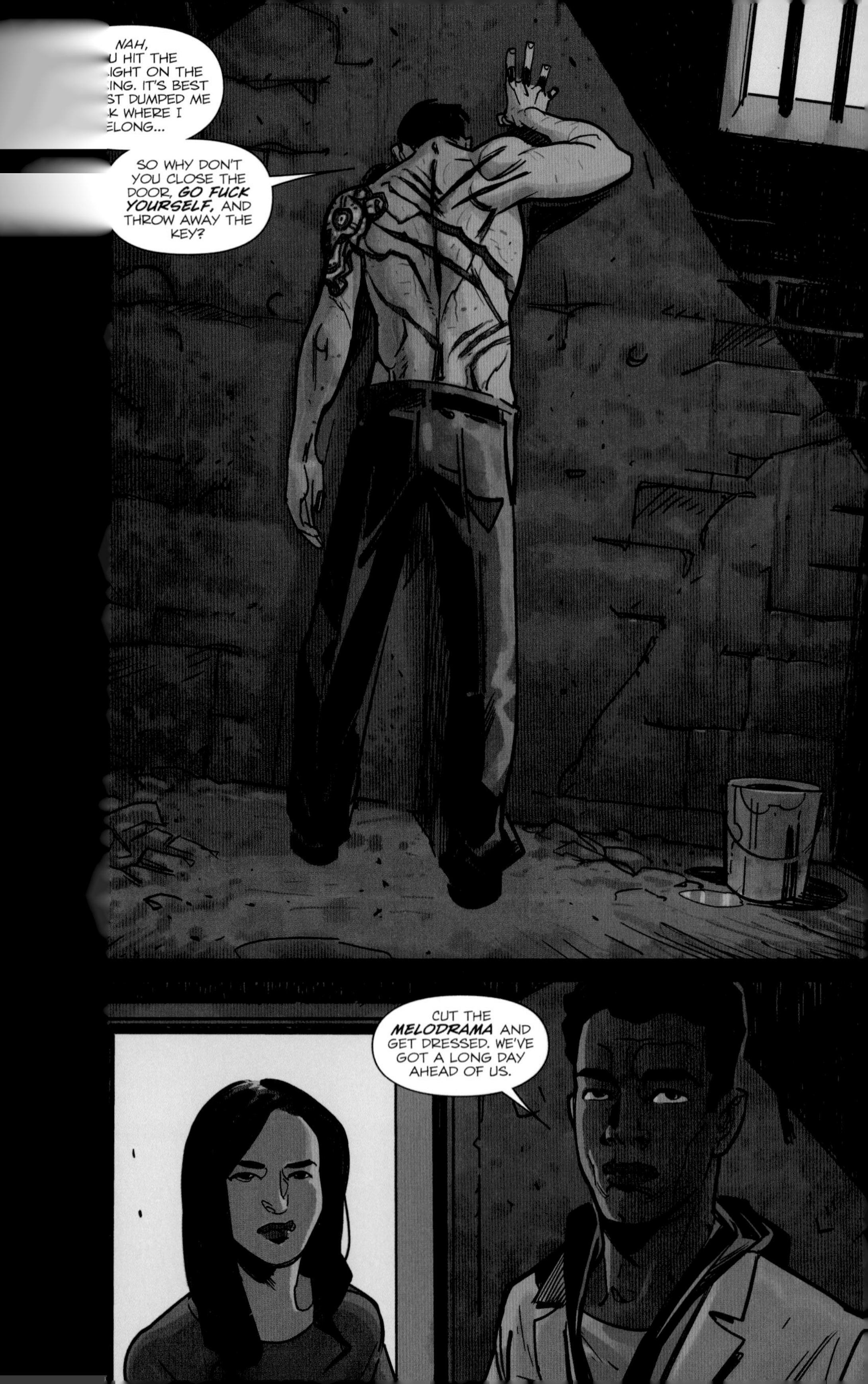
NAH,
U HIT THE
IGHT ON THE
ING. IT'S BEST
ST DUMPED ME
K WHERE I
ELONG...
SO WHY DON'T YOU CLOSE THE DOOR, GO FUCK YOURSELF, AND THROW AWAY THE KEY?
CUT THE MELODRAMA AND GET DRESSED. WE'VE GOT A LONG DAY AHEAD OF US.

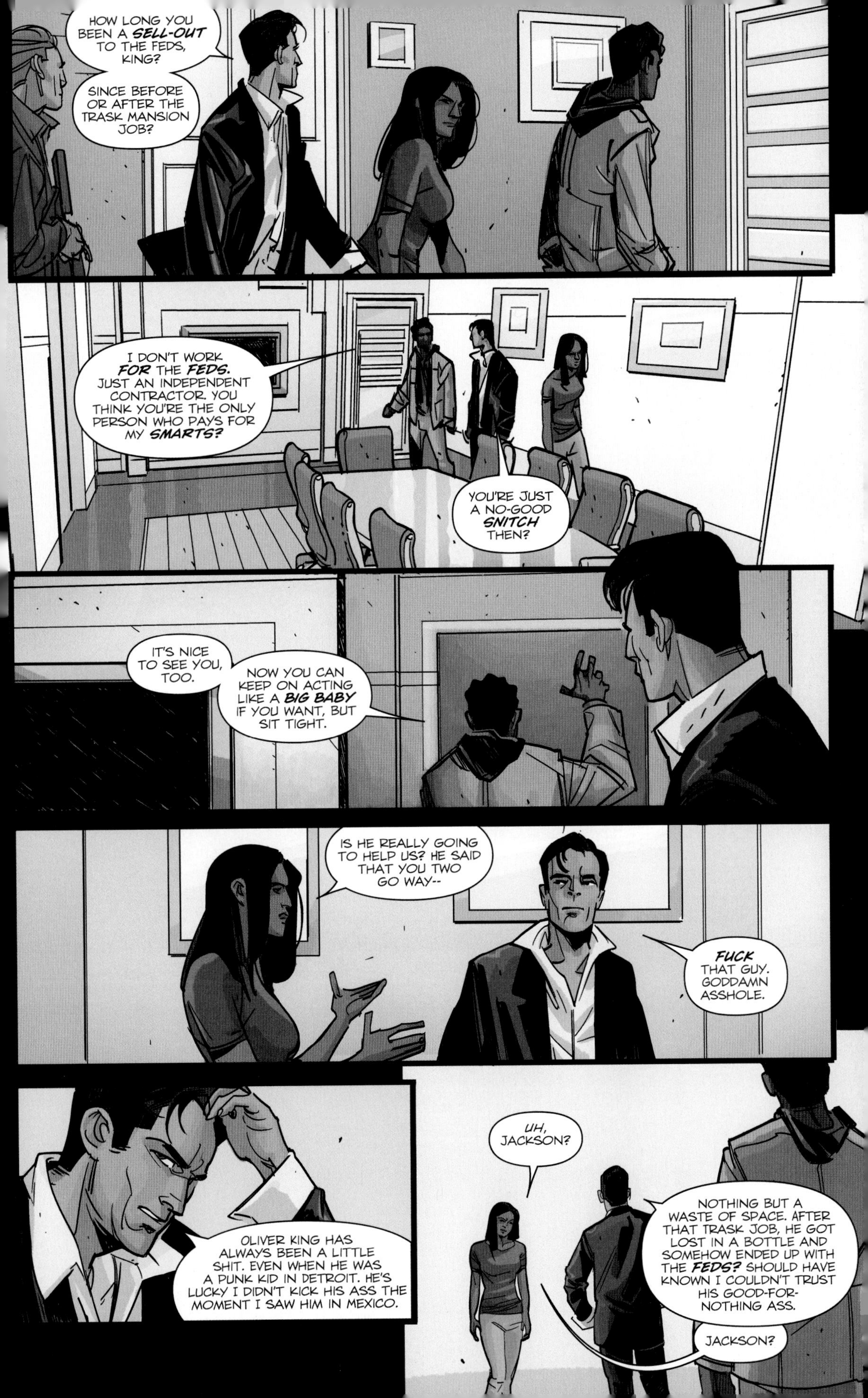
HOW LONG YOU BEEN A SELL-OUT TO THE FEDS, KING?
SINCE BEFORE OR AFTER THE TRASK MANSION JOB?
I DON'T WORK FOR THE FEDS. JUST AN INDEPENDENT CONTRACTOR. YOU THINK YOU'RE THE ONLY PERSON WHO PAYS FOR MY SMARTS?
YOU'RE JUST A NO-GOOD SNITCH THEN?
IT'S NICE TO SEE YOU, TOO.
NOW YOU CAN KEEP ON ACTING LIKE A BIG BABY IF YOU WANT, BUT SIT TIGHT.
IS HE REALLY GOING TO HELP US? HE SAID THAT YOU TWO GO WAY--
FUCK THAT GUY. GODDAMN ASSHOLE.
OLIVER KING HAS ALWAYS BEEN A LITTLE SHIT. EVEN WHEN HE WAS A PUNK KID IN DETROIT. HE'S LUCKY I DIDN'T KICK HIS ASS THE MOMENT I SAW HIM IN MEXICO.
UH, JACKSON?
NOTHING BUT A WASTE OF SPACE. AFTER THAT TRASK JOB, HE GOT LOST IN A BOTTLE AND SOMEHOW ENDED UP WITH THE FEDS? SHOULD HAVE KNOWN I COULDN'T TRUST HIS GOOD-FOR-NOTHING ASS.
JACKSON?

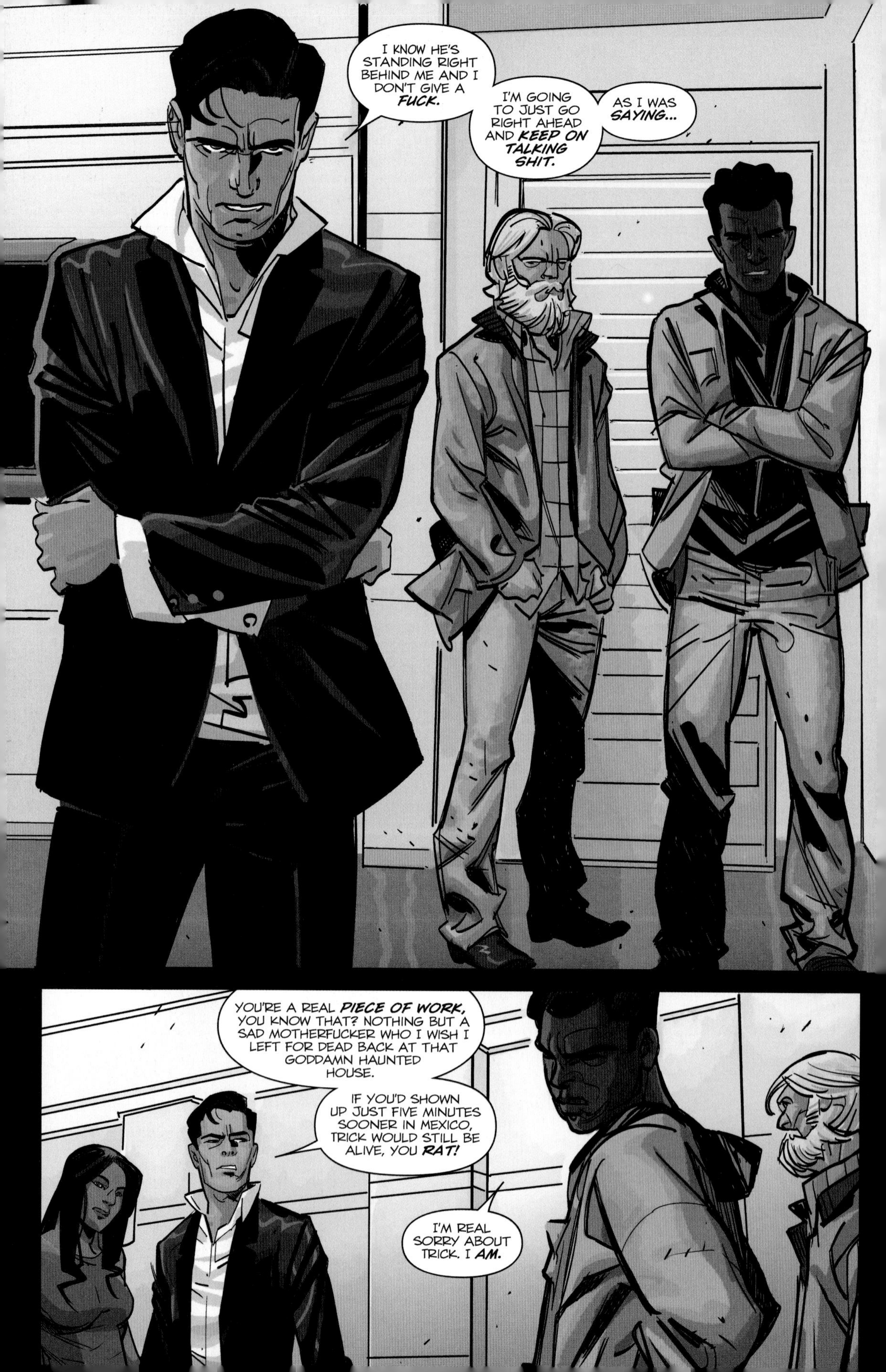
I KNOW HE'S STANDING RIGHT BEHIND ME AND I DON'T GIVE A ***FUCK.***
I'M GOING TO JUST GO RIGHT AHEAD AND ***KEEP ON TALKING SHIT.***
AS I WAS ***SAYING...***
YOU'RE A REAL ***PIECE OF WORK,*** YOU KNOW THAT? NOTHING BUT A SAD MOTHERFUCKER WHO I WISH I LEFT FOR DEAD BACK AT THAT GODDAMN HAUNTED HOUSE.
IF YOU'D SHOWN UP JUST FIVE MINUTES SOONER IN MEXICO, TRICK WOULD STILL BE ALIVE, YOU ***RAT!***
I'M REAL SORRY ABOUT TRICK. I ***AM.***

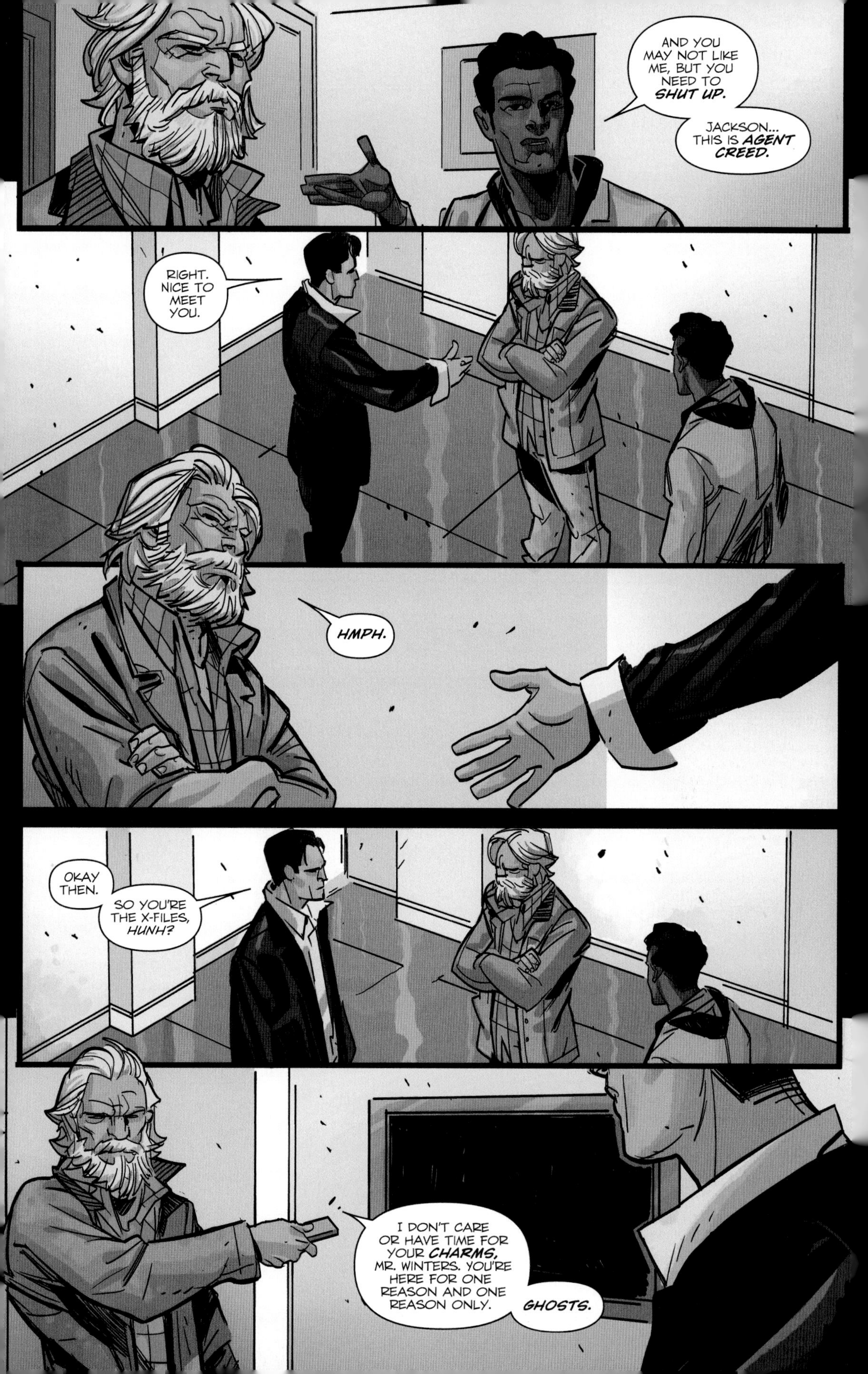
AND YOU MAY NOT LIKE ME, BUT YOU NEED TO SHUT UP.
JACKSON... THIS IS AGENT CREED.
RIGHT. NICE TO MEET YOU.
HMPH.
OKAY THEN.
SO YOU'RE THE X-FILES, HUNH?
I DON'T CARE OR HAVE TIME FOR YOUR CHARMS, MR. WINTERS. YOU'RE HERE FOR ONE REASON AND ONE REASON ONLY.
GHOSTS.

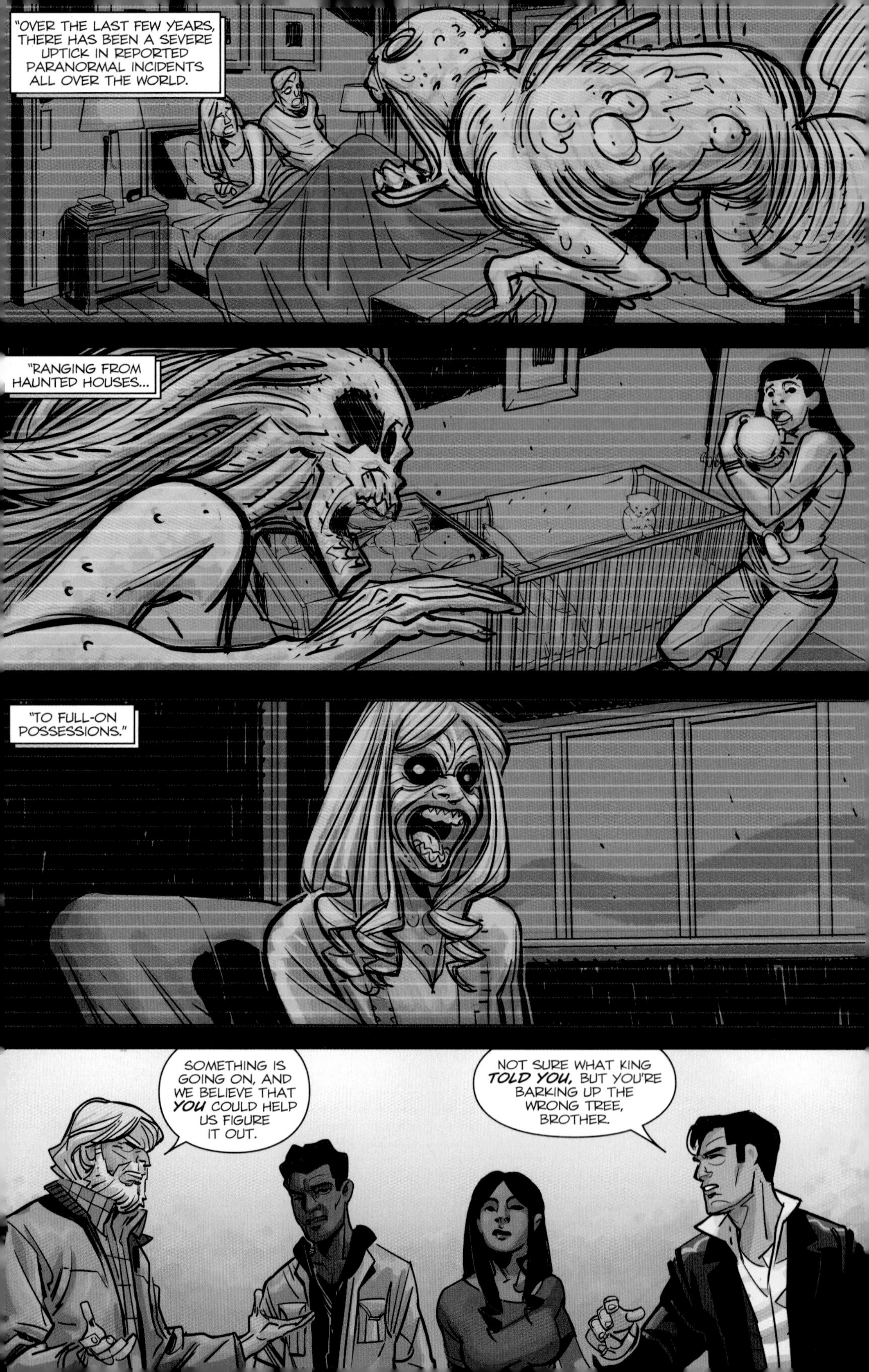
"OVER THE LAST FEW YEARS, THERE HAS BEEN A SEVERE UPTICK IN REPORTED PARANORMAL INCIDENTS ALL OVER THE WORLD.
"RANGING FROM HAUNTED HOUSES...
"TO FULL-ON POSSESSIONS."
SOMETHING IS GOING ON, AND WE BELIEVE THAT YOU COULD HELP US FIGURE IT OUT.
NOT SURE WHAT KING TOLD YOU, BUT YOU'RE BARKING UP THE WRONG TREE, BROTHER.

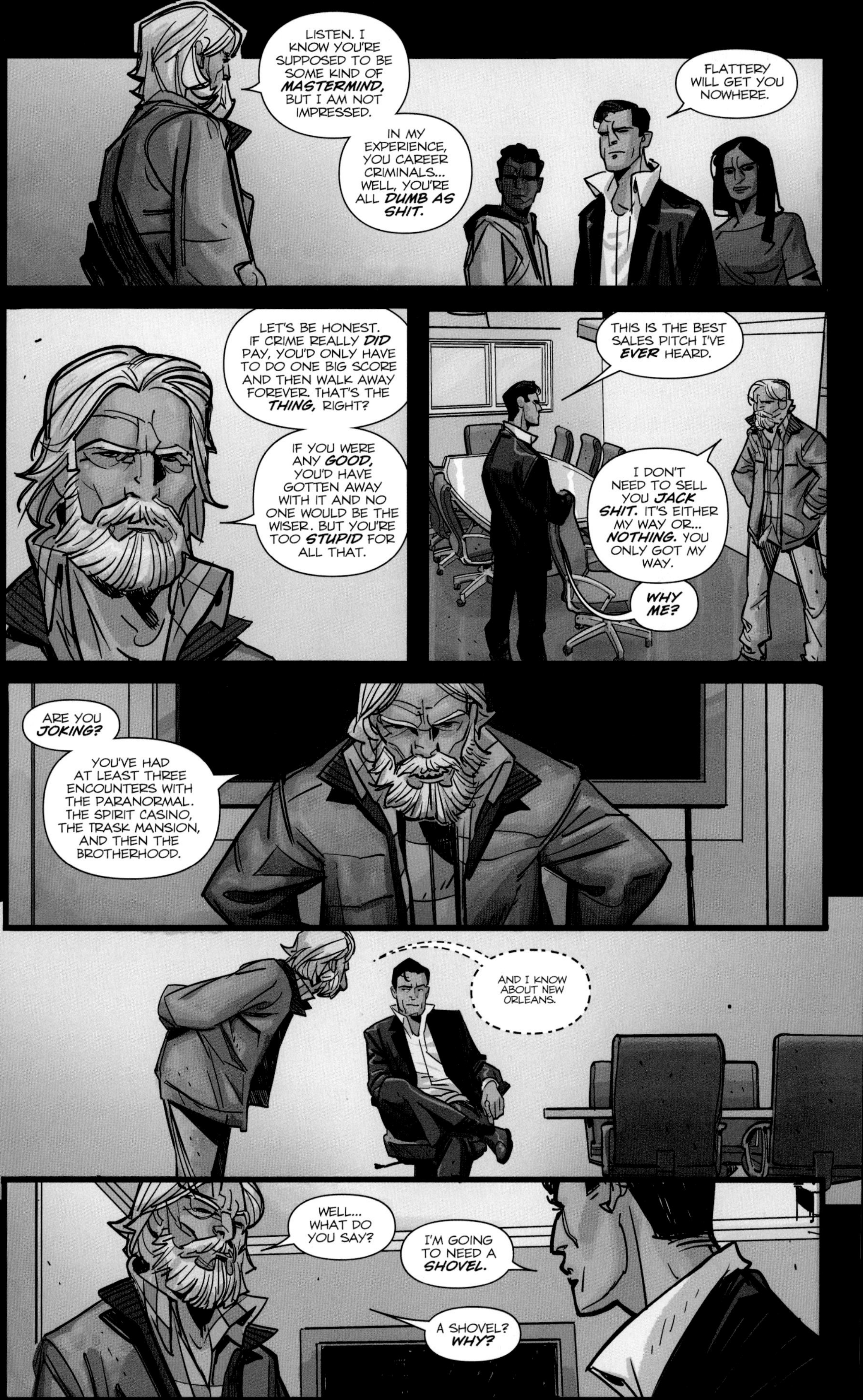
LISTEN. I KNOW YOU'RE SUPPOSED TO BE SOME KIND OF MASTERMIND, BUT I AM NOT IMPRESSED.
IN MY EXPERIENCE, YOU CAREER CRIMINALS... WELL, YOU'RE ALL DUMB AS SHIT.
FLATTERY WILL GET YOU NOWHERE.
LET'S BE HONEST. IF CRIME REALLY DID PAY, YOU'D ONLY HAVE TO DO ONE BIG SCORE AND THEN WALK AWAY FOREVER. THAT'S THE THING, RIGHT?
IF YOU WERE ANY GOOD, YOU'D HAVE GOTTEN AWAY WITH IT AND NO ONE WOULD BE THE WISER. BUT YOU'RE TOO STUPID FOR ALL THAT.
THIS IS THE BEST SALES PITCH I'VE EVER HEARD.
I DON'T NEED TO SELL YOU JACK SHIT. IT'S EITHER MY WAY OR... NOTHING. YOU ONLY GOT MY WAY.
WHY ME?
ARE YOU JOKING?
YOU'VE HAD AT LEAST THREE ENCOUNTERS WITH THE PARANORMAL. THE SPIRIT CASINO, THE TRASK MANSION, AND THEN THE BROTHERHOOD.
AND I KNOW ABOUT NEW ORLEANS.
WELL... WHAT DO YOU SAY?
I'M GOING TO NEED A SHOVEL.
A SHOVEL? WHY?

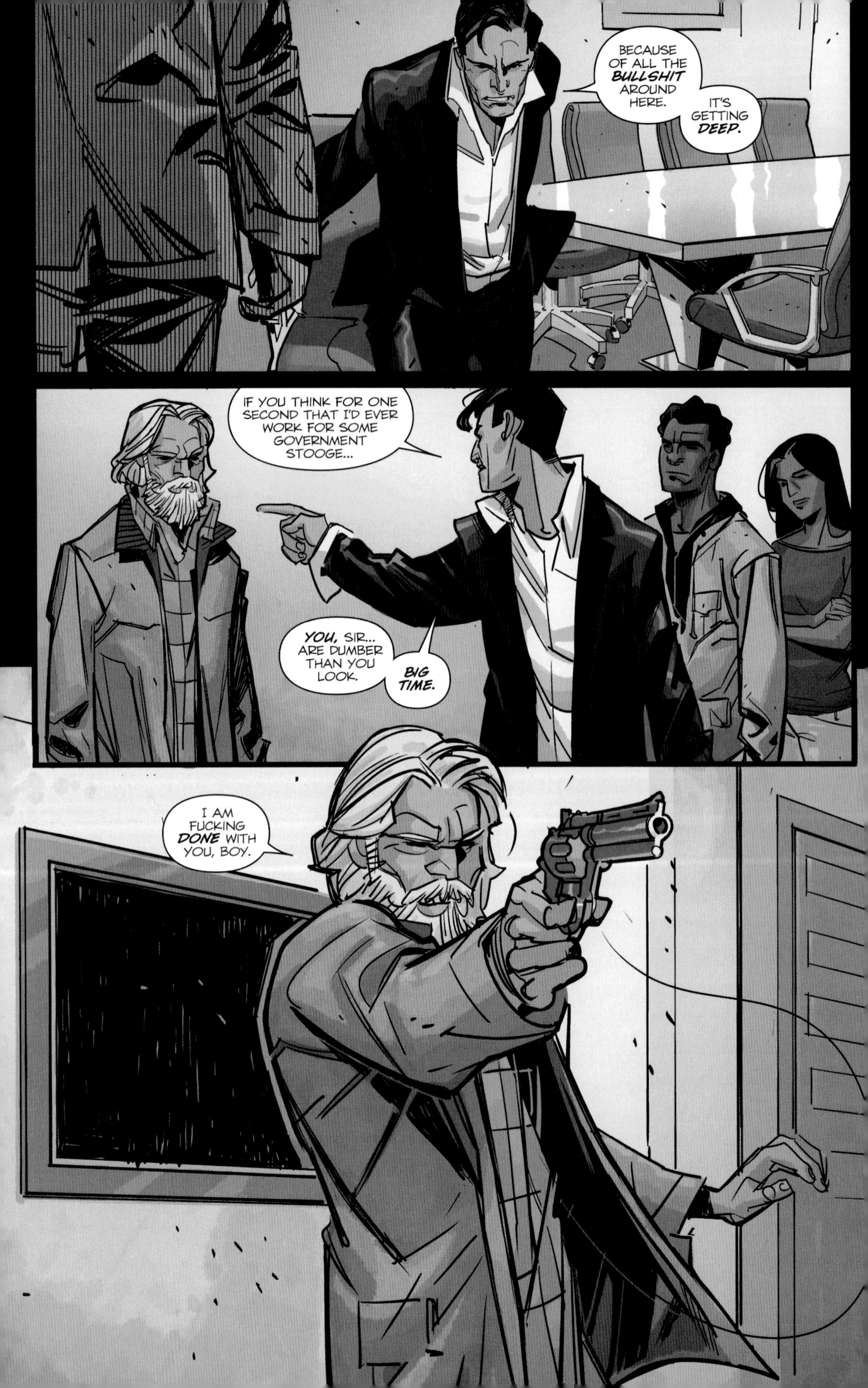
BECAUSE OF ALL THE BULLSHIT AROUND HERE.
IT'S GETTING DEEP.
IF YOU THINK FOR ONE SECOND THAT I'D EVER WORK FOR SOME GOVERNMENT STOOGE...
YOU, SIR... ARE DUMBER THAN YOU LOOK.
BIG TIME.
I AM FUCKING DONE WITH YOU, BOY.

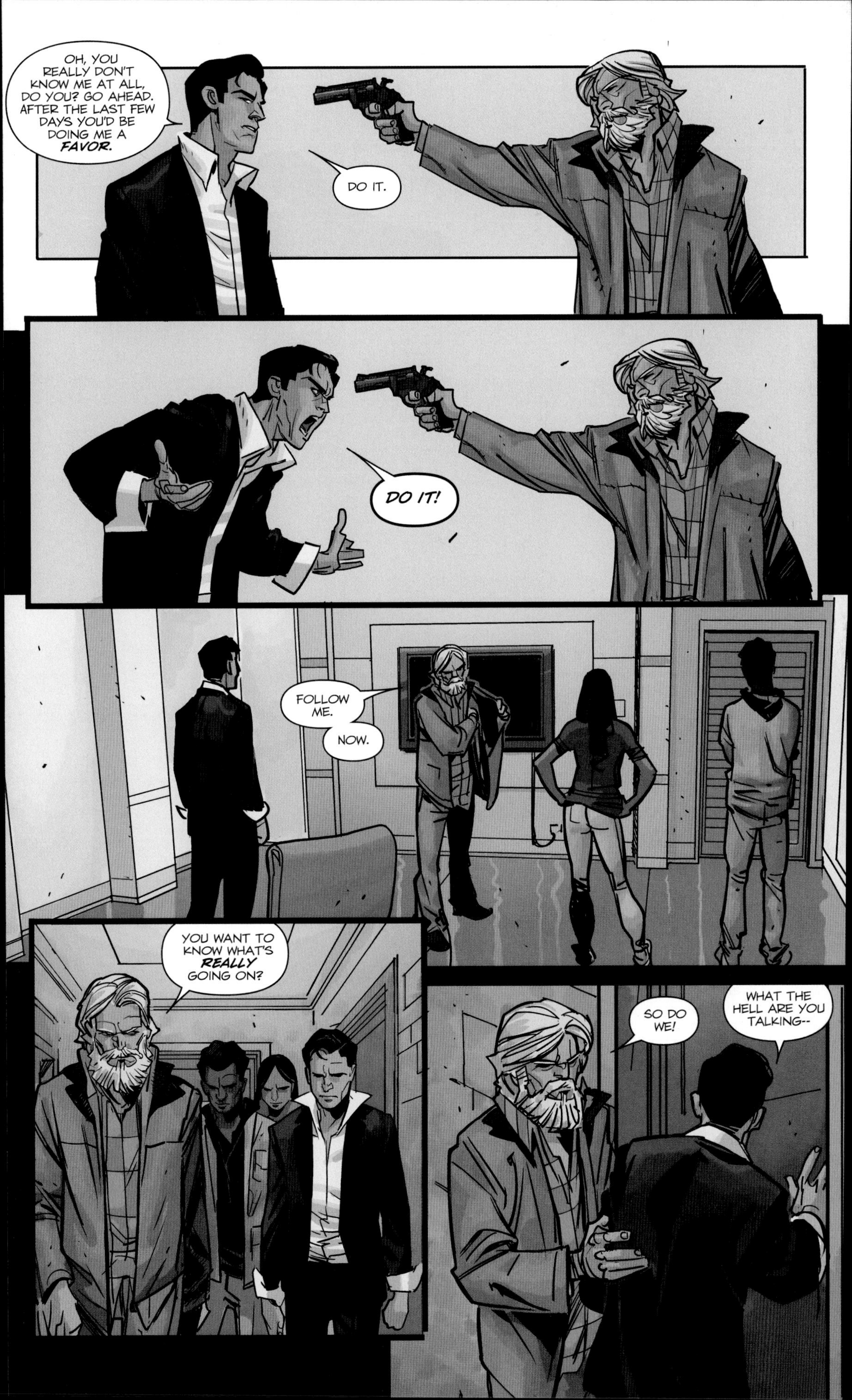
OH, YOU REALLY DON'T KNOW ME AT ALL, DO YOU? GO AHEAD. AFTER THE LAST FEW DAYS YOU'D BE DOING ME A FAVOR.
DO IT.
DO IT!
FOLLOW ME.
NOW.
YOU WANT TO KNOW WHAT'S REALLY GOING ON?
SO DO WE!
WHAT THE HELL ARE YOU TALKING--

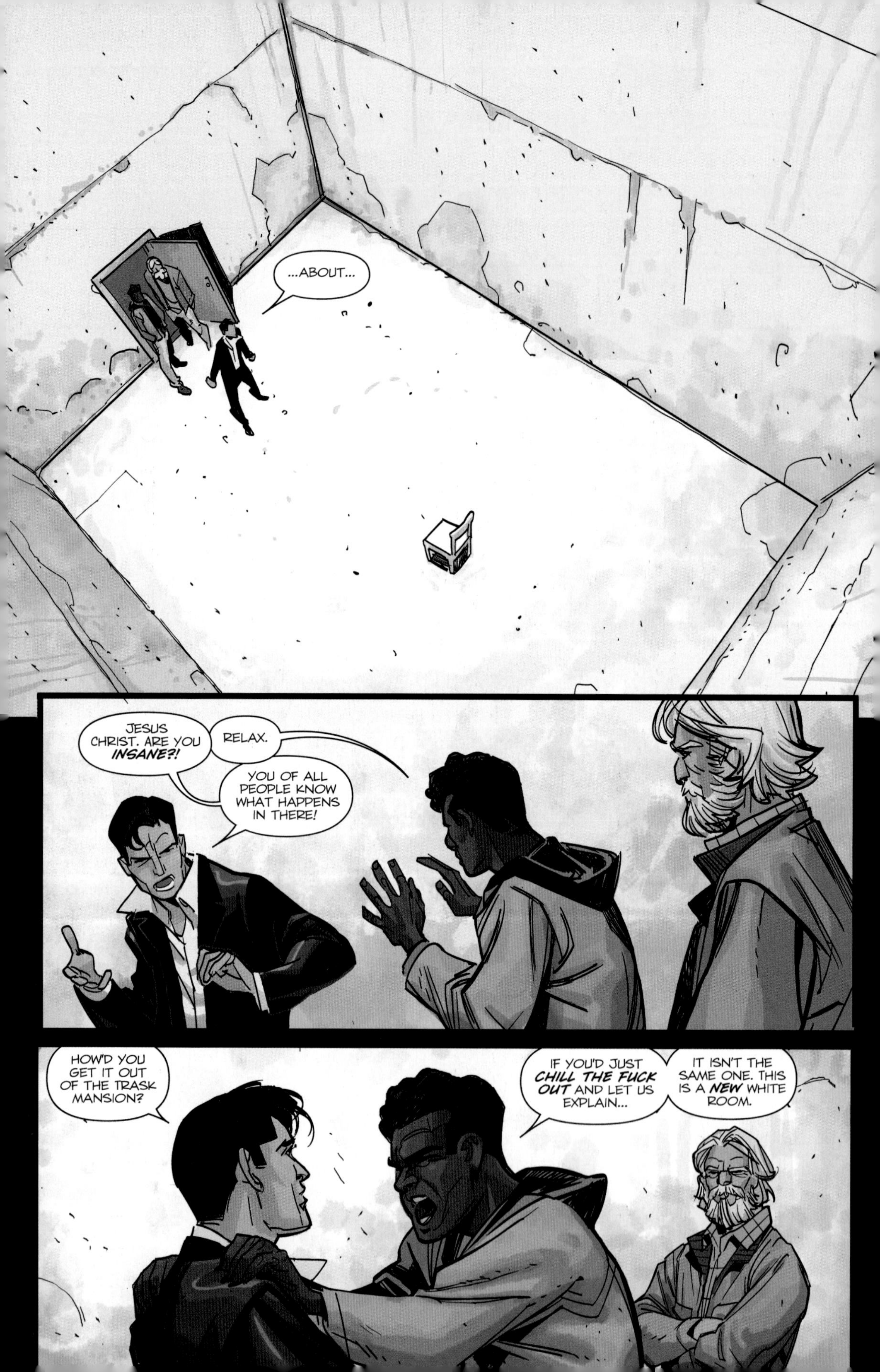
...ABOUT...
JESUS CHRIST. ARE YOU *INSANE?!*
RELAX.
YOU OF ALL PEOPLE KNOW WHAT HAPPENS IN THERE!
HOW'D YOU GET IT OUT OF THE TRASK MANSION?
IF YOU'D JUST *CHILL THE FUCK OUT* AND LET US EXPLAIN...
IT ISN'T THE SAME ONE. THIS IS A *NEW* WHITE ROOM.

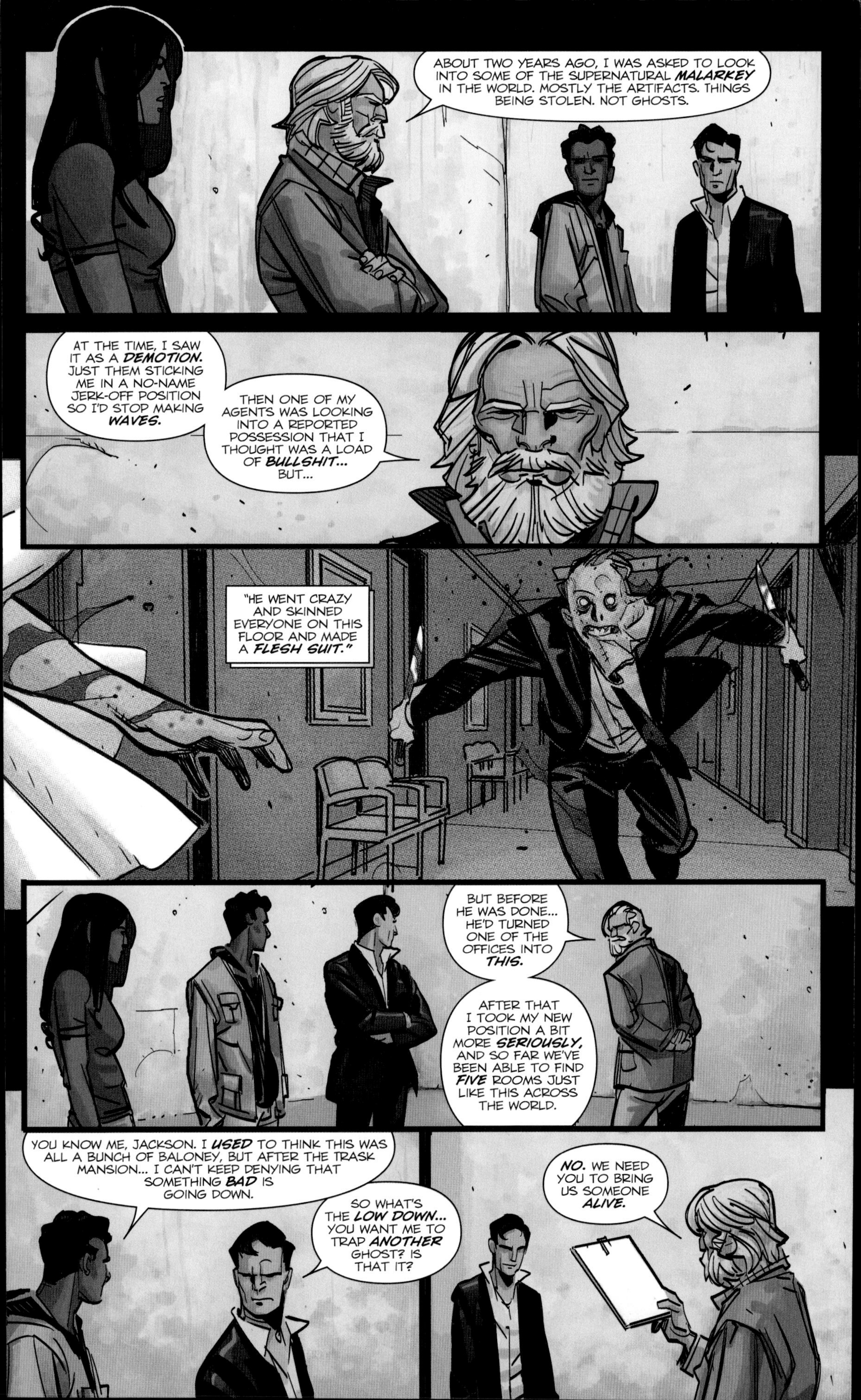
ABOUT TWO YEARS AGO, I WAS ASKED TO LOOK INTO SOME OF THE SUPERNATURAL MALARKEY IN THE WORLD. MOSTLY THE ARTIFACTS. THINGS BEING STOLEN. NOT GHOSTS.
AT THE TIME, I SAW IT AS A DEMOTION. JUST THEM STICKING ME IN A NO-NAME JERK-OFF POSITION SO I'D STOP MAKING WAVES.
THEN ONE OF MY AGENTS WAS LOOKING INTO A REPORTED POSSESSION THAT I THOUGHT WAS A LOAD OF BULLSHIT... BUT...
"HE WENT CRAZY AND SKINNED EVERYONE ON THIS FLOOR AND MADE A FLESH SUIT."
BUT BEFORE HE WAS DONE... HE'D TURNED ONE OF THE OFFICES INTO THIS.
AFTER THAT I TOOK MY NEW POSITION A BIT MORE SERIOUSLY, AND SO FAR WE'VE BEEN ABLE TO FIND FIVE ROOMS JUST LIKE THIS ACROSS THE WORLD.
YOU KNOW ME, JACKSON. I USED TO THINK THIS WAS ALL A BUNCH OF BALONEY, BUT AFTER THE TRASK MANSION... I CAN'T KEEP DENYING THAT SOMETHING BAD IS GOING DOWN.
SO WHAT'S THE LOW DOWN... YOU WANT ME TO TRAP ANOTHER GHOST? IS THAT IT?
NO. WE NEED YOU TO BRING US SOMEONE ALIVE.

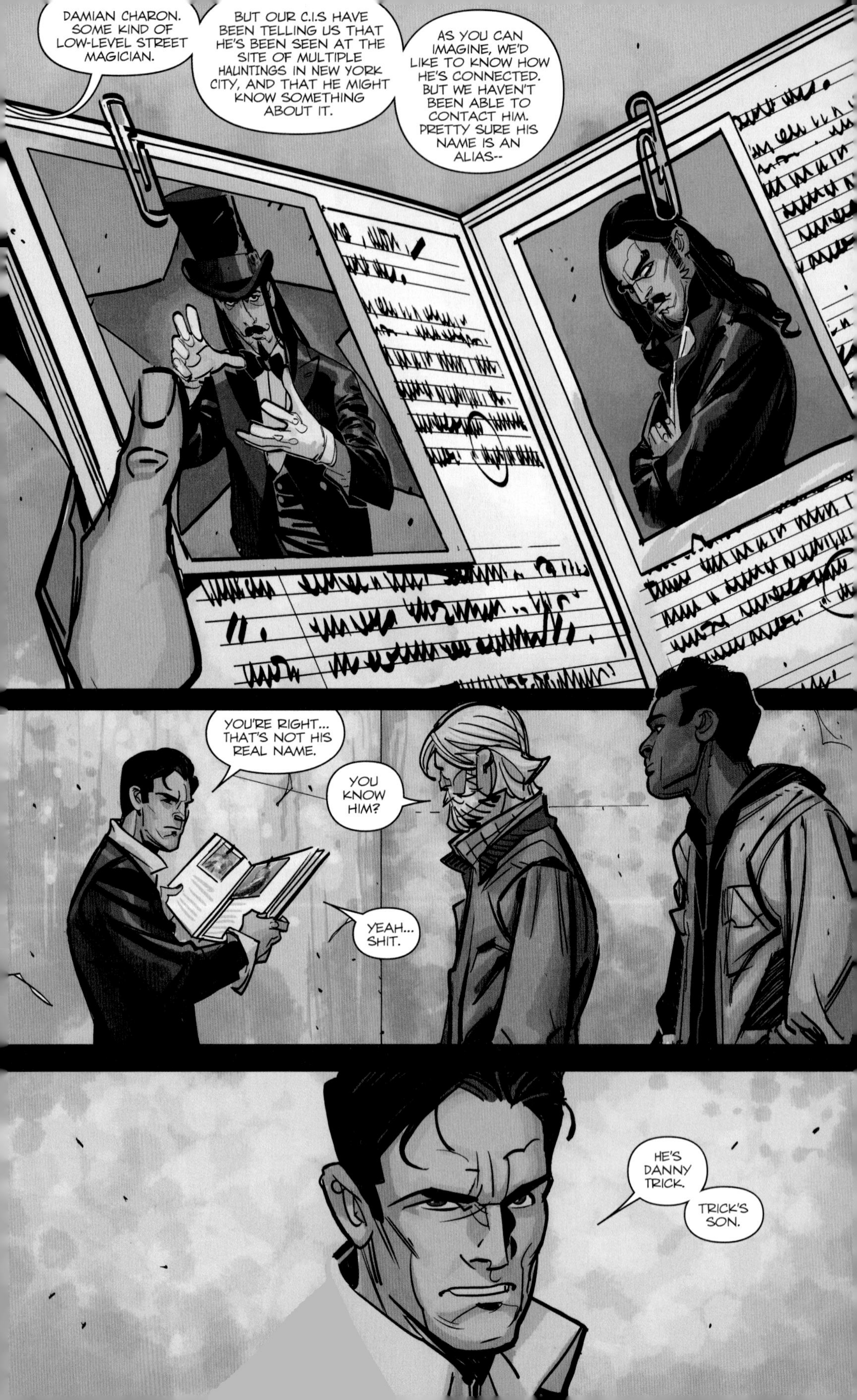
DAMIAN CHARON. SOME KIND OF LOW-LEVEL STREET MAGICIAN.
BUT OUR C.I.S HAVE BEEN TELLING US THAT HE'S BEEN SEEN AT THE SITE OF MULTIPLE HAUNTINGS IN NEW YORK CITY, AND THAT HE MIGHT KNOW SOMETHING ABOUT IT.
AS YOU CAN IMAGINE, WE'D LIKE TO KNOW HOW HE'S CONNECTED. BUT WE HAVEN'T BEEN ABLE TO CONTACT HIM. PRETTY SURE HIS NAME IS AN ALIAS--
YOU'RE RIGHT... THAT'S NOT HIS REAL NAME.
YOU KNOW HIM?
YEAH... SHIT.
HE'S DANNY TRICK.
TRICK'S SON.

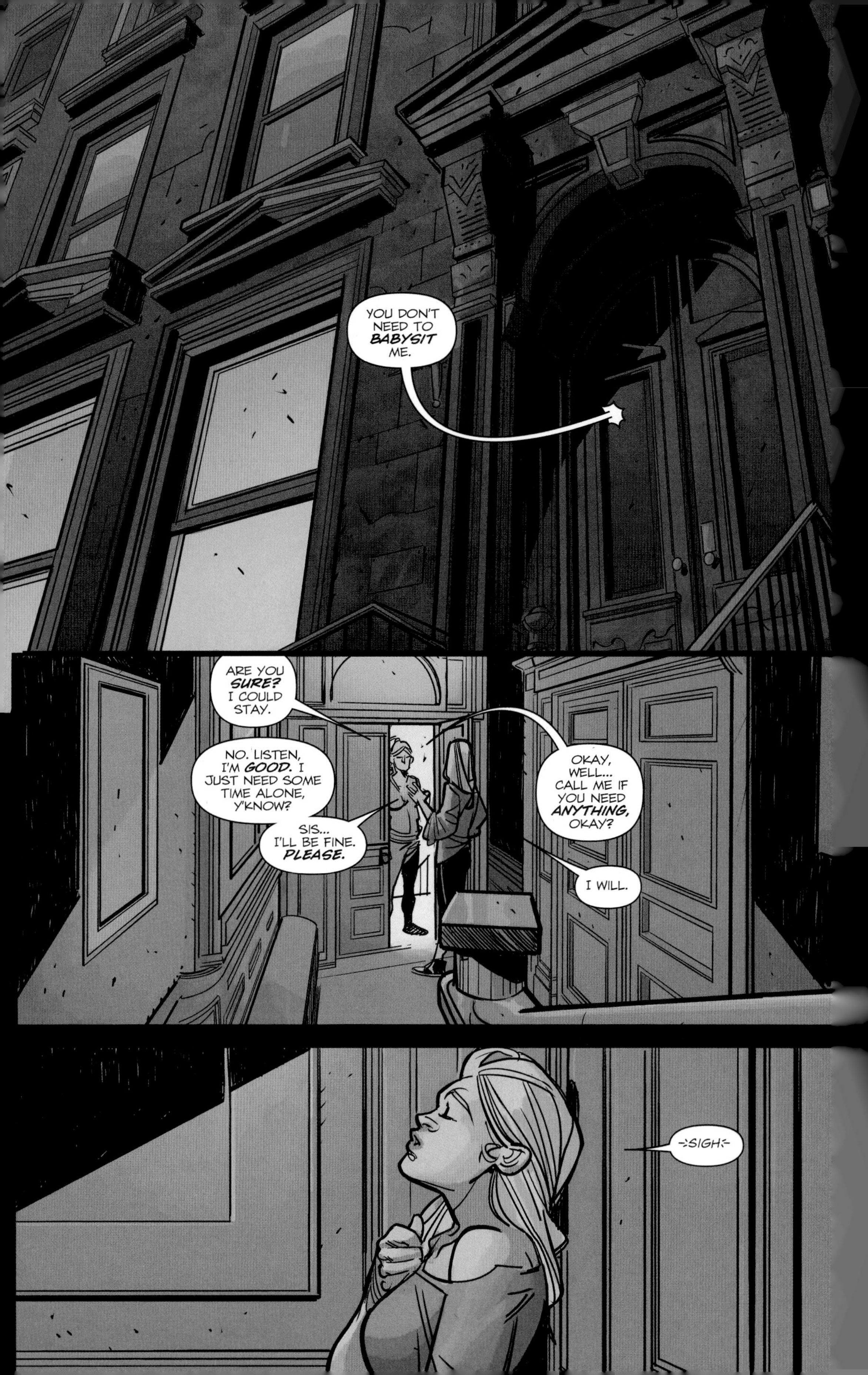
YOU DON'T NEED TO BABYSIT ME.
ARE YOU SURE? I COULD STAY.
NO. LISTEN, I'M GOOD. I JUST NEED SOME TIME ALONE, Y'KNOW?
SIS... I'LL BE FINE. PLEASE.
OKAY, WELL... CALL ME IF YOU NEED ANYTHING, OKAY?
I WILL.
-SIGH-

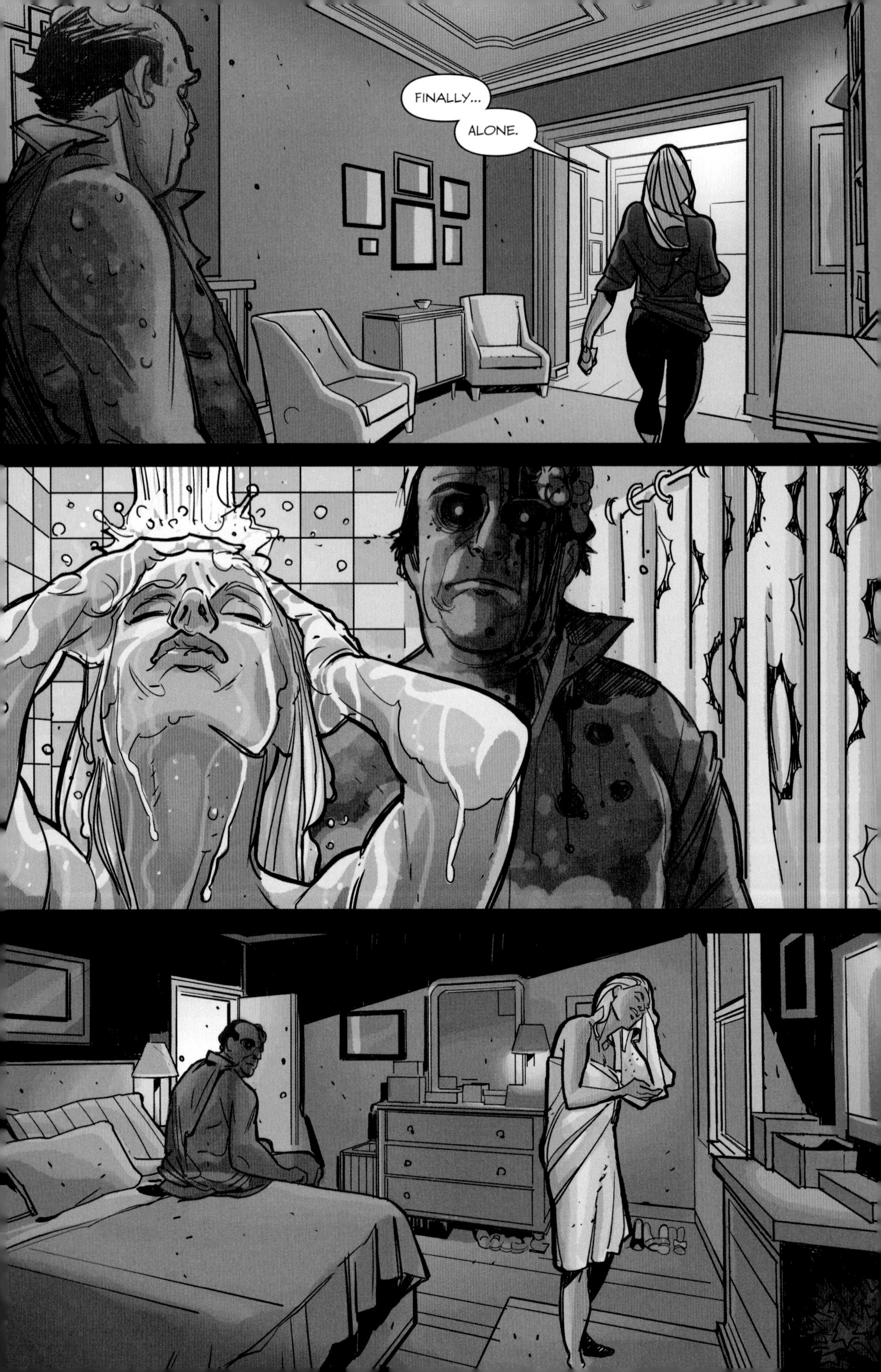
FINALLY...
ALONE.

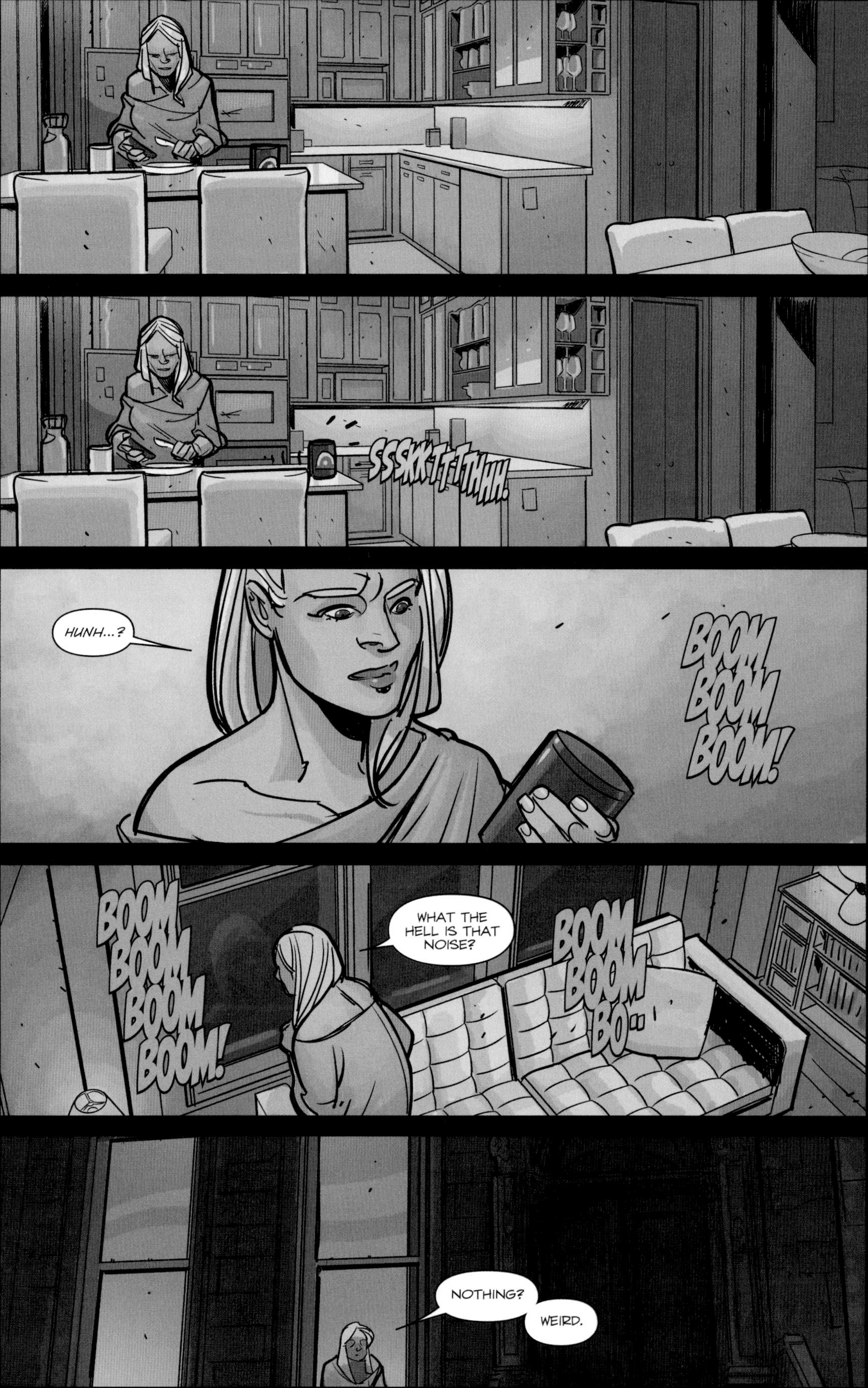
SSSKKTTTTHHH!
HUNH...?
BOOM BOOM BOOM!
BOOM BOOM BOOM BOOM!
WHAT THE HELL IS THAT NOISE?
BOOM BOOM BO..
NOTHING?
WEIRD.

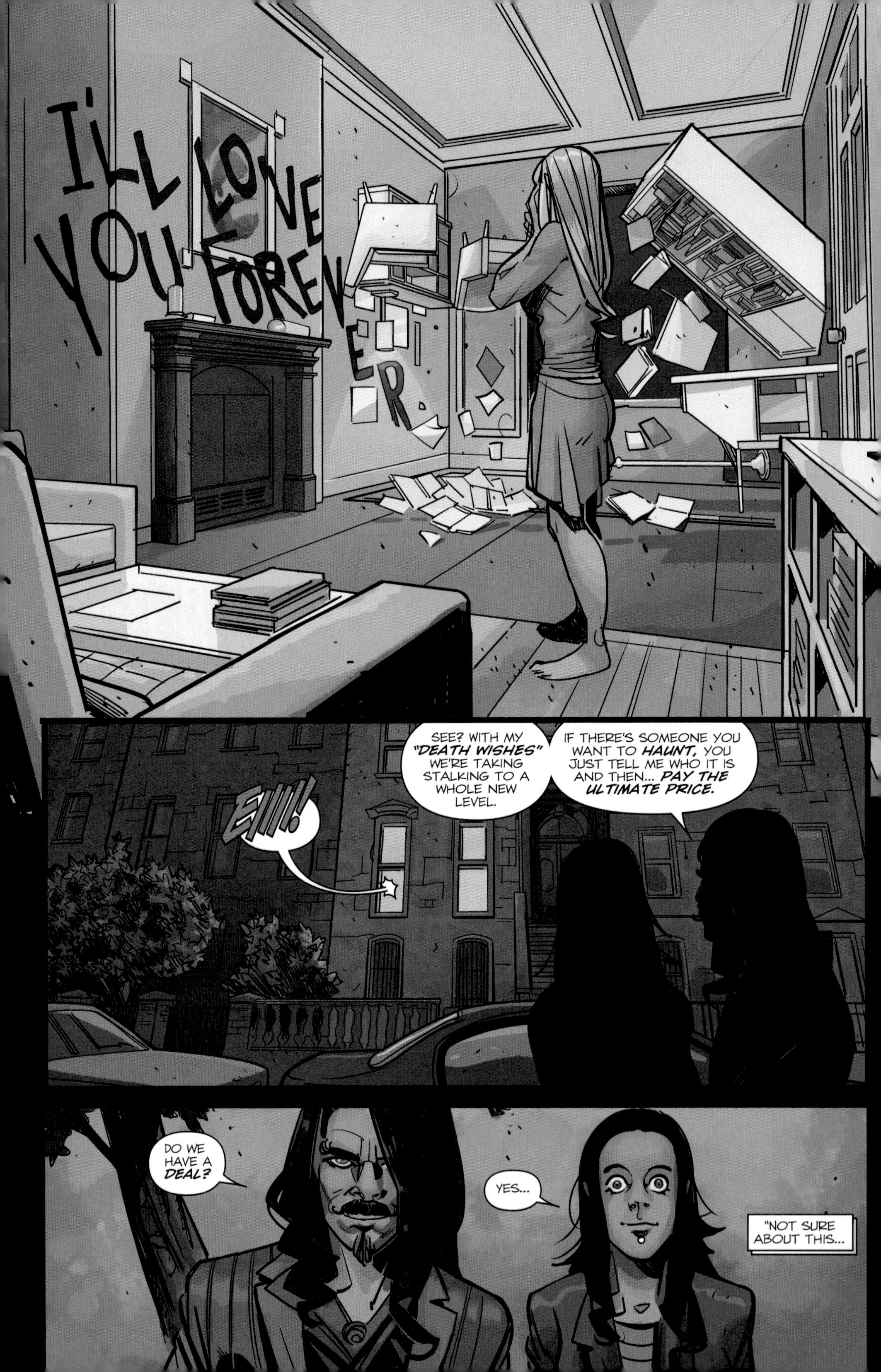

I'LL LOVE YOU FOREVER
SEE? WITH MY "DEATH WISHES" WE'RE TAKING STALKING TO A WHOLE NEW LEVEL.
IF THERE'S SOMEONE YOU WANT TO HAUNT, YOU JUST TELL ME WHO IT IS AND THEN... PAY THE ULTIMATE PRICE.
EIII!
DO WE HAVE A DEAL?
YES...
"NOT SURE ABOUT THIS...

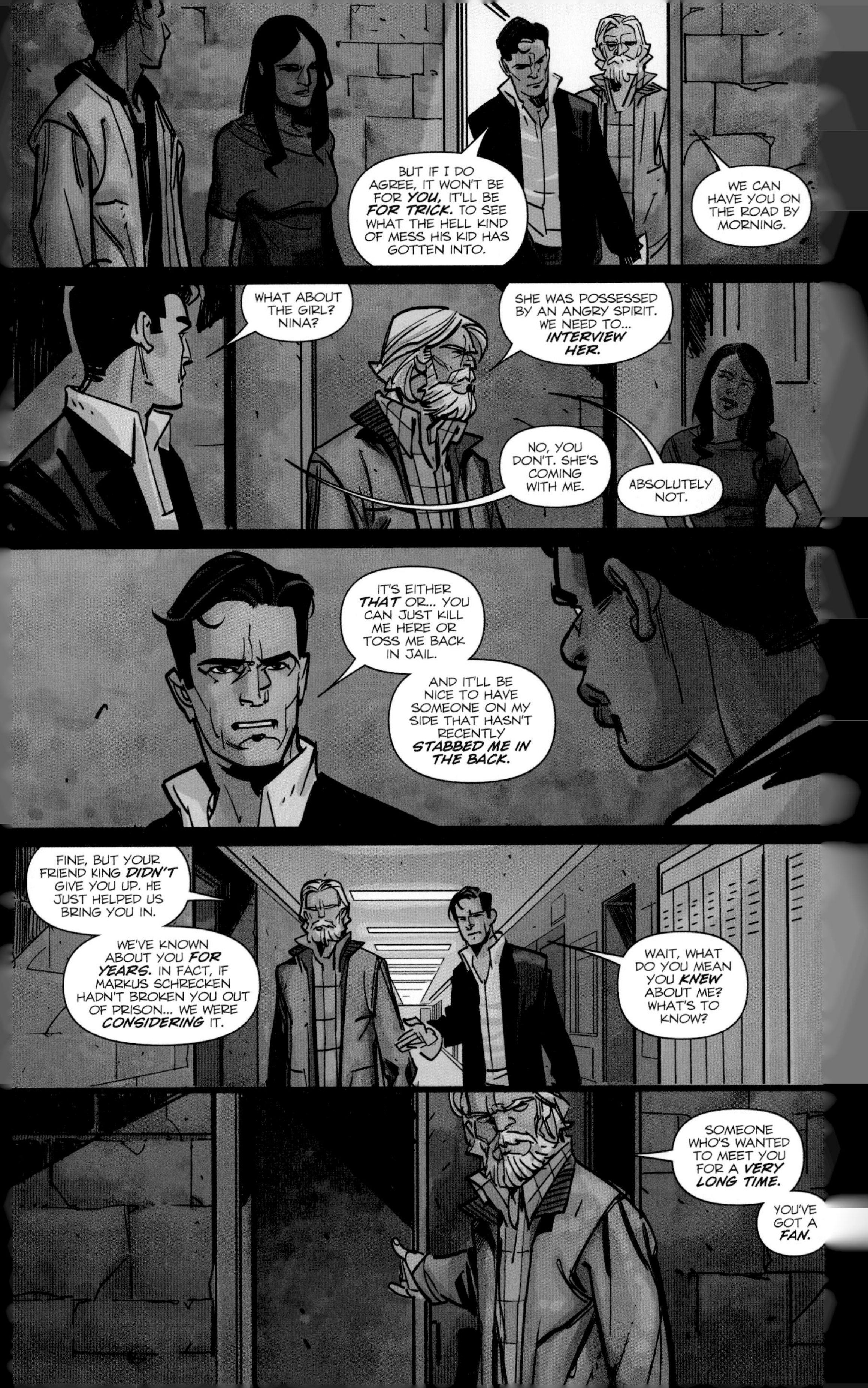
BUT IF I DO AGREE, IT WON'T BE FOR YOU, IT'LL BE FOR TRICK. TO SEE WHAT THE HELL KIND OF MESS HIS KID HAS GOTTEN INTO.
WE CAN HAVE YOU ON THE ROAD BY MORNING.
WHAT ABOUT THE GIRL? NINA?
SHE WAS POSSESSED BY AN ANGRY SPIRIT. WE NEED TO... INTERVIEW HER.
NO, YOU DON'T. SHE'S COMING WITH ME.
ABSOLUTELY NOT.
IT'S EITHER THAT OR... YOU CAN JUST KILL ME HERE OR TOSS ME BACK IN JAIL.
AND IT'LL BE NICE TO HAVE SOMEONE ON MY SIDE THAT HASN'T RECENTLY STABBED ME IN THE BACK.
FINE, BUT YOUR FRIEND KING DIDN'T GIVE YOU UP. HE JUST HELPED US BRING YOU IN.
WE'VE KNOWN ABOUT YOU FOR YEARS. IN FACT, IF MARKUS SCHRECKEN HADN'T BROKEN YOU OUT OF PRISON... WE WERE CONSIDERING IT.
WAIT, WHAT DO YOU MEAN YOU KNEW ABOUT ME? WHAT'S TO KNOW?
SOMEONE WHO'S WANTED TO MEET YOU FOR A VERY LONG TIME.
YOU'VE GOT A FAN.

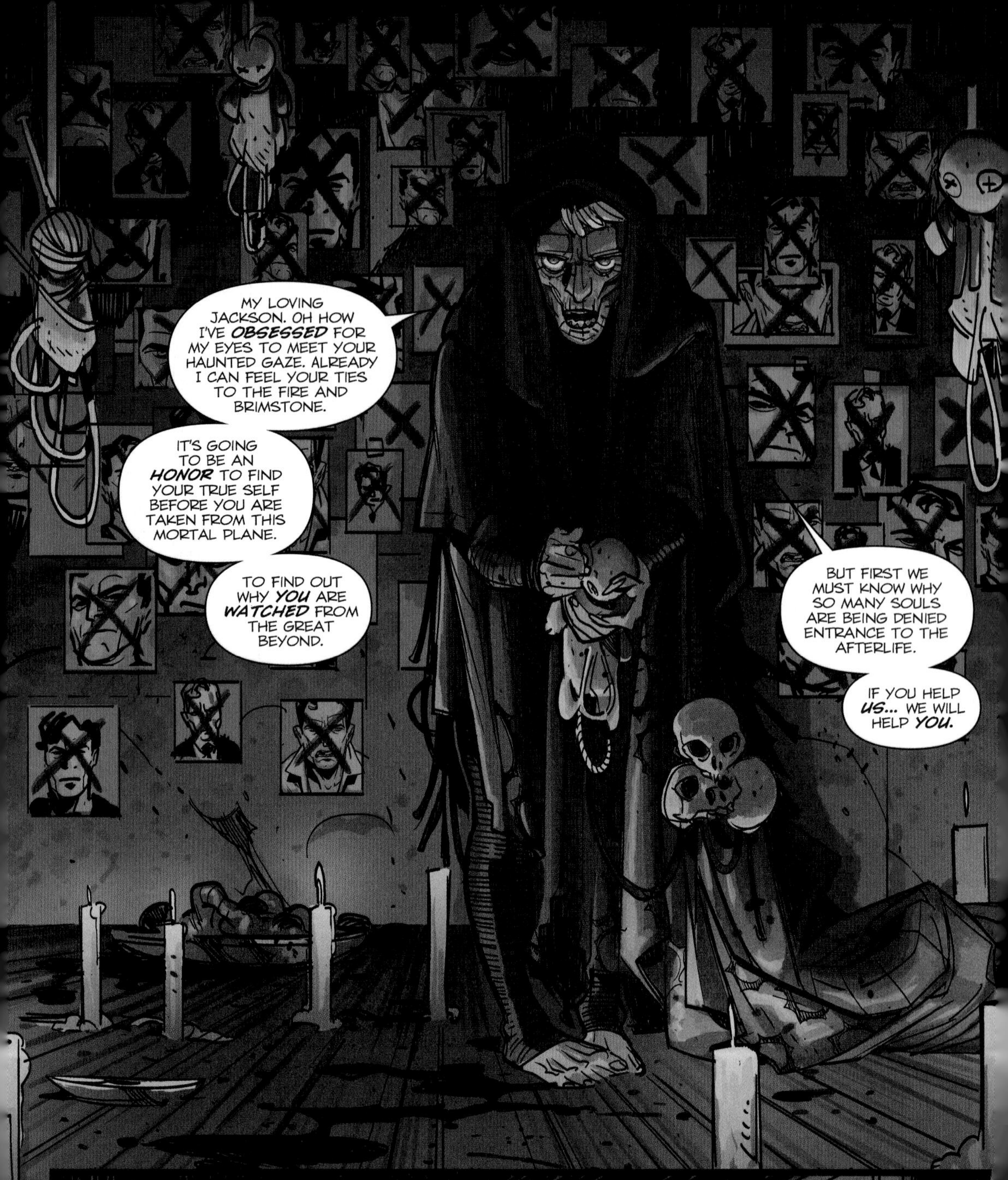
MY LOVING JACKSON. OH HOW I'VE **OBSESSED** FOR MY EYES TO MEET YOUR HAUNTED GAZE. ALREADY I CAN FEEL YOUR TIES TO THE FIRE AND BRIMSTONE.
IT'S GOING TO BE AN **HONOR** TO FIND YOUR TRUE SELF BEFORE YOU ARE TAKEN FROM THIS MORTAL PLANE.
TO FIND OUT WHY **YOU** ARE **WATCHED** FROM THE GREAT BEYOND.
BUT FIRST WE MUST KNOW WHY SO MANY SOULS ARE BEING DENIED ENTRANCE TO THE AFTERLIFE.
IF YOU HELP **US...** WE WILL HELP **YOU.**

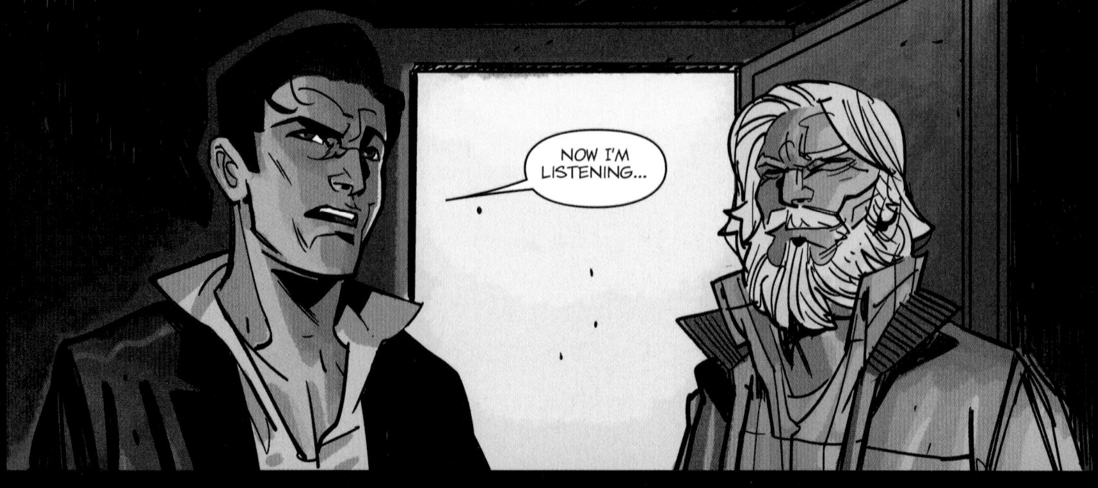
NOW I'M LISTENING...

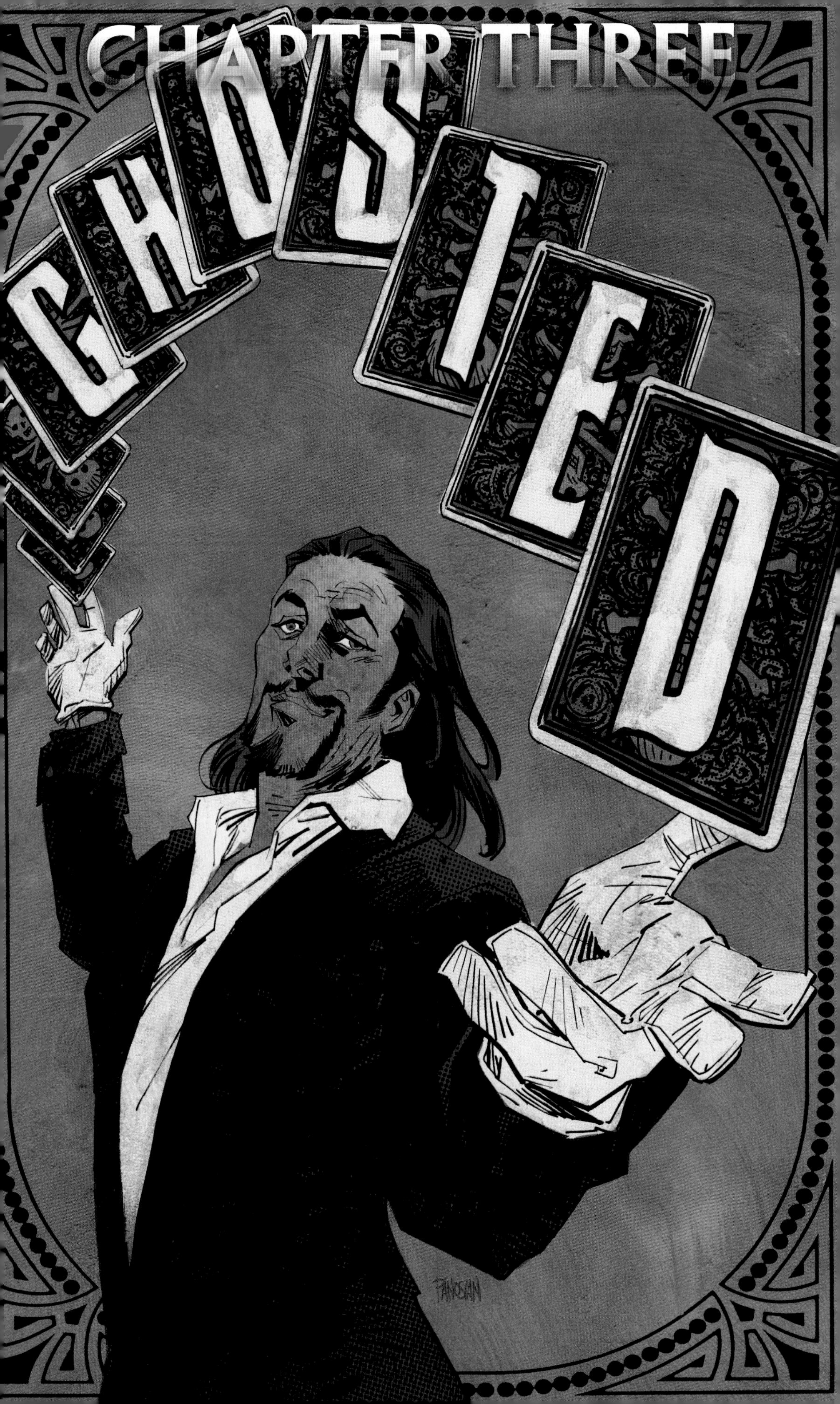
CHAPTER THREE
GHOSTED
PANOSIAN

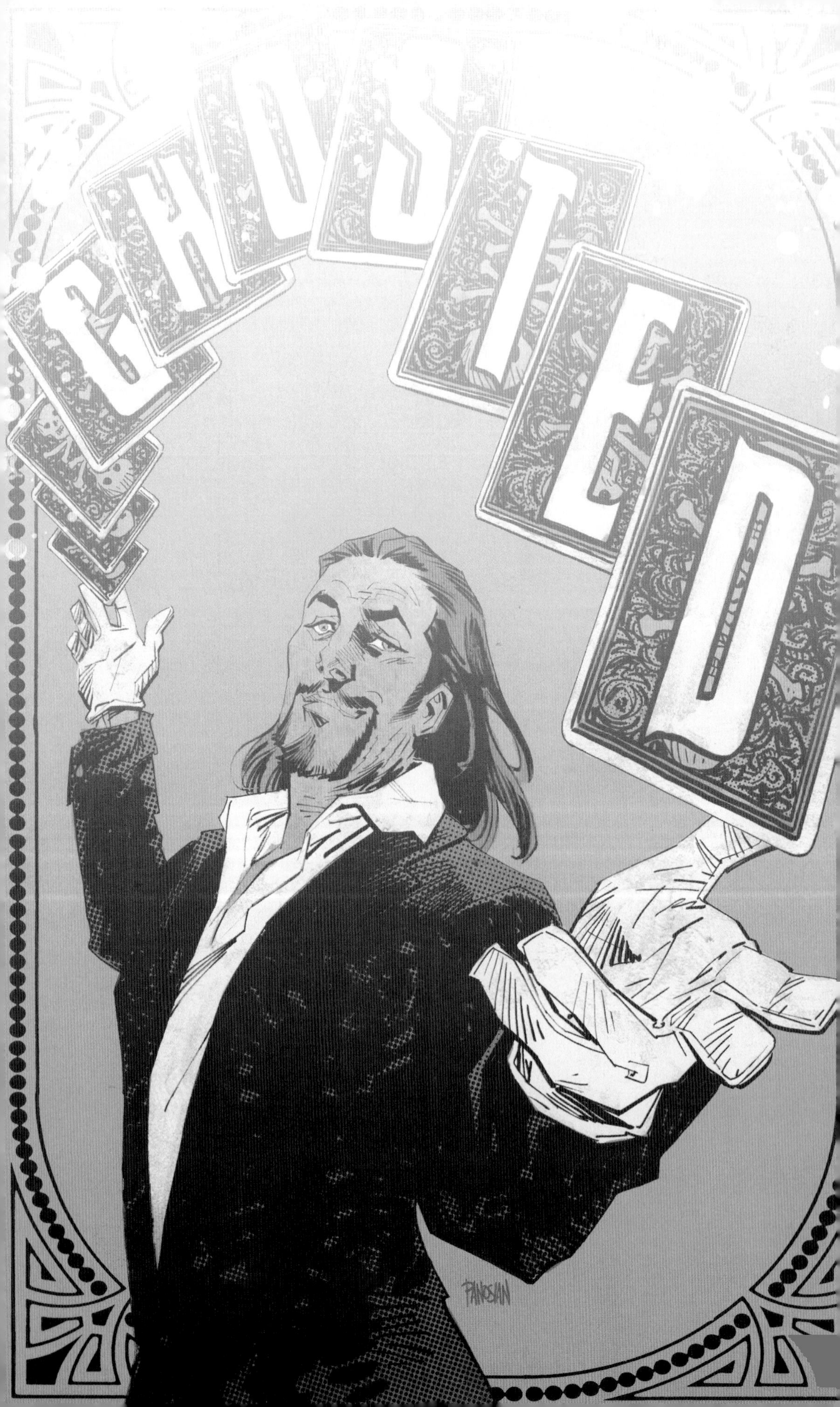
GHOSTED
PANOSIAN

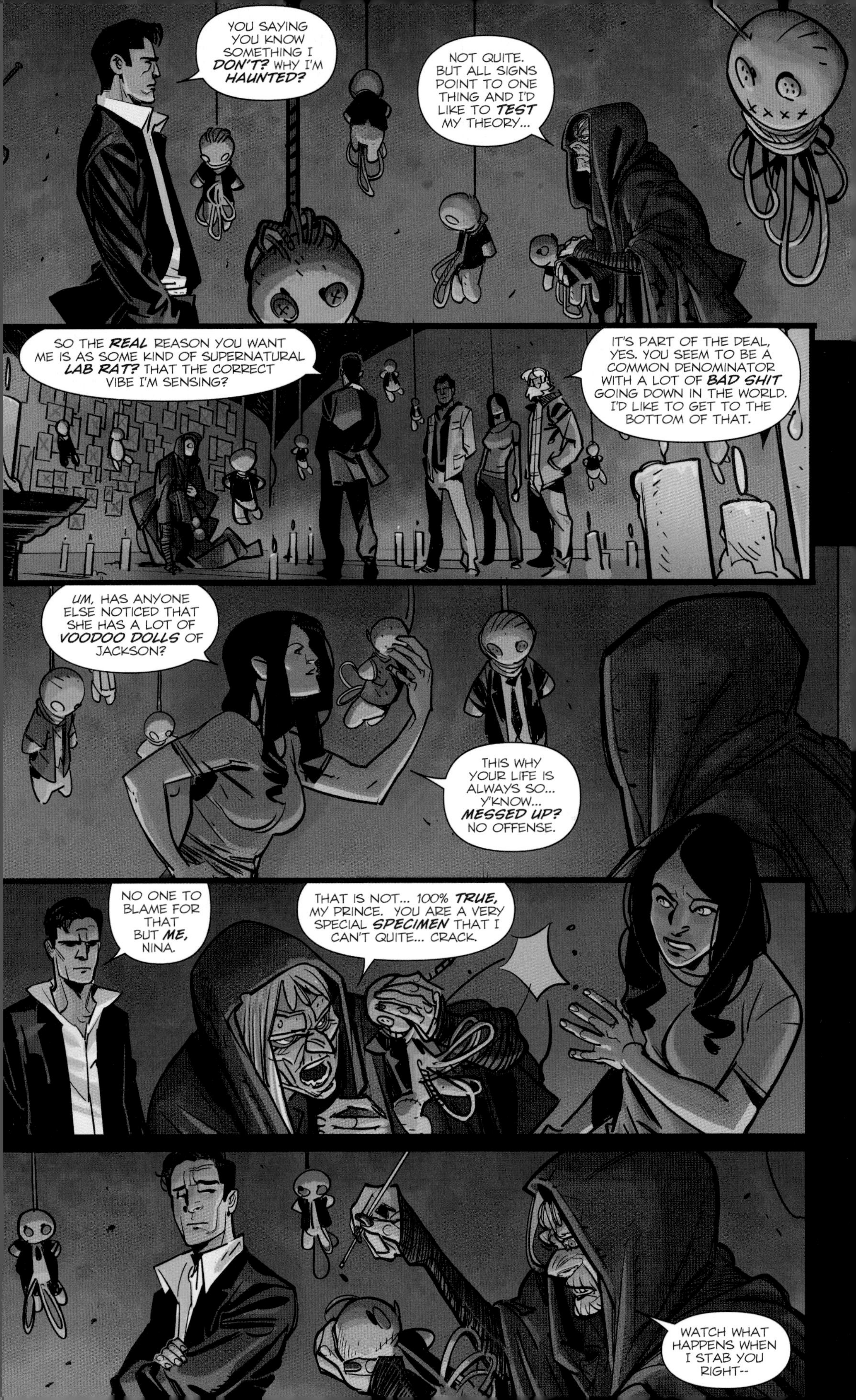
YOU SAYING YOU KNOW SOMETHING I DON'T? WHY I'M HAUNTED?
NOT QUITE. BUT ALL SIGNS POINT TO ONE THING AND I'D LIKE TO TEST MY THEORY...
SO THE REAL REASON YOU WANT ME IS AS SOME KIND OF SUPERNATURAL LAB RAT? THAT THE CORRECT VIBE I'M SENSING?
IT'S PART OF THE DEAL, YES. YOU SEEM TO BE A COMMON DENOMINATOR WITH A LOT OF BAD SHIT GOING DOWN IN THE WORLD. I'D LIKE TO GET TO THE BOTTOM OF THAT.
UM, HAS ANYONE ELSE NOTICED THAT SHE HAS A LOT OF VOODOO DOLLS OF JACKSON?
THIS WHY YOUR LIFE IS ALWAYS SO... Y'KNOW... MESSED UP? NO OFFENSE.
NO ONE TO BLAME FOR THAT BUT ME, NINA.
THAT IS NOT... 100% TRUE, MY PRINCE. YOU ARE A VERY SPECIAL SPECIMEN THAT I CAN'T QUITE... CRACK.
WATCH WHAT HAPPENS WHEN I STAB YOU RIGHT--

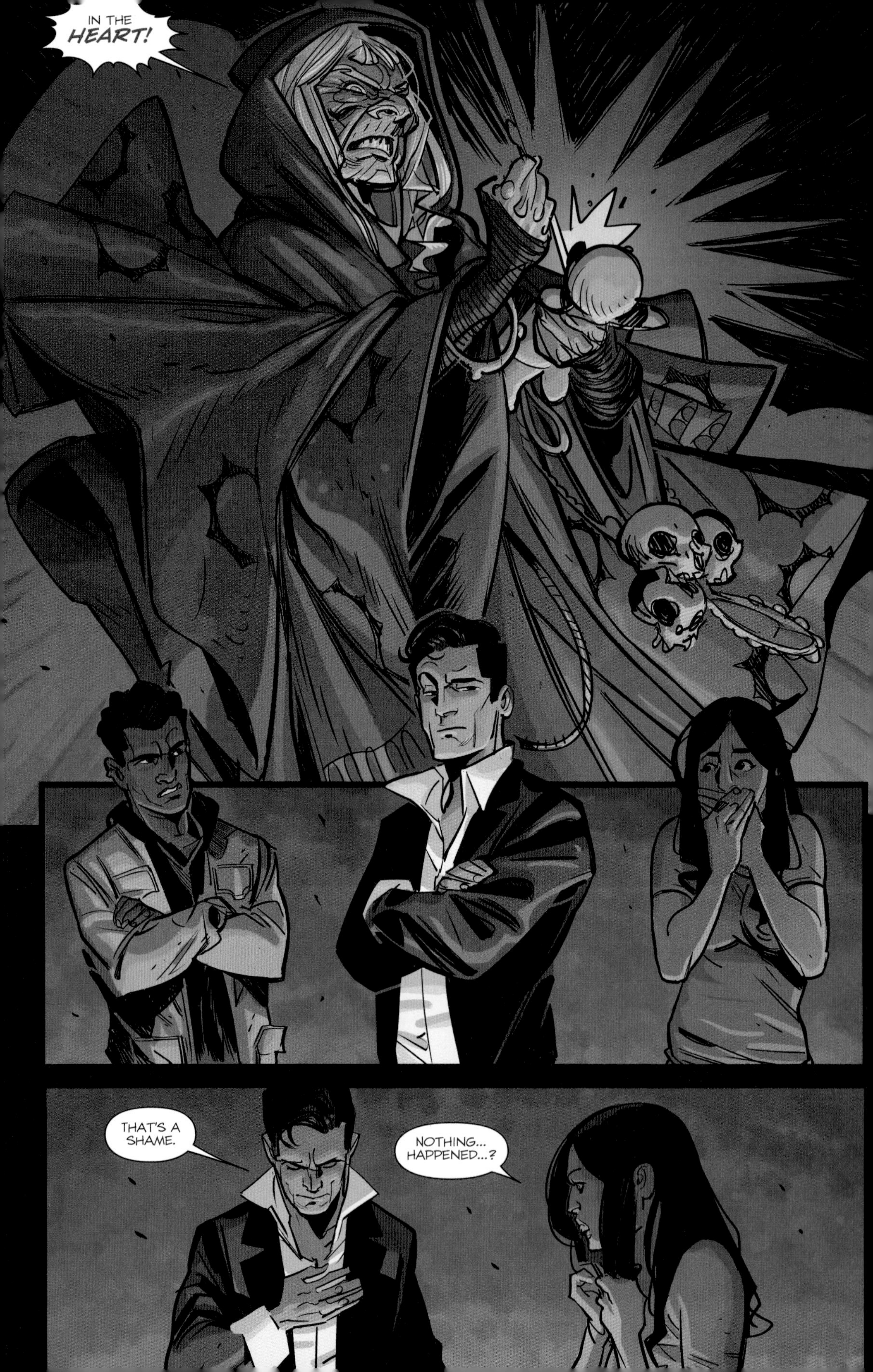
IN THE HEART!
THAT'S A SHAME.
NOTHING... HAPPENED...?

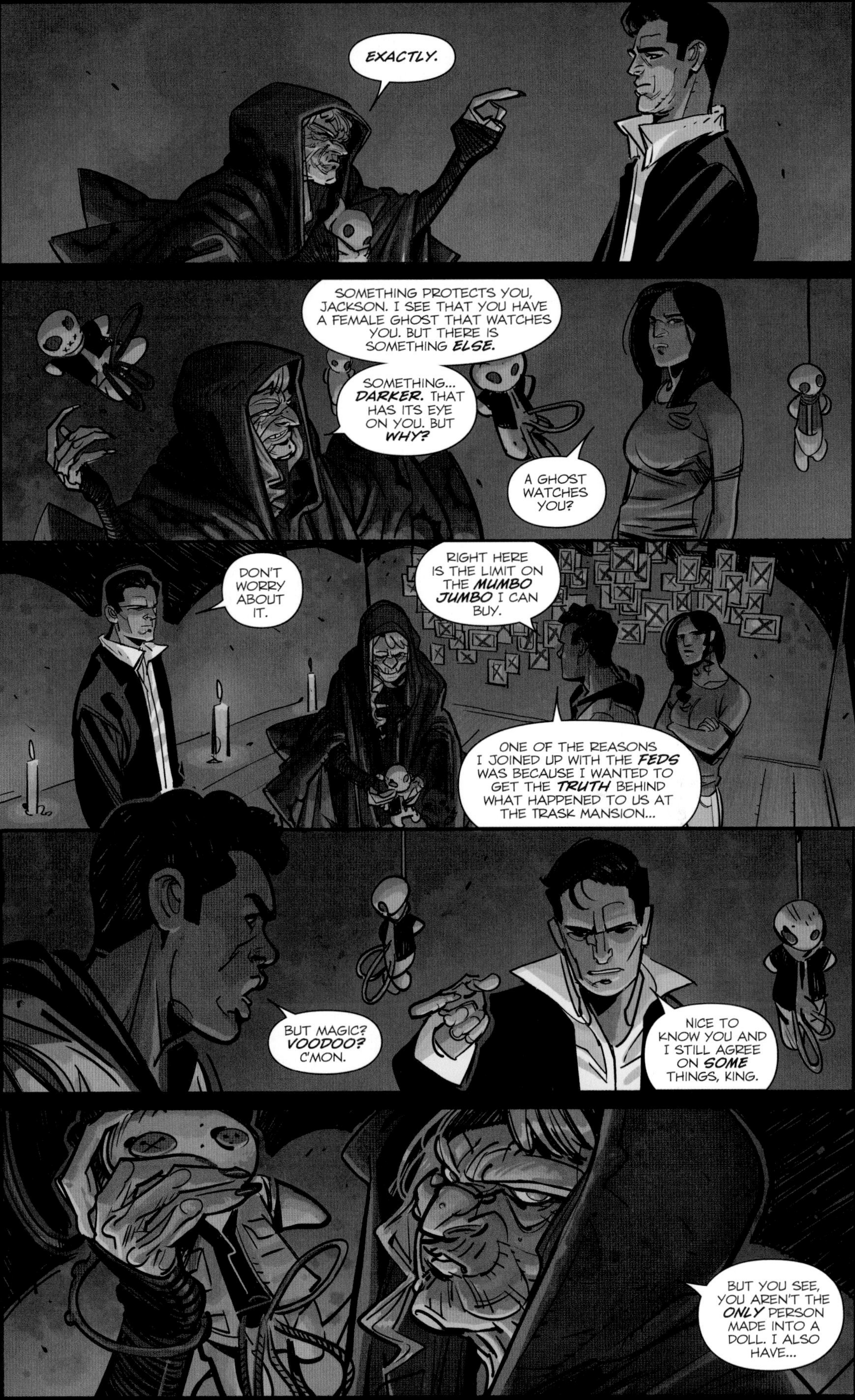
EXACTLY.
SOMETHING PROTECTS YOU, JACKSON. I SEE THAT YOU HAVE A FEMALE GHOST THAT WATCHES YOU. BUT THERE IS SOMETHING ELSE.
SOMETHING... DARKER. THAT HAS ITS EYE ON YOU. BUT WHY?
A GHOST WATCHES YOU?
DON'T WORRY ABOUT IT.
RIGHT HERE IS THE LIMIT ON THE MUMBO JUMBO I CAN BUY.
ONE OF THE REASONS I JOINED UP WITH THE FEDS WAS BECAUSE I WANTED TO GET THE TRUTH BEHIND WHAT HAPPENED TO US AT THE TRASK MANSION...
BUT MAGIC? VOODOO? C'MON.
NICE TO KNOW YOU AND I STILL AGREE ON SOME THINGS, KING.
BUT YOU SEE, YOU AREN'T THE ONLY PERSON MADE INTO A DOLL. I ALSO HAVE...

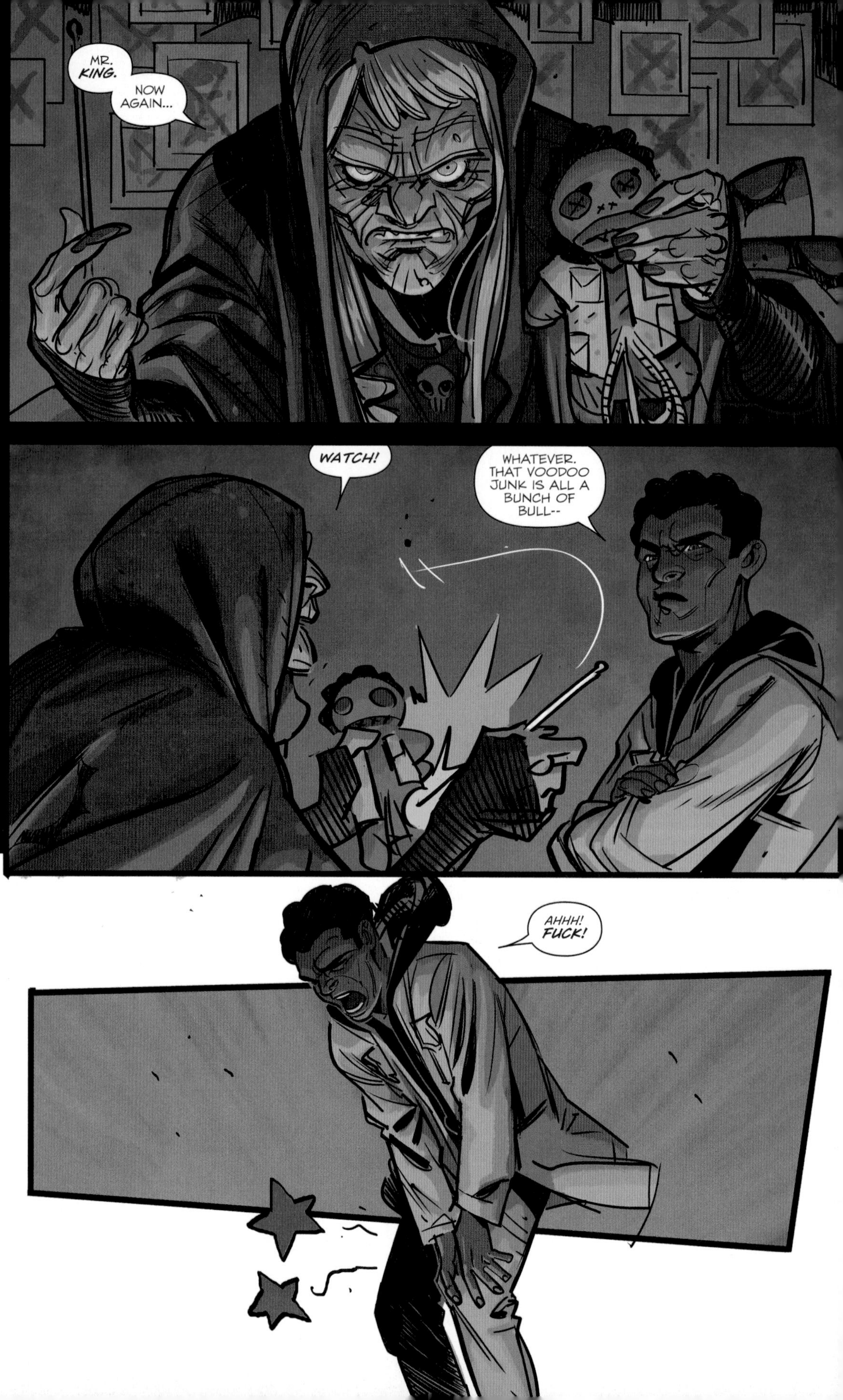
MR. KING.
NOW AGAIN...
WATCH!
WHATEVER. THAT VOODOO JUNK IS ALL A BUNCH OF BULL--
AHHH! FUCK!

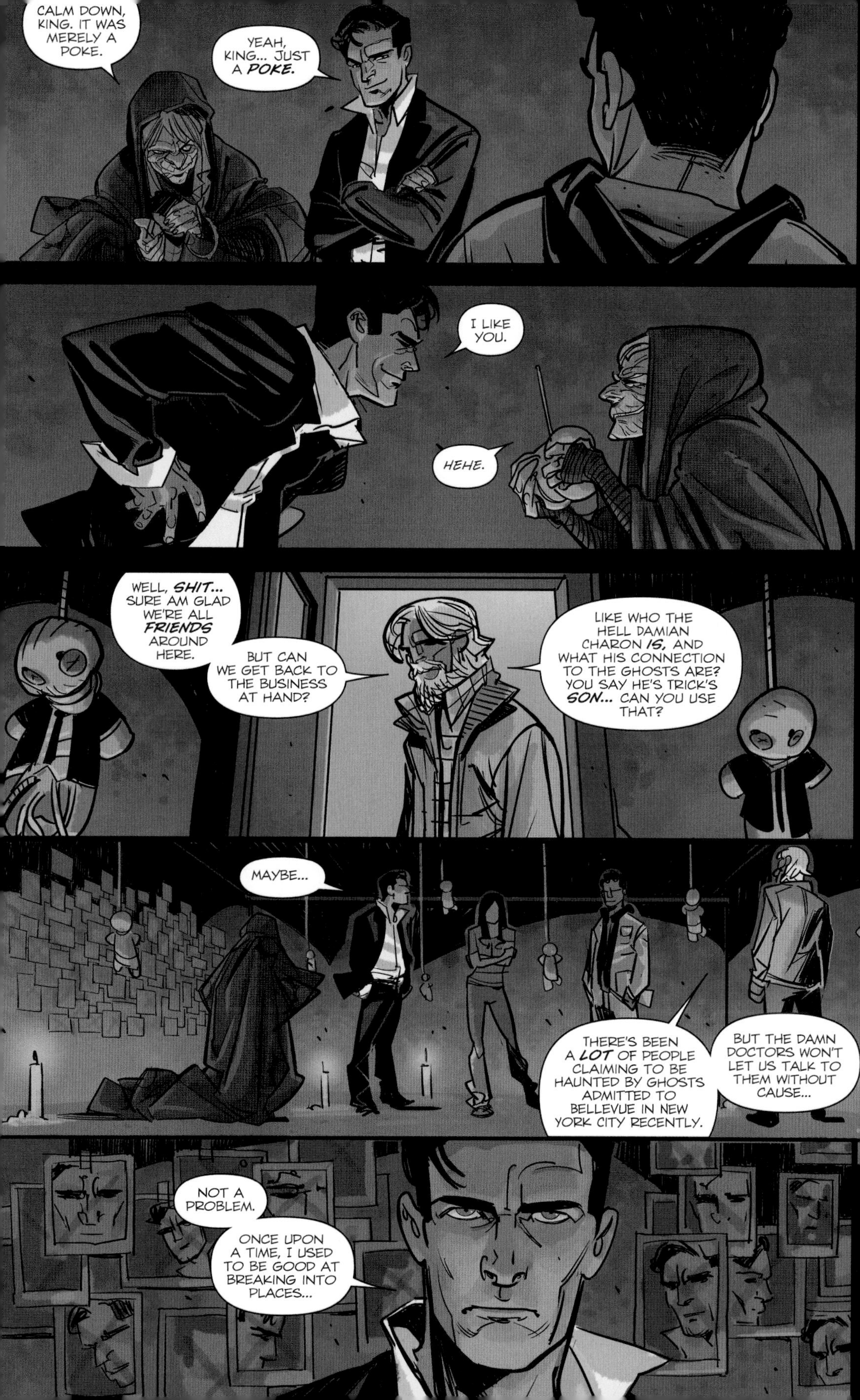
CALM DOWN, KING. IT WAS MERELY A POKE.
YEAH, KING... JUST A POKE.
I LIKE YOU.
HEHE.
WELL, SHIT... SURE AM GLAD WE'RE ALL FRIENDS AROUND HERE.
BUT CAN WE GET BACK TO THE BUSINESS AT HAND?
LIKE WHO THE HELL DAMIAN CHARON IS, AND WHAT HIS CONNECTION TO THE GHOSTS ARE? YOU SAY HE'S TRICK'S SON... CAN YOU USE THAT?
MAYBE...
THERE'S BEEN A LOT OF PEOPLE CLAIMING TO BE HAUNTED BY GHOSTS ADMITTED TO BELLEVUE IN NEW YORK CITY RECENTLY.
BUT THE DAMN DOCTORS WON'T LET US TALK TO THEM WITHOUT CAUSE...
NOT A PROBLEM.
ONCE UPON A TIME, I USED TO BE GOOD AT BREAKING INTO PLACES...

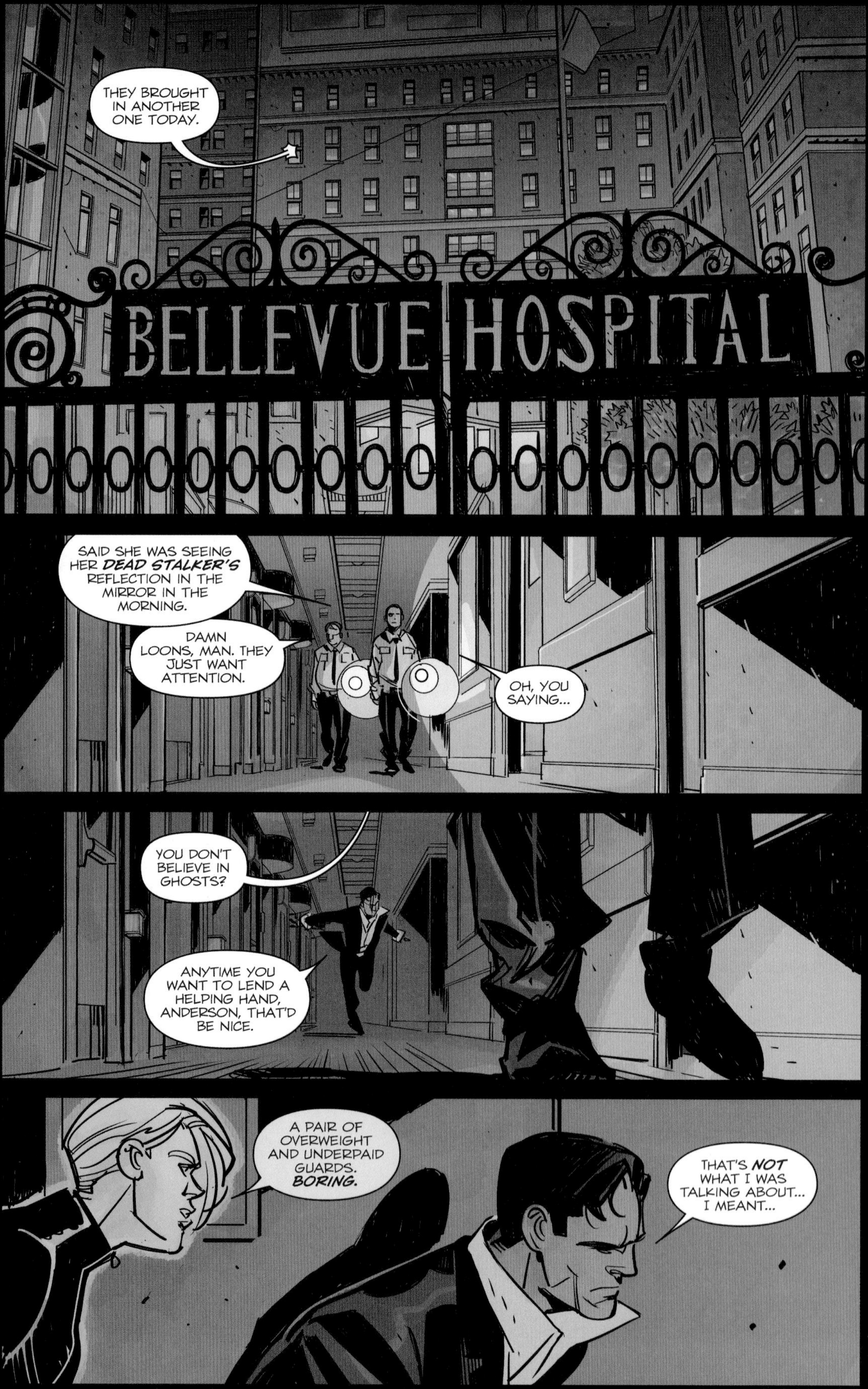
BELLEVUE HOSPITAL
THEY BROUGHT IN ANOTHER ONE TODAY.
SAID SHE WAS SEEING HER *DEAD STALKER'S* REFLECTION IN THE MIRROR IN THE MORNING.
DAMN LOONS, MAN. THEY JUST WANT ATTENTION.
OH, YOU SAYING...
YOU DON'T BELIEVE IN GHOSTS?
ANYTIME YOU WANT TO LEND A HELPING HAND, ANDERSON, THAT'D BE NICE.
A PAIR OF OVERWEIGHT AND UNDERPAID GUARDS. *BORING.*
THAT'S *NOT* WHAT I WAS TALKING ABOUT... I MEANT...

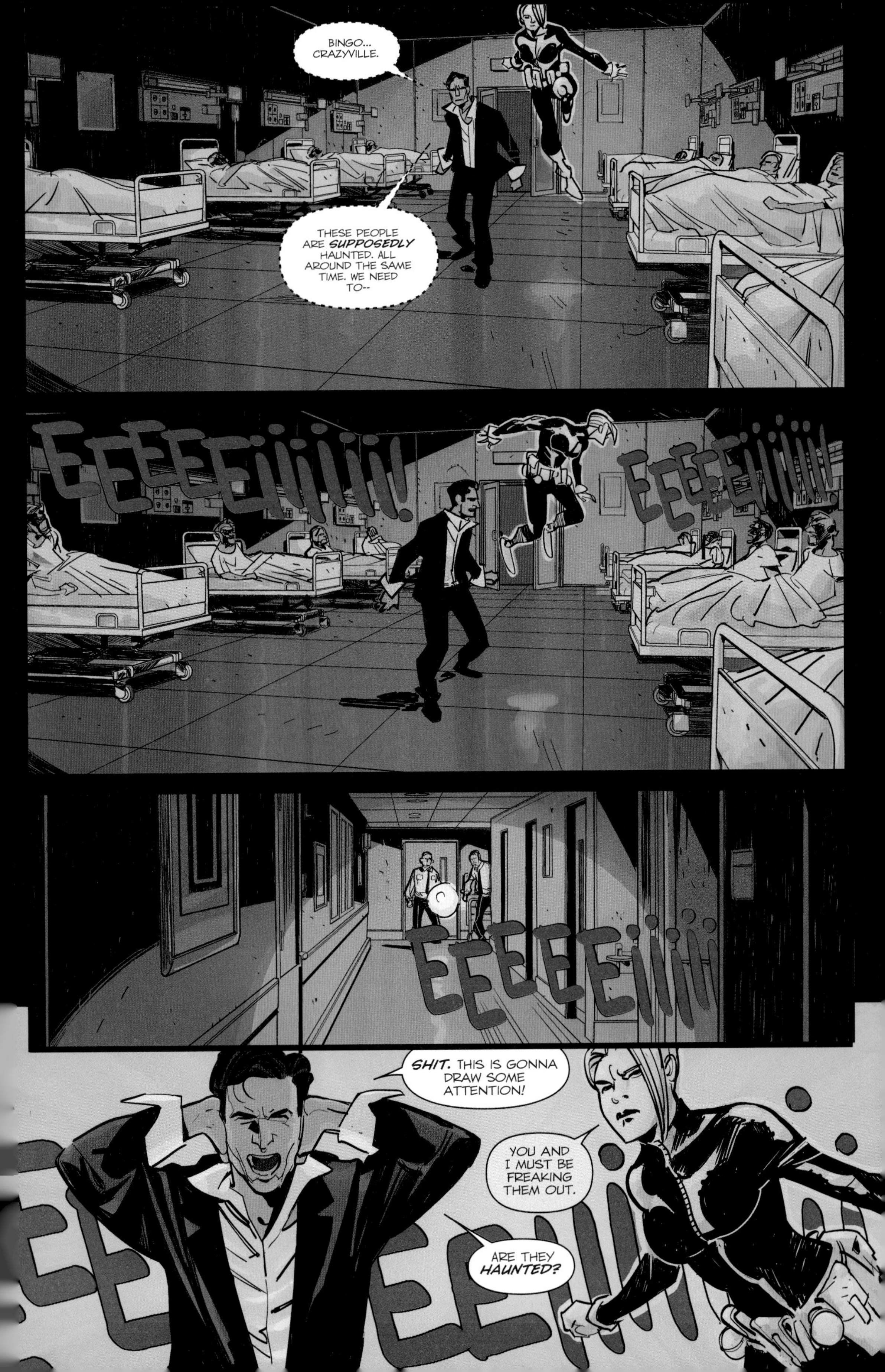

BINGO... CRAZYVILLE.
THESE PEOPLE ARE SUPPOSEDLY HAUNTED. ALL AROUND THE SAME TIME. WE NEED TO--
EEEEEiiiiiii!
EEEEEiiiiiii!
EEEEEiiiiiii
SHIT. THIS IS GONNA DRAW SOME ATTENTION!
YOU AND I MUST BE FREAKING THEM OUT.
ARE THEY HAUNTED?

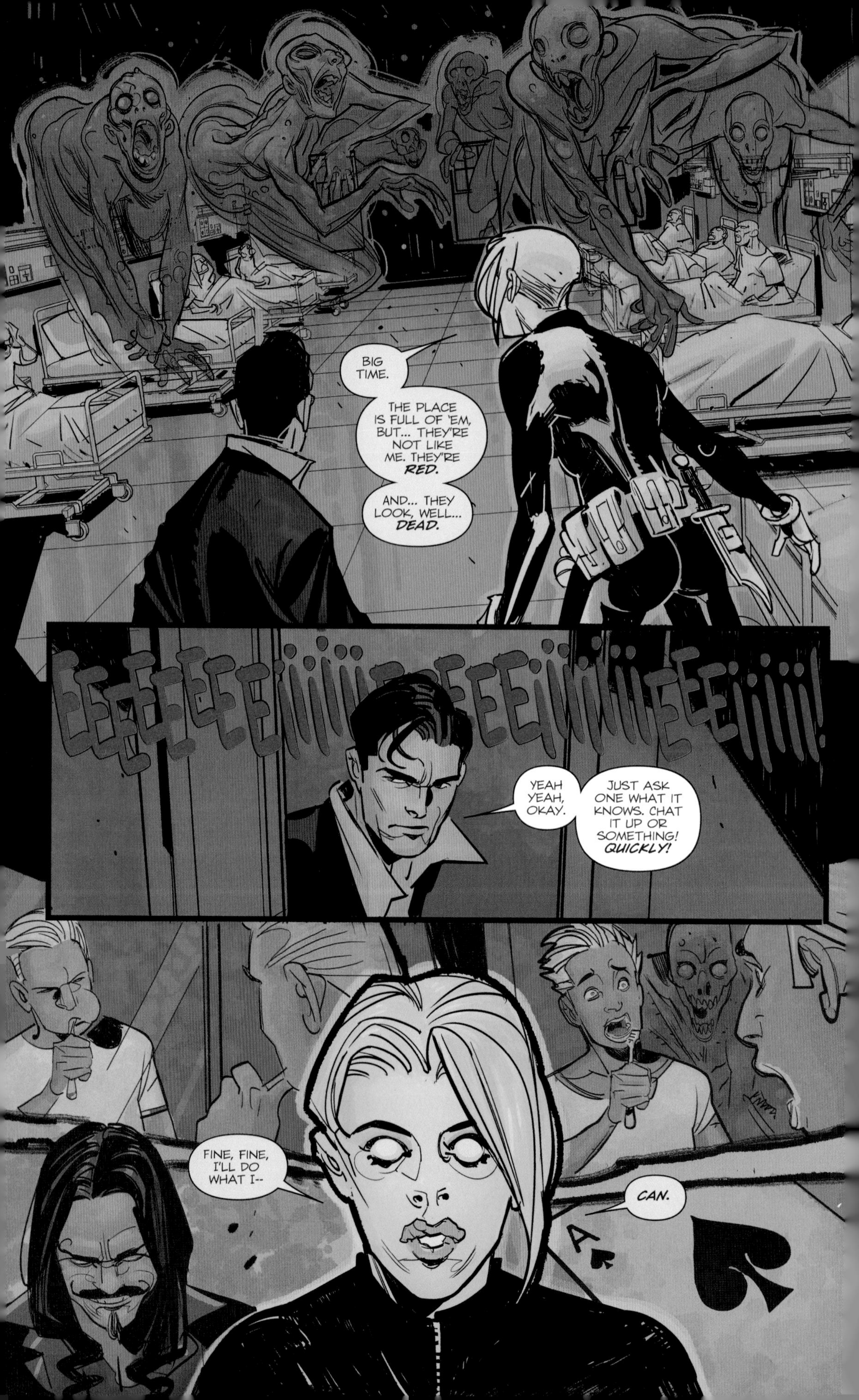
BIG TIME.
THE PLACE IS FULL OF 'EM, BUT... THEY'RE NOT LIKE ME. THEY'RE RED.
AND... THEY LOOK, WELL... DEAD.
YEAH YEAH, OKAY.
JUST ASK ONE WHAT IT KNOWS. CHAT IT UP OR SOMETHING! QUICKLY!
FINE, FINE, I'LL DO WHAT I--
CAN.

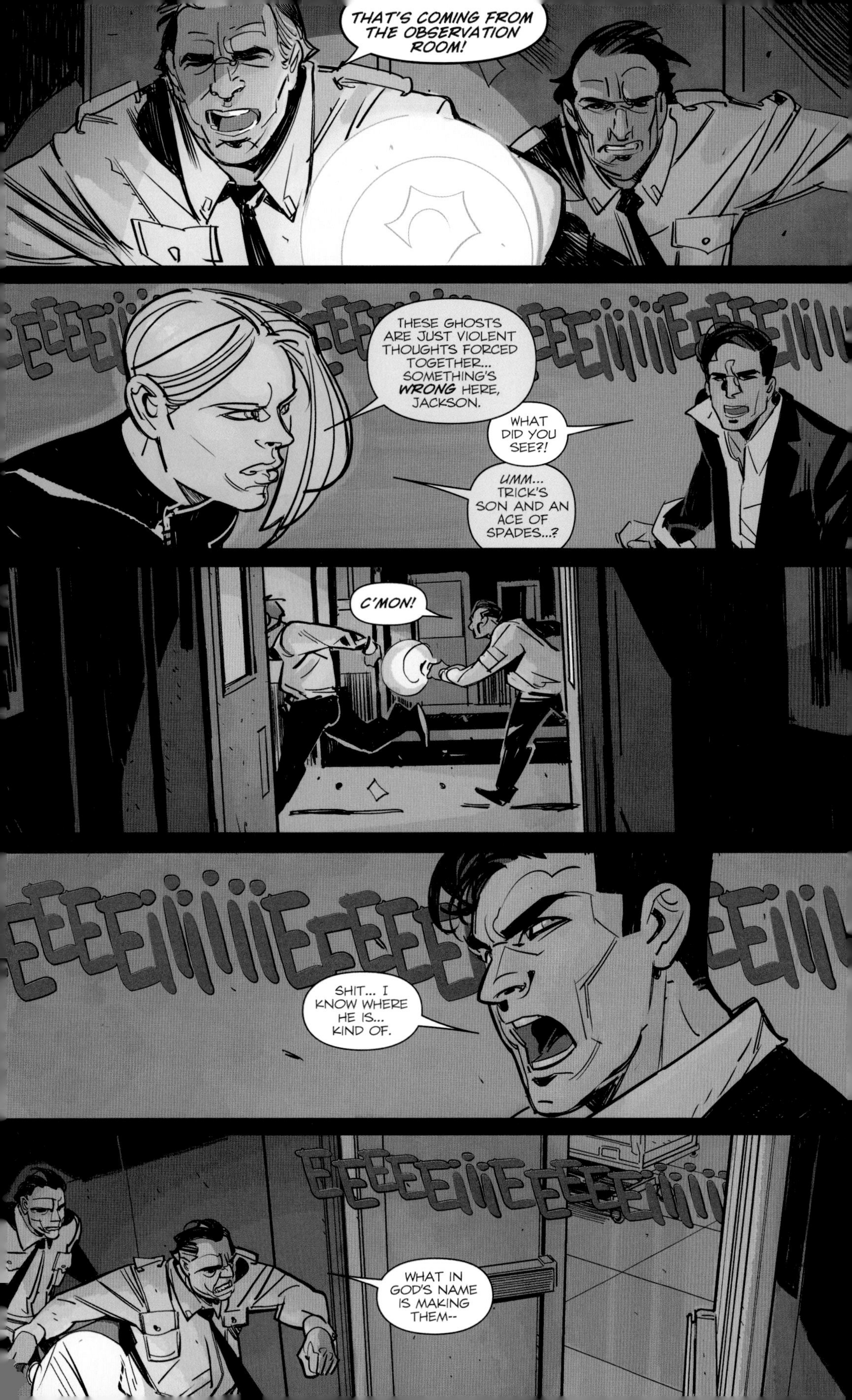
THAT'S COMING FROM THE OBSERVATION ROOM!
EEEEIIIIEEEEIIIIEEEEEIIII
THESE GHOSTS ARE JUST VIOLENT THOUGHTS FORCED TOGETHER... SOMETHING'S **WRONG** HERE, JACKSON.
WHAT DID YOU SEE?!
UMM... TRICK'S SON AND AN ACE OF SPADES...?
C'MON!
EEEEIIIIEEEEIIII
SHIT... I KNOW WHERE HE IS... KIND OF.
EEEEIIIIEEEEEIIII
WHAT IN GOD'S NAME IS MAKING THEM--

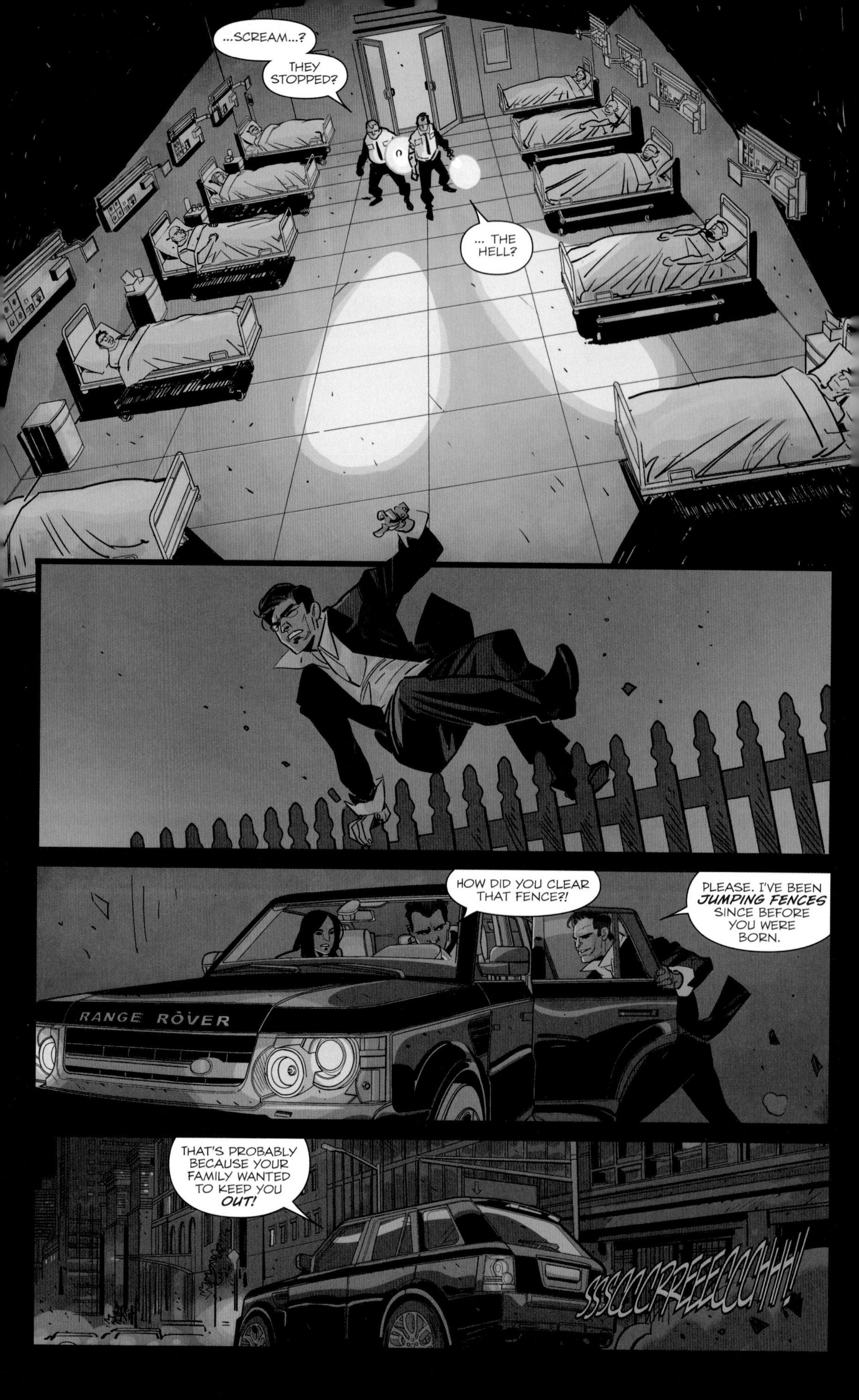
...SCREAM...?
THEY STOPPED?
... THE HELL?
HOW DID YOU CLEAR THAT FENCE?!
PLEASE. I'VE BEEN JUMPING FENCES SINCE BEFORE YOU WERE BORN.
RANGE RÖVER
THAT'S PROBABLY BECAUSE YOUR FAMILY WANTED TO KEEP YOU OUT!
SSSCCCCRREEECCCHHH!

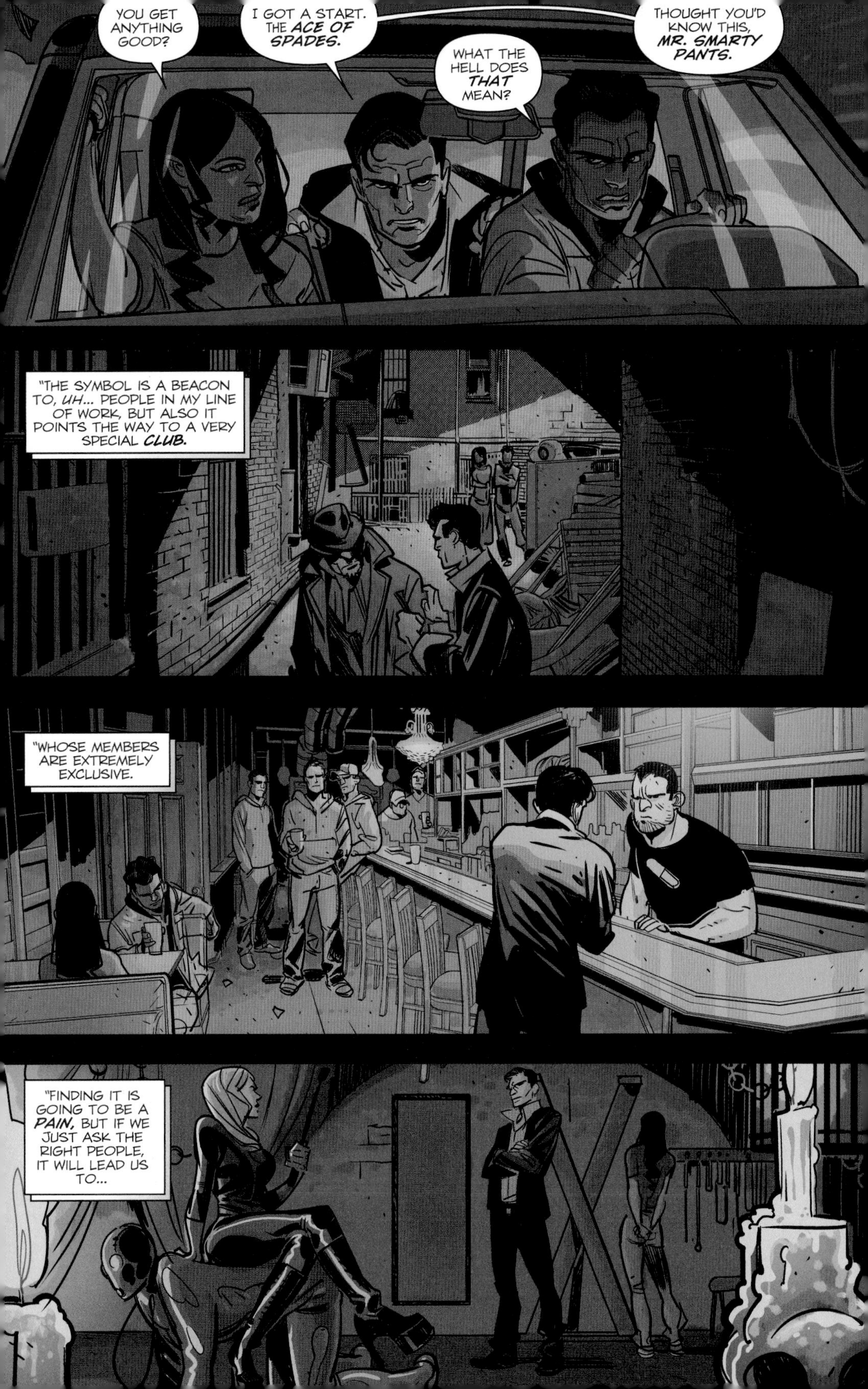

YOU GET ANYTHING GOOD?
I GOT A START. THE ACE OF SPADES.
WHAT THE HELL DOES THAT MEAN?
THOUGHT YOU'D KNOW THIS, MR. SMARTY PANTS.
"THE SYMBOL IS A BEACON TO, UH... PEOPLE IN MY LINE OF WORK, BUT ALSO IT POINTS THE WAY TO A VERY SPECIAL CLUB.
"WHOSE MEMBERS ARE EXTREMELY EXCLUSIVE.
"FINDING IT IS GOING TO BE A PAIN, BUT IF WE JUST ASK THE RIGHT PEOPLE, IT WILL LEAD US TO...

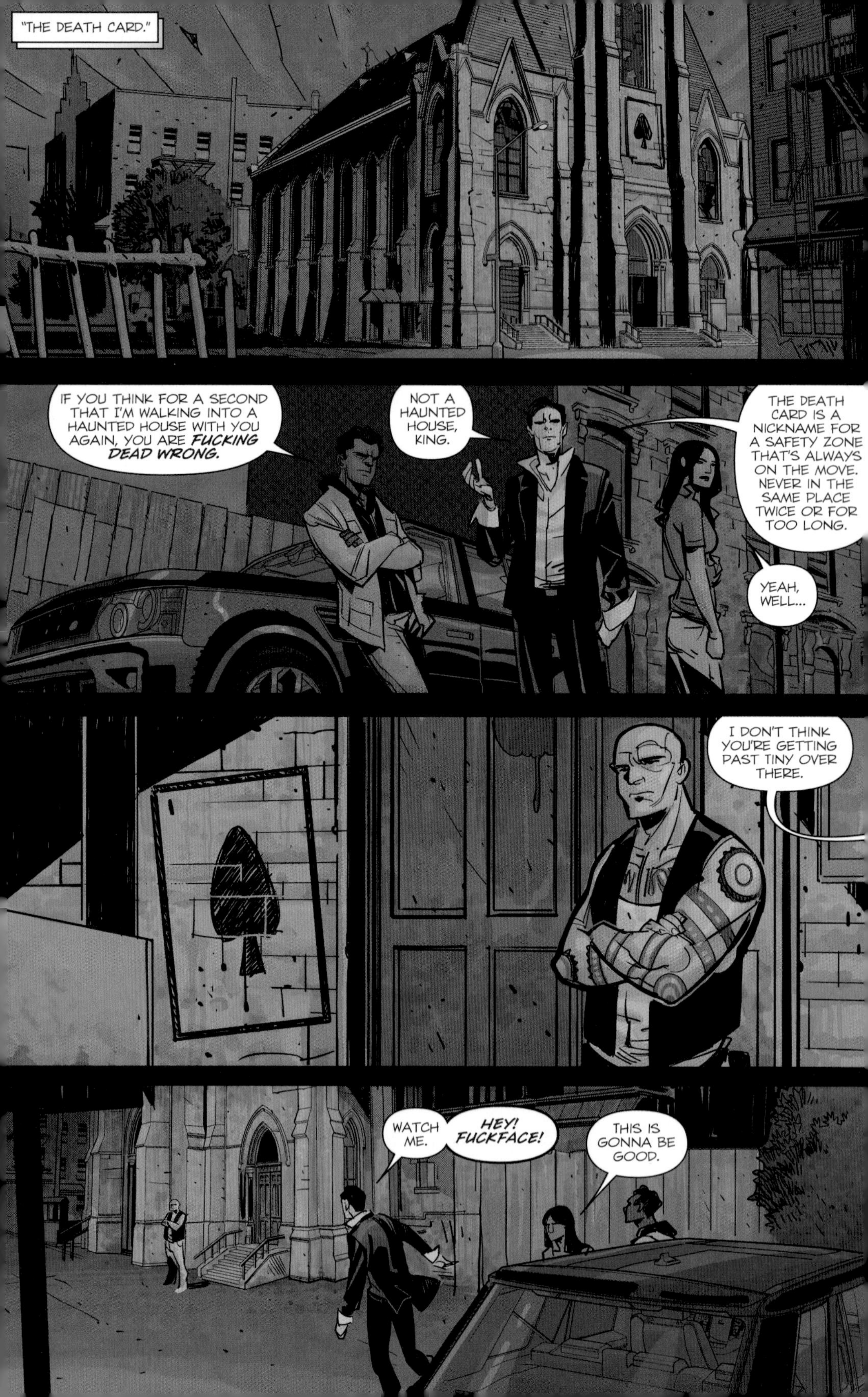
"THE DEATH CARD."
IF YOU THINK FOR A SECOND THAT I'M WALKING INTO A HAUNTED HOUSE WITH YOU AGAIN, YOU ARE ***FUCKING DEAD WRONG.***
NOT A HAUNTED HOUSE, KING.
THE DEATH CARD IS A NICKNAME FOR A SAFETY ZONE THAT'S ALWAYS ON THE MOVE. NEVER IN THE SAME PLACE TWICE OR FOR TOO LONG.
YEAH, WELL...
I DON'T THINK YOU'RE GETTING PAST TINY OVER THERE.
WATCH ME.
HEY! FUCKFACE!
THIS IS GONNA BE GOOD.

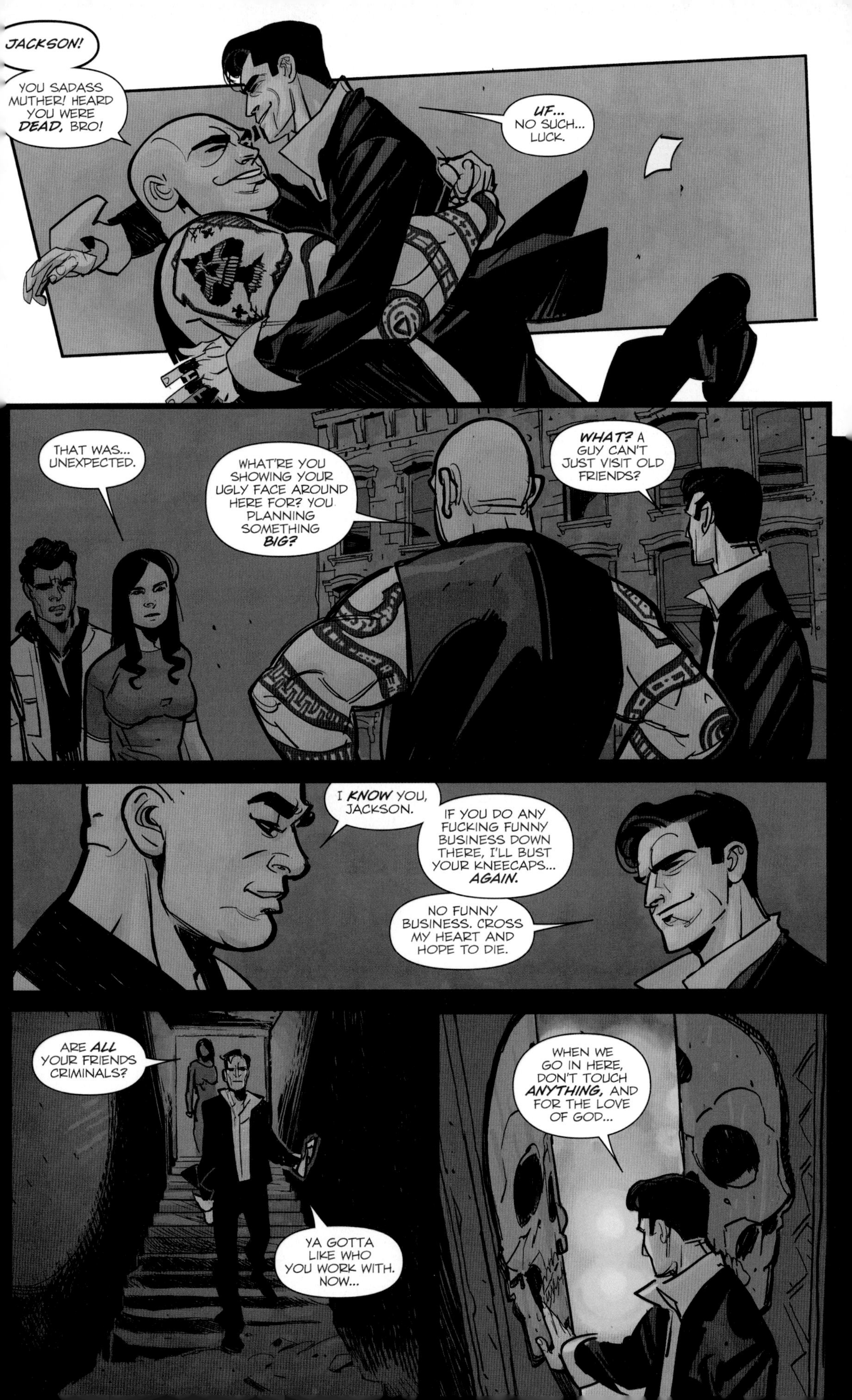
JACKSON!
YOU SADASS MUTHER! HEARD YOU WERE **DEAD,** BRO!
UF... NO SUCH... LUCK.
THAT WAS... UNEXPECTED.
WHAT'RE YOU SHOWING YOUR UGLY FACE AROUND HERE FOR? YOU PLANNING SOMETHING **BIG?**
WHAT? A GUY CAN'T JUST VISIT OLD FRIENDS?
I **KNOW** YOU, JACKSON.
IF YOU DO ANY FUCKING FUNNY BUSINESS DOWN THERE, I'LL BUST YOUR KNEECAPS... **AGAIN.**
NO FUNNY BUSINESS. CROSS MY HEART AND HOPE TO DIE.
ARE **ALL** YOUR FRIENDS CRIMINALS?
YA GOTTA LIKE WHO YOU WORK WITH. NOW...
WHEN WE GO IN HERE, DON'T TOUCH **ANYTHING,** AND FOR THE LOVE OF GOD...

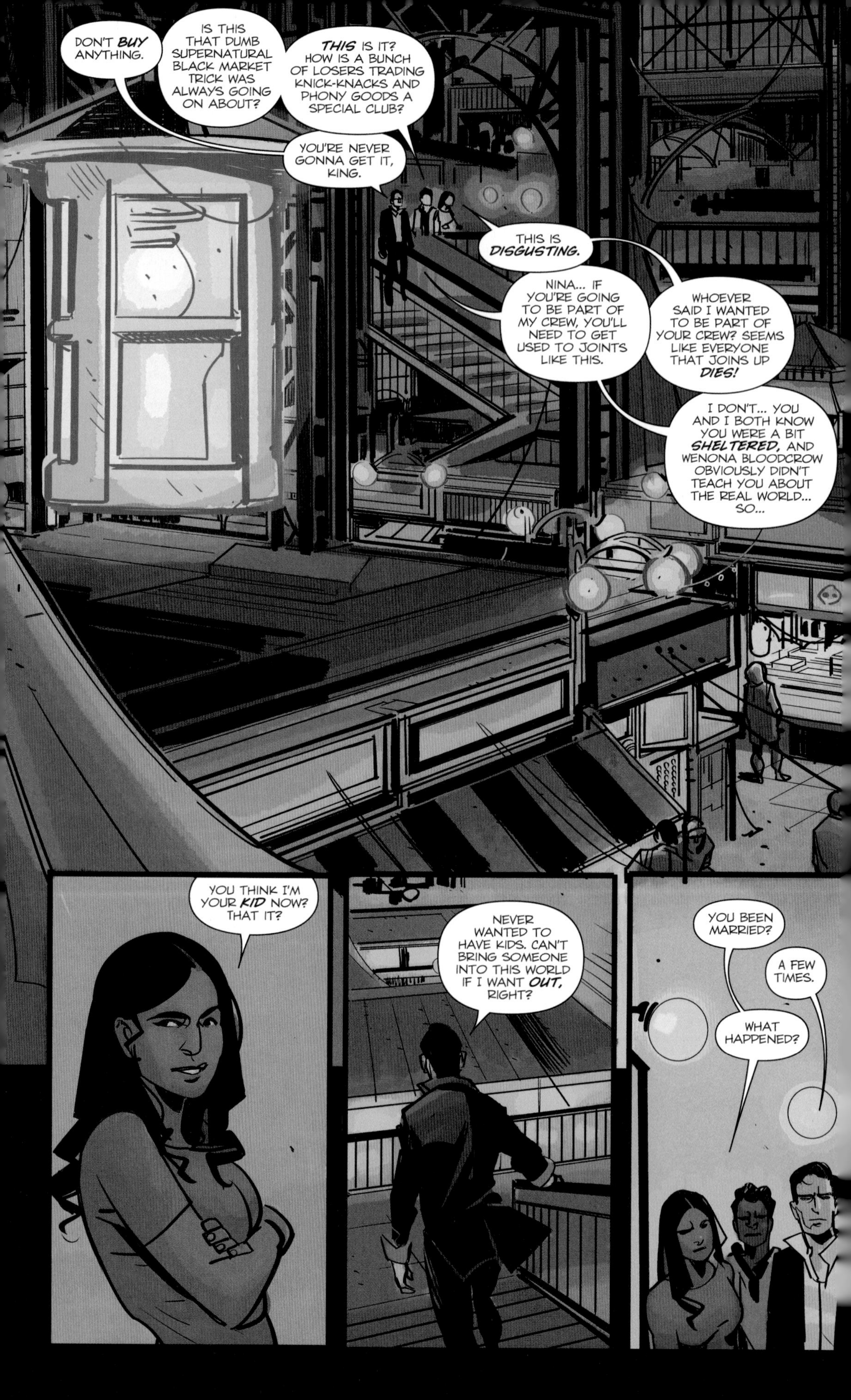
DON'T **BUY** ANYTHING.
IS THIS THAT DUMB SUPERNATURAL BLACK MARKET TRICK WAS ALWAYS GOING ON ABOUT?
THIS IS IT? HOW IS A BUNCH OF LOSERS TRADING KNICK-KNACKS AND PHONY GOODS A SPECIAL CLUB?
YOU'RE NEVER GONNA GET IT, KING.
THIS IS **DISGUSTING.**
NINA... IF YOU'RE GOING TO BE PART OF MY CREW, YOU'LL NEED TO GET USED TO JOINTS LIKE THIS.
WHOEVER SAID I WANTED TO BE PART OF YOUR CREW? SEEMS LIKE EVERYONE THAT JOINS UP **DIES!**
I DON'T... YOU AND I BOTH KNOW YOU WERE A BIT **SHELTERED,** AND WENONA BLOODCROW OBVIOUSLY DIDN'T TEACH YOU ABOUT THE REAL WORLD... SO...
YOU THINK I'M YOUR **KID** NOW? THAT IT?
NEVER WANTED TO HAVE KIDS. CAN'T BRING SOMEONE INTO THIS WORLD IF I WANT **OUT,** RIGHT?
YOU BEEN MARRIED?
A FEW TIMES.
WHAT HAPPENED?

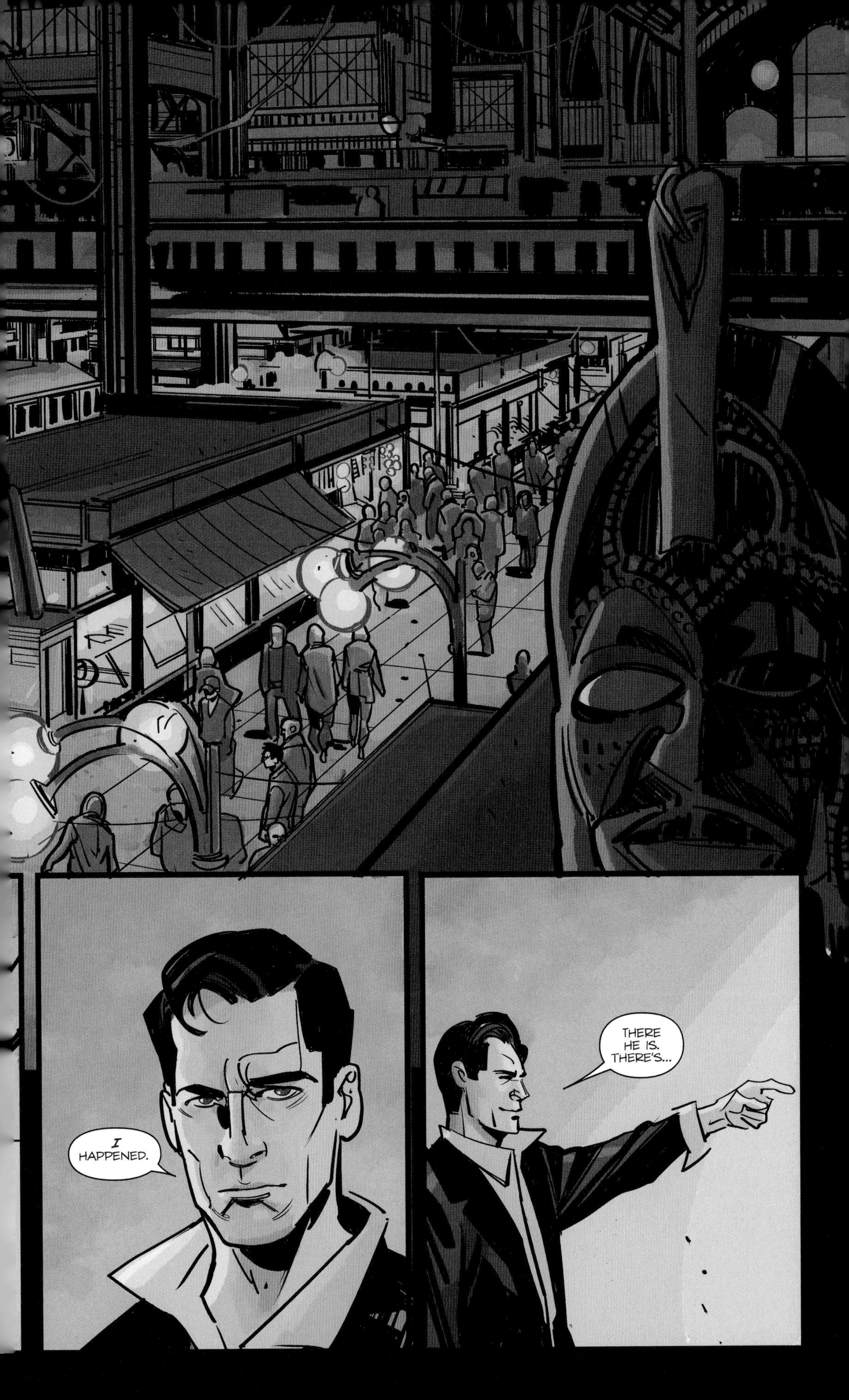
I HAPPENED.
THERE HE IS. THERE'S...

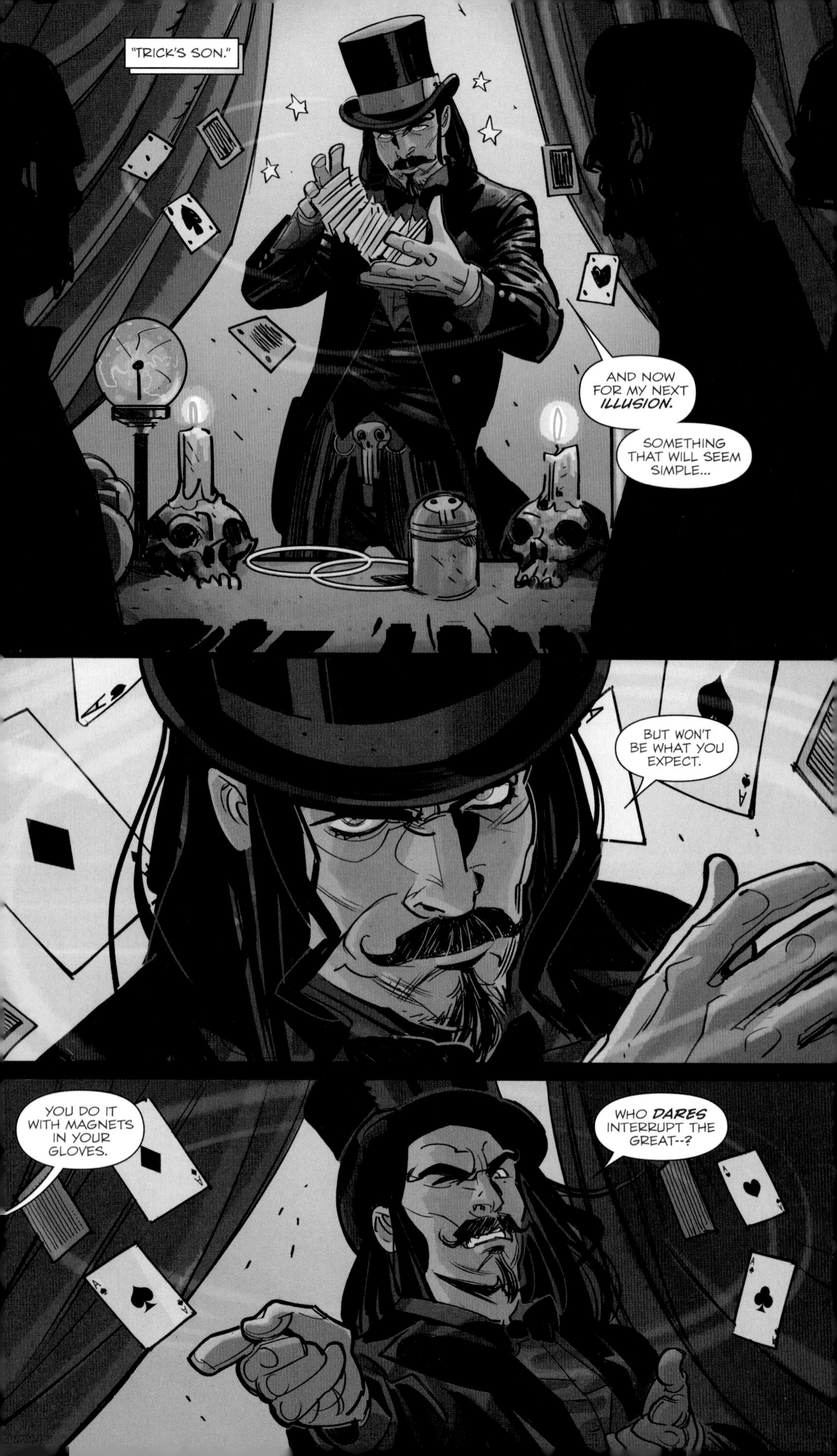
"TRICK'S SON."
AND NOW FOR MY NEXT *ILLUSION.*
SOMETHING THAT WILL SEEM SIMPLE...
BUT WON'T BE WHAT YOU EXPECT.
YOU DO IT WITH MAGNETS IN YOUR GLOVES.
WHO *DARES* INTERRUPT THE GREAT--?

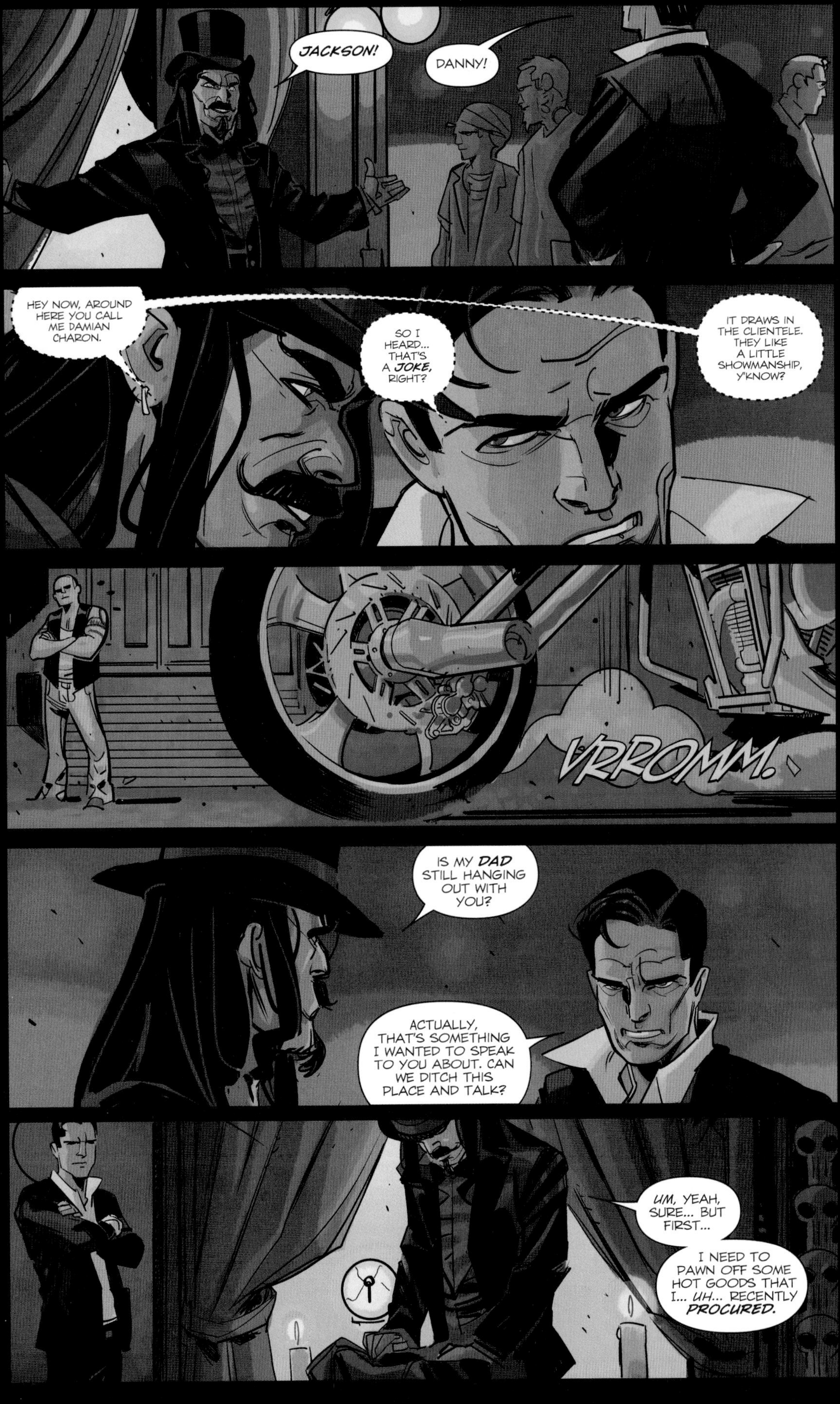
JACKSON!
DANNY!
HEY NOW, AROUND HERE YOU CALL ME DAMIAN CHARON.
SO I HEARD... THAT'S A JOKE, RIGHT?
IT DRAWS IN THE CLIENTELE. THEY LIKE A LITTLE SHOWMANSHIP, Y'KNOW?
VRROMM.
IS MY DAD STILL HANGING OUT WITH YOU?
ACTUALLY, THAT'S SOMETHING I WANTED TO SPEAK TO YOU ABOUT. CAN WE DITCH THIS PLACE AND TALK?
UM, YEAH, SURE... BUT FIRST...
I NEED TO PAWN OFF SOME HOT GOODS THAT I... UH... RECENTLY PROCURED.

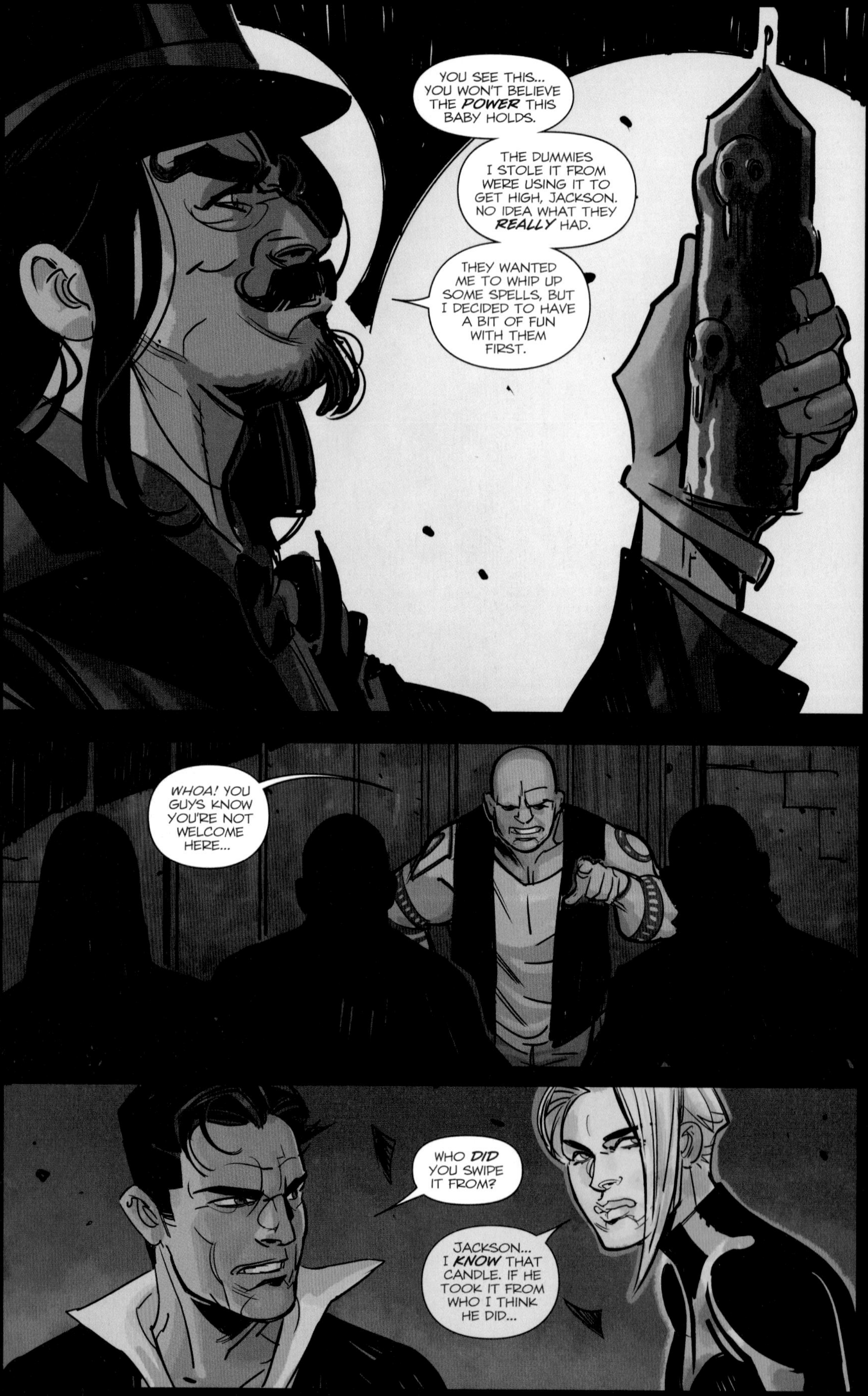
YOU SEE THIS... YOU WON'T BELIEVE THE **POWER** THIS BABY HOLDS.
THE DUMMIES I STOLE IT FROM WERE USING IT TO GET HIGH, JACKSON. NO IDEA WHAT THEY **REALLY** HAD.
THEY WANTED ME TO WHIP UP SOME SPELLS, BUT I DECIDED TO HAVE A BIT OF FUN WITH THEM FIRST.
WHOA! YOU GUYS KNOW YOU'RE NOT WELCOME HERE...
WHO **DID** YOU SWIPE IT FROM?
JACKSON... I **KNOW** THAT CANDLE. IF HE TOOK IT FROM WHO I THINK HE DID...

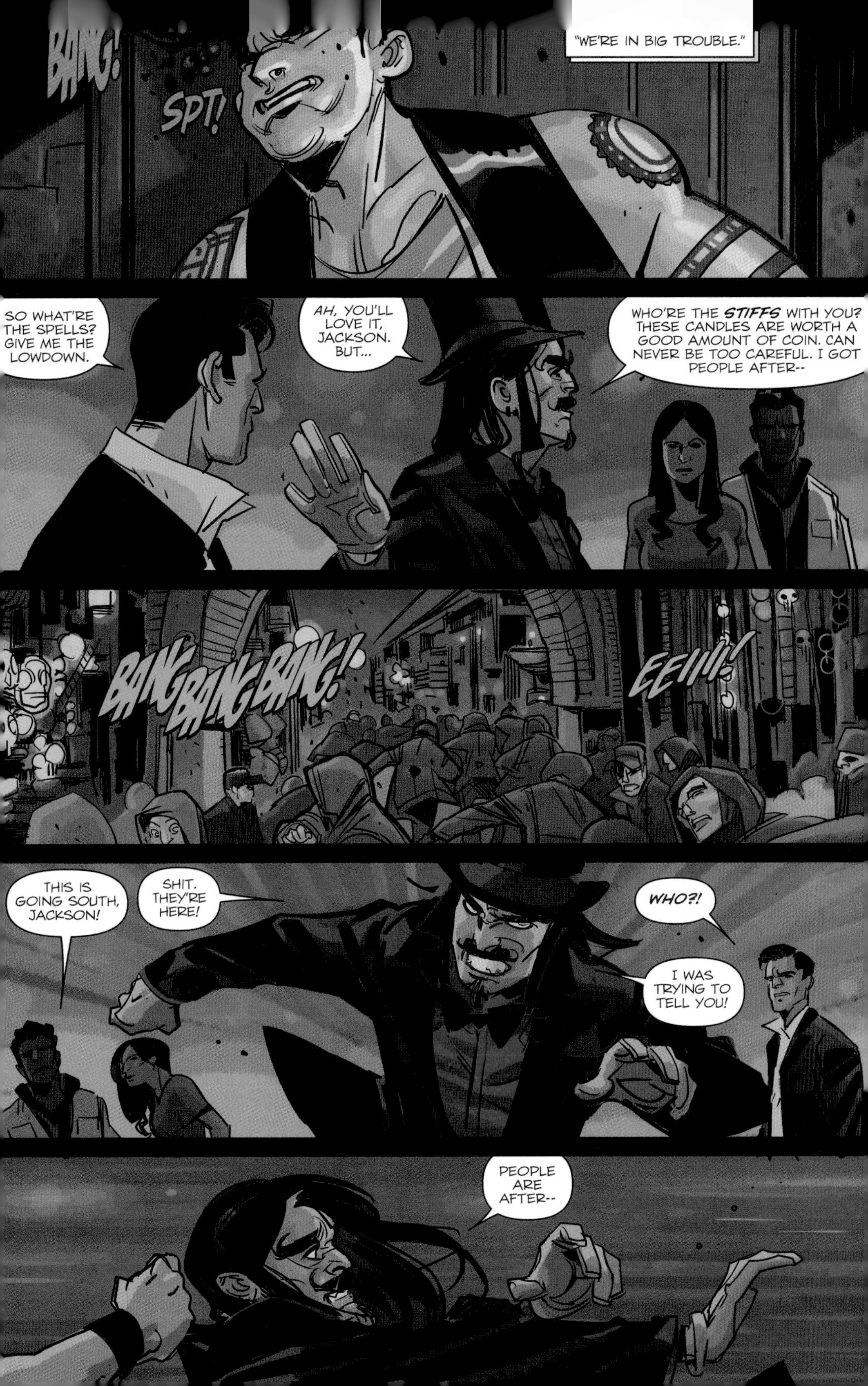
BANG!
SPT!
"WE'RE IN BIG TROUBLE."
SO WHAT'RE THE SPELLS? GIVE ME THE LOWDOWN.
AH, YOU'LL LOVE IT, JACKSON. BUT...
WHO'RE THE STIFFS WITH YOU? THESE CANDLES ARE WORTH A GOOD AMOUNT OF COIN. CAN NEVER BE TOO CAREFUL. I GOT PEOPLE AFTER--
BANG BANG BANG!
EEIII!
THIS IS GOING SOUTH, JACKSON!
SHIT. THEY'RE HERE!
WHO?!
I WAS TRYING TO TELL YOU!
PEOPLE ARE AFTER--

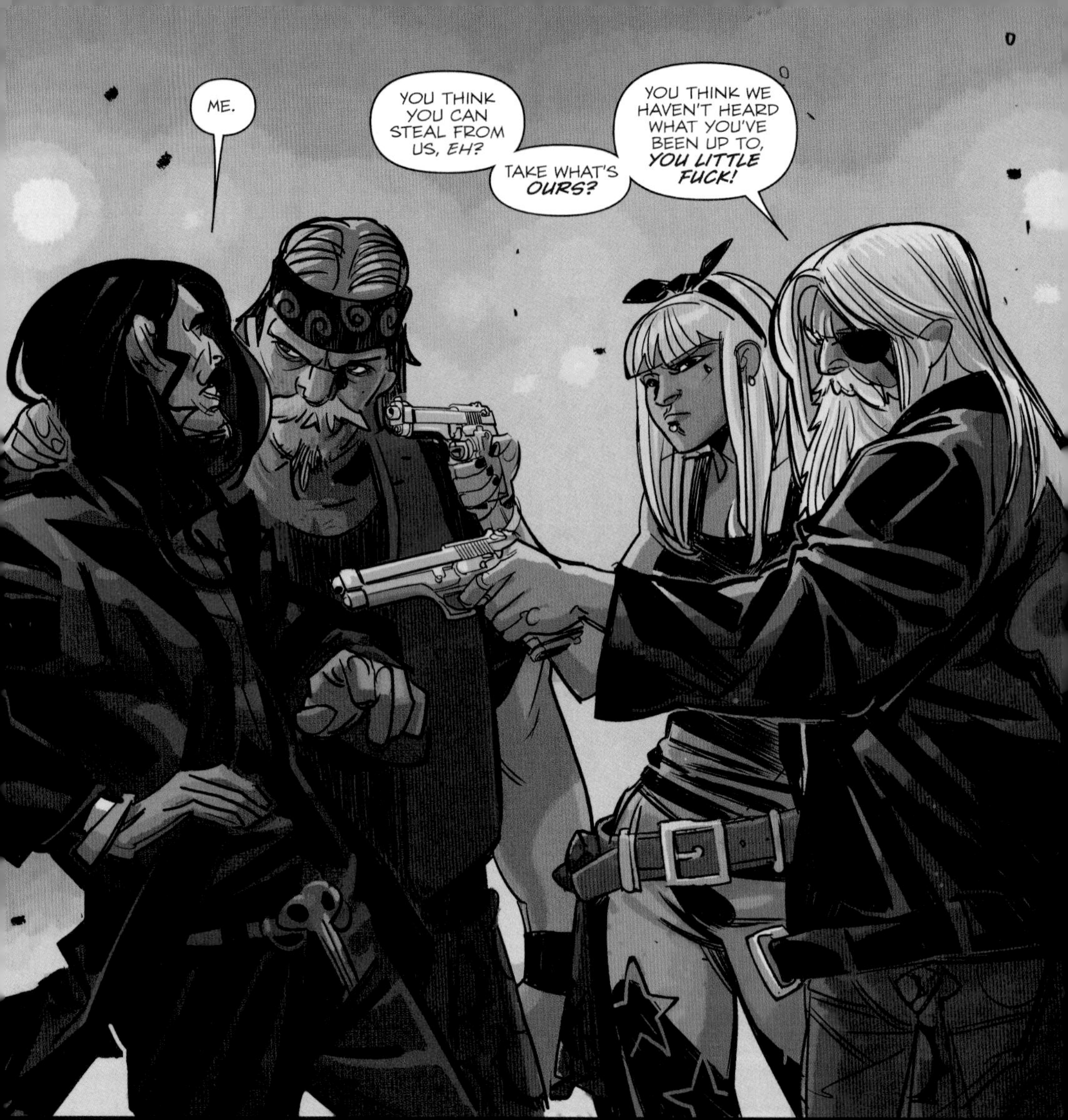
ME.
YOU THINK YOU CAN STEAL FROM US, *EH?*
TAKE WHAT'S ***OURS?***
YOU THINK WE HAVEN'T HEARD WHAT YOU'VE BEEN UP TO, ***YOU LITTLE FUCK!***

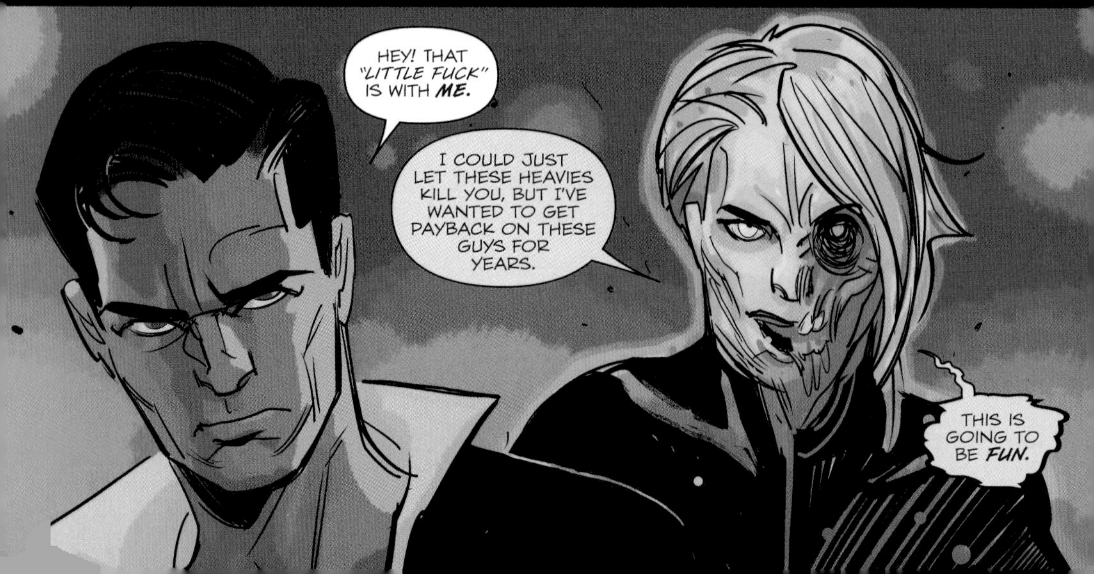
HEY! THAT *"LITTLE FUCK"* IS WITH ***ME.***
I COULD JUST LET THESE HEAVIES KILL YOU, BUT I'VE WANTED TO GET PAYBACK ON THESE GUYS FOR YEARS.
THIS IS GOING TO BE ***FUN.***

CHAPTER FOUR

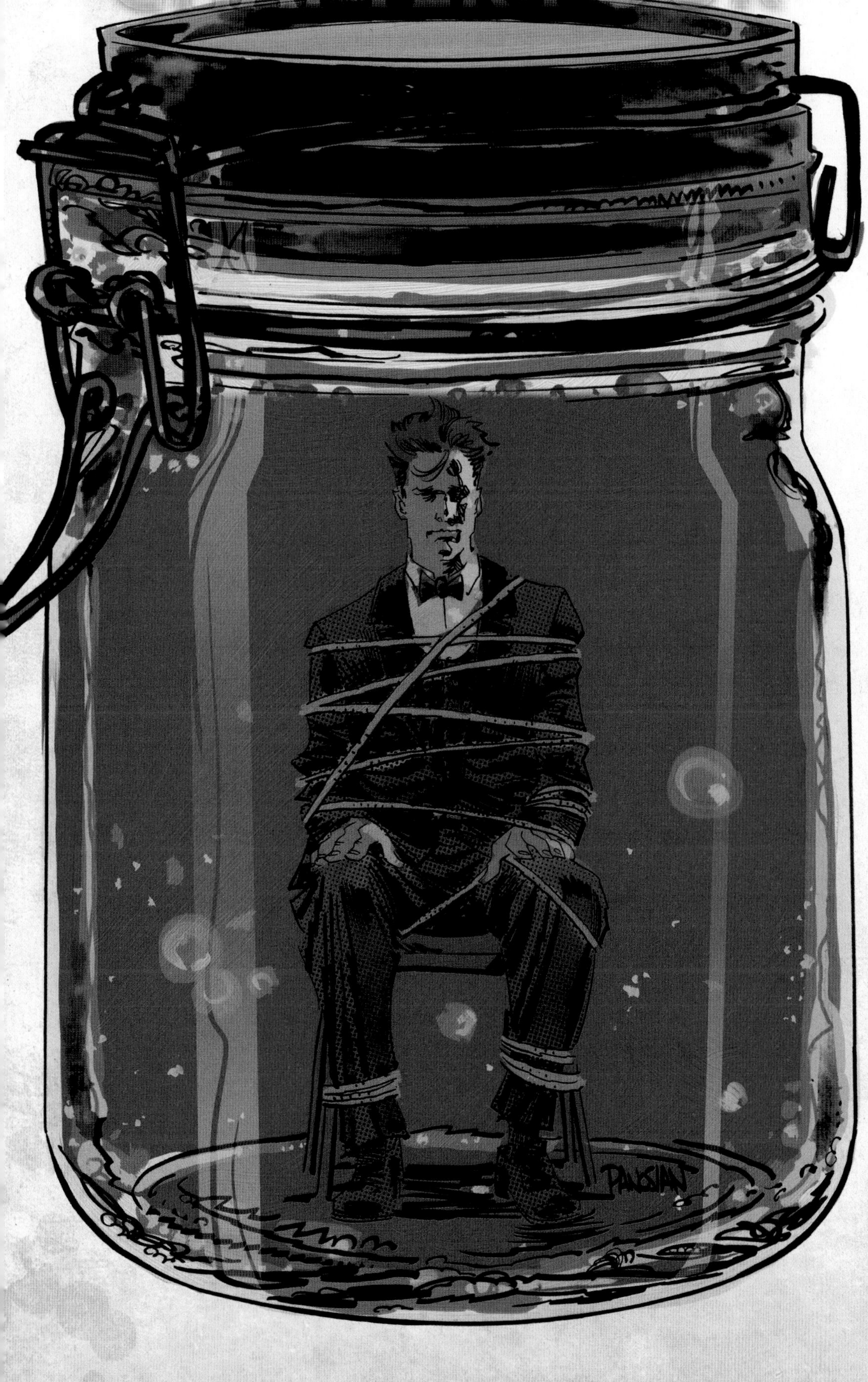
PANOSIAN

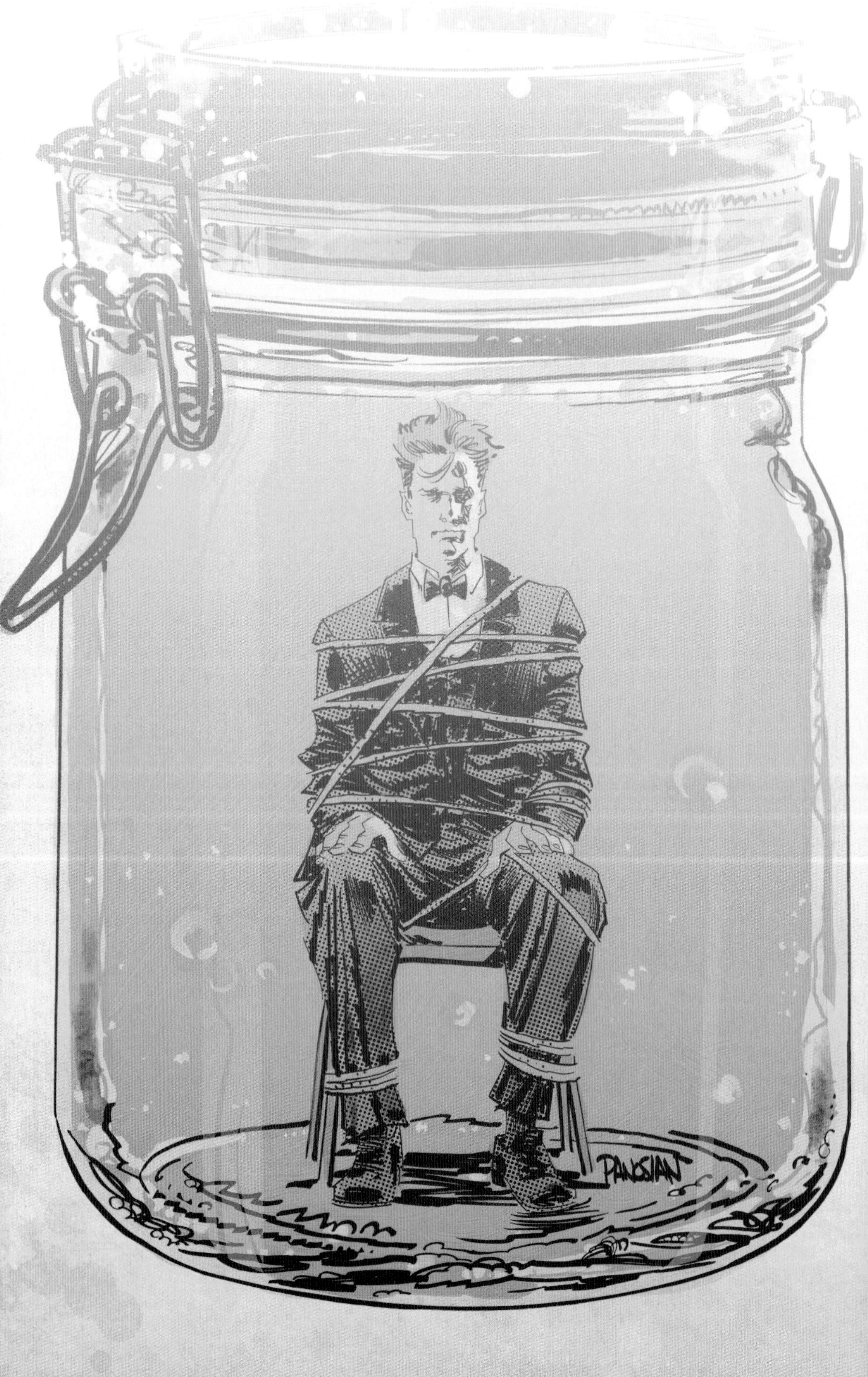
PANOSIAN

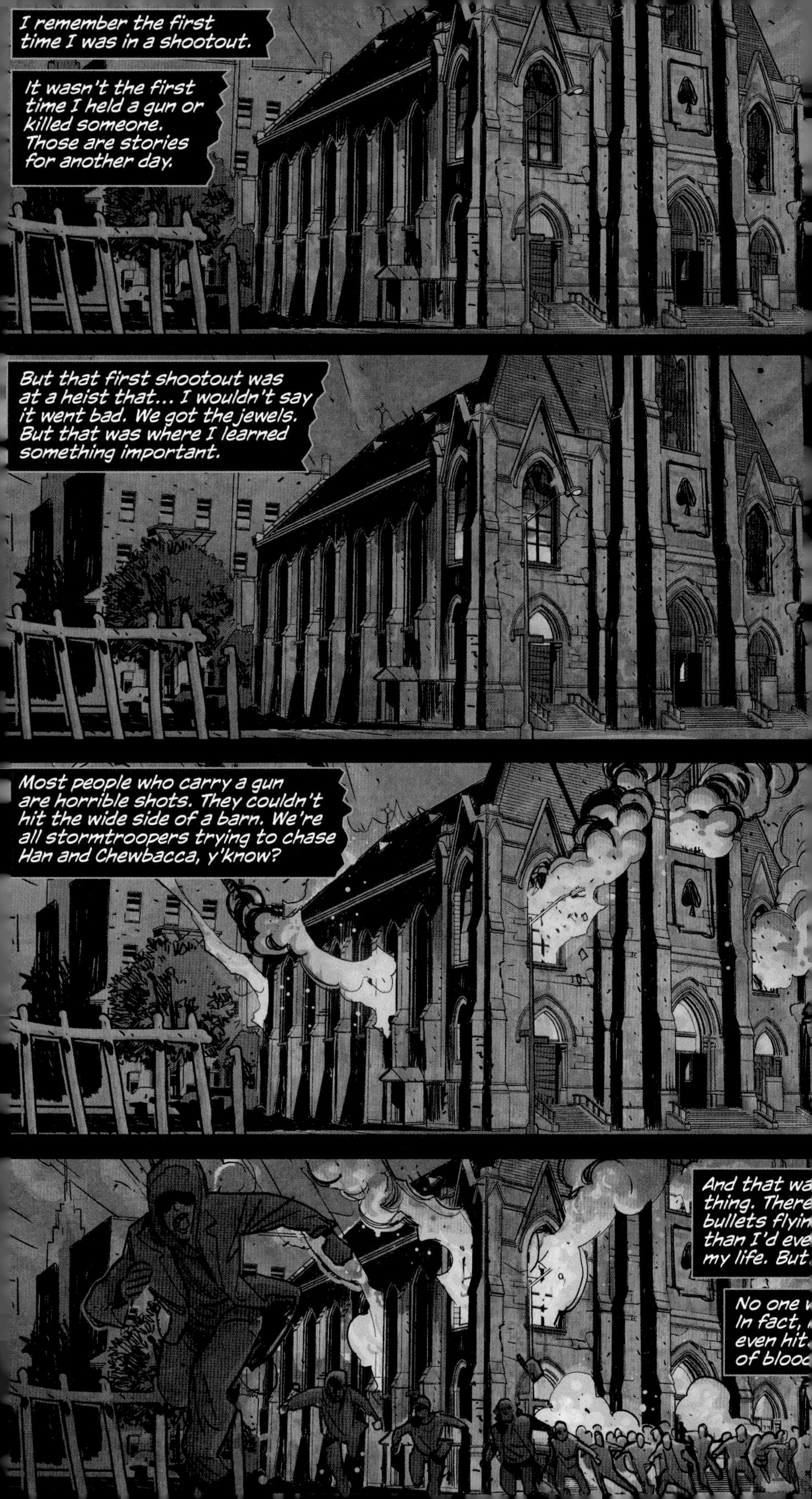
I remember the first time I was in a shootout.
It wasn't the first time I held a gun or killed someone. Those are stories for another day.
But that first shootout was at a heist that... I wouldn't say it went bad. We got the jewels. But that was where I learned something important.
Most people who carry a gun are horrible shots. They couldn't hit the wide side of a barn. We're all stormtroopers trying to chase Han and Chewbacca, y'know?
And that wa
thing. There
bullets flyin
than I'd eve
my life. But
No one
In fact,
even hit
of blood

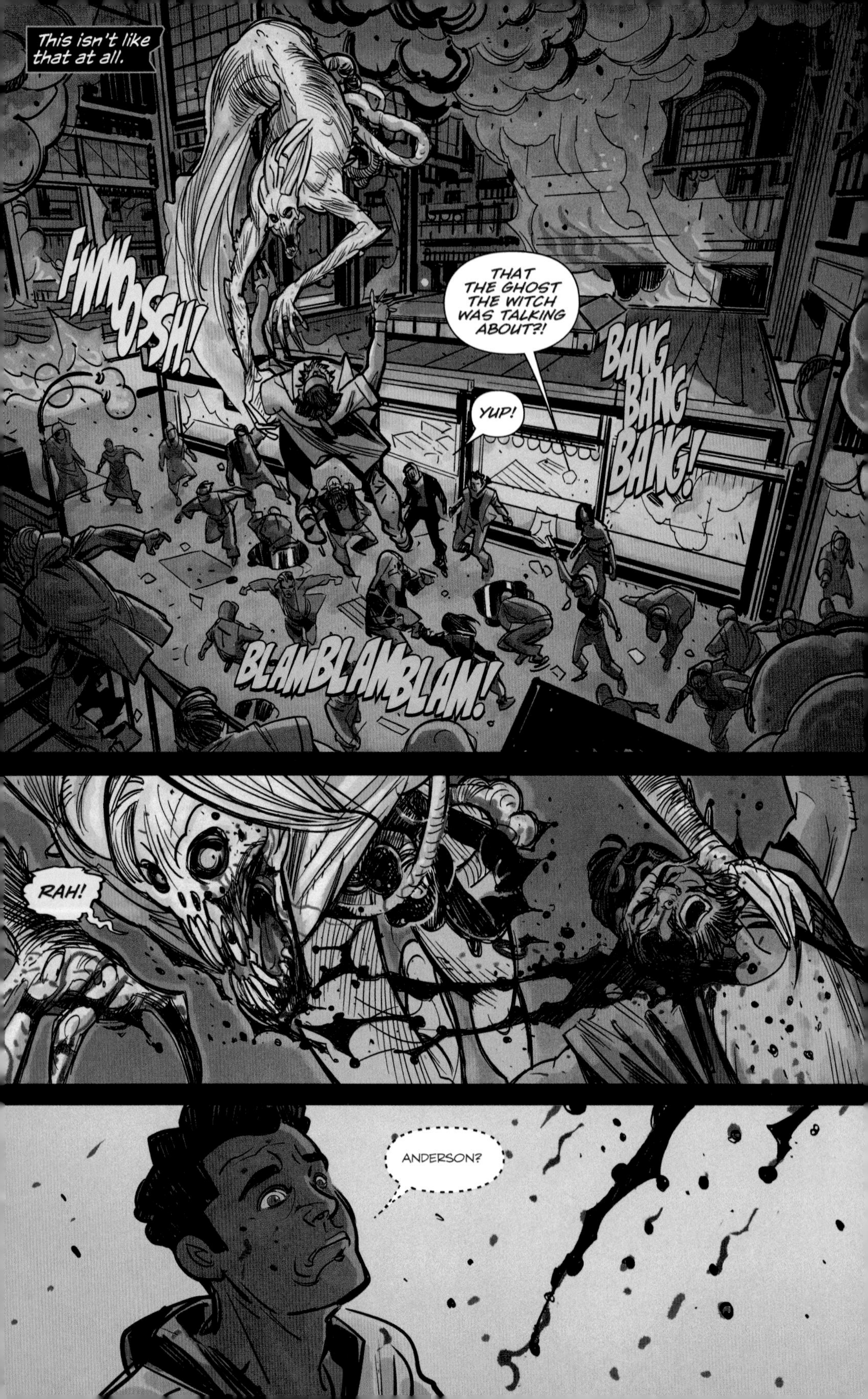
This isn't like that at all.
FWWOOSSH!
THAT THE GHOST THE WITCH WAS TALKING ABOUT?!
YUP!
BANG BANG BANG!
BLAMBLAMBLAM!
RAH!
ANDERSON?

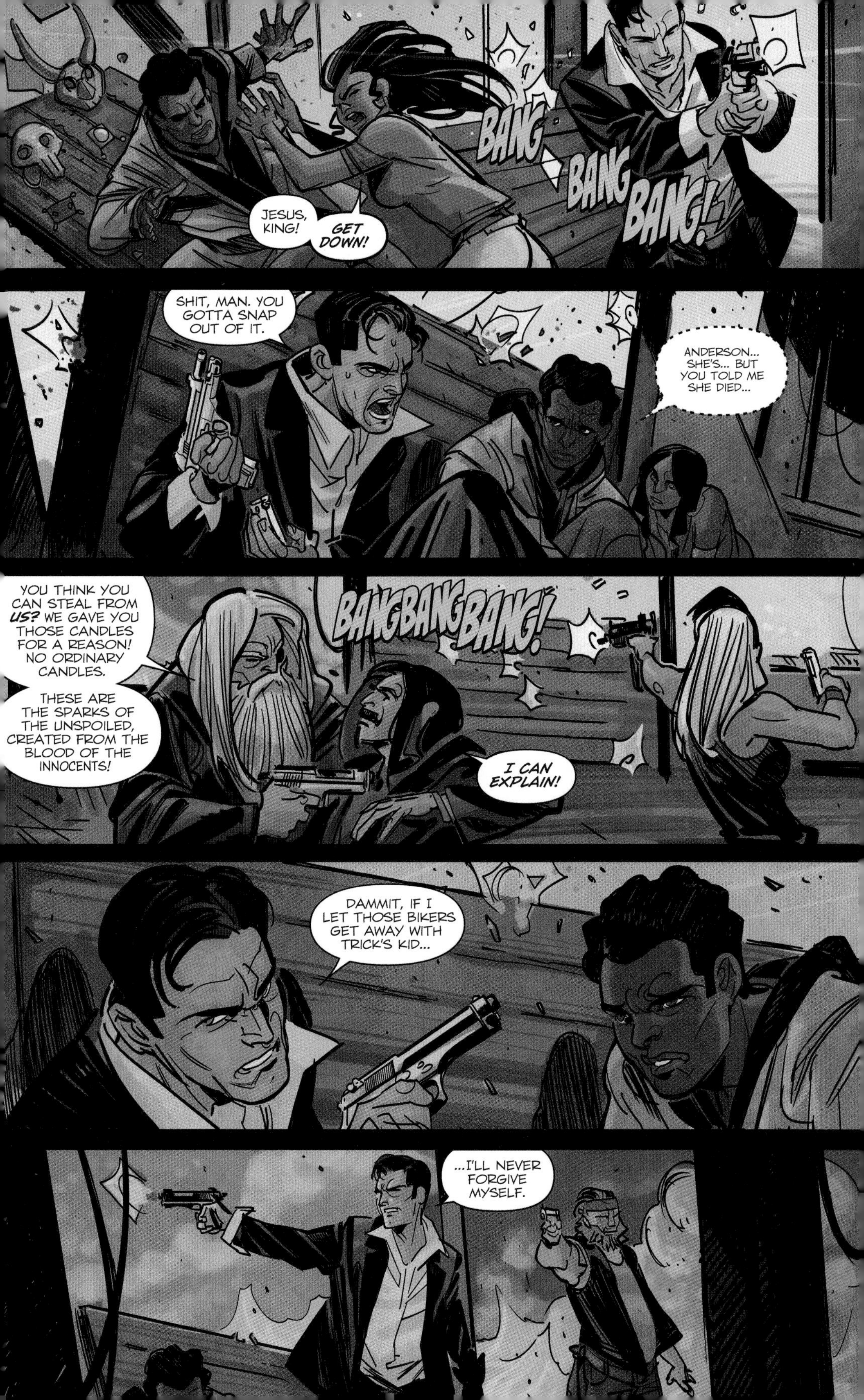

JESUS, KING!
GET DOWN!
BANG BANG BANG!
SHIT, MAN. YOU GOTTA SNAP OUT OF IT.
ANDERSON... SHE'S... BUT YOU TOLD ME SHE DIED...
YOU THINK YOU CAN STEAL FROM US? WE GAVE YOU THOSE CANDLES FOR A REASON! NO ORDINARY CANDLES.
THESE ARE THE SPARKS OF THE UNSPOILED, CREATED FROM THE BLOOD OF THE INNOCENTS!
BANGBANGBANG!
I CAN EXPLAIN!
DAMMIT, IF I LET THOSE BIKERS GET AWAY WITH TRICK'S KID...
...I'LL NEVER FORGIVE MYSELF.

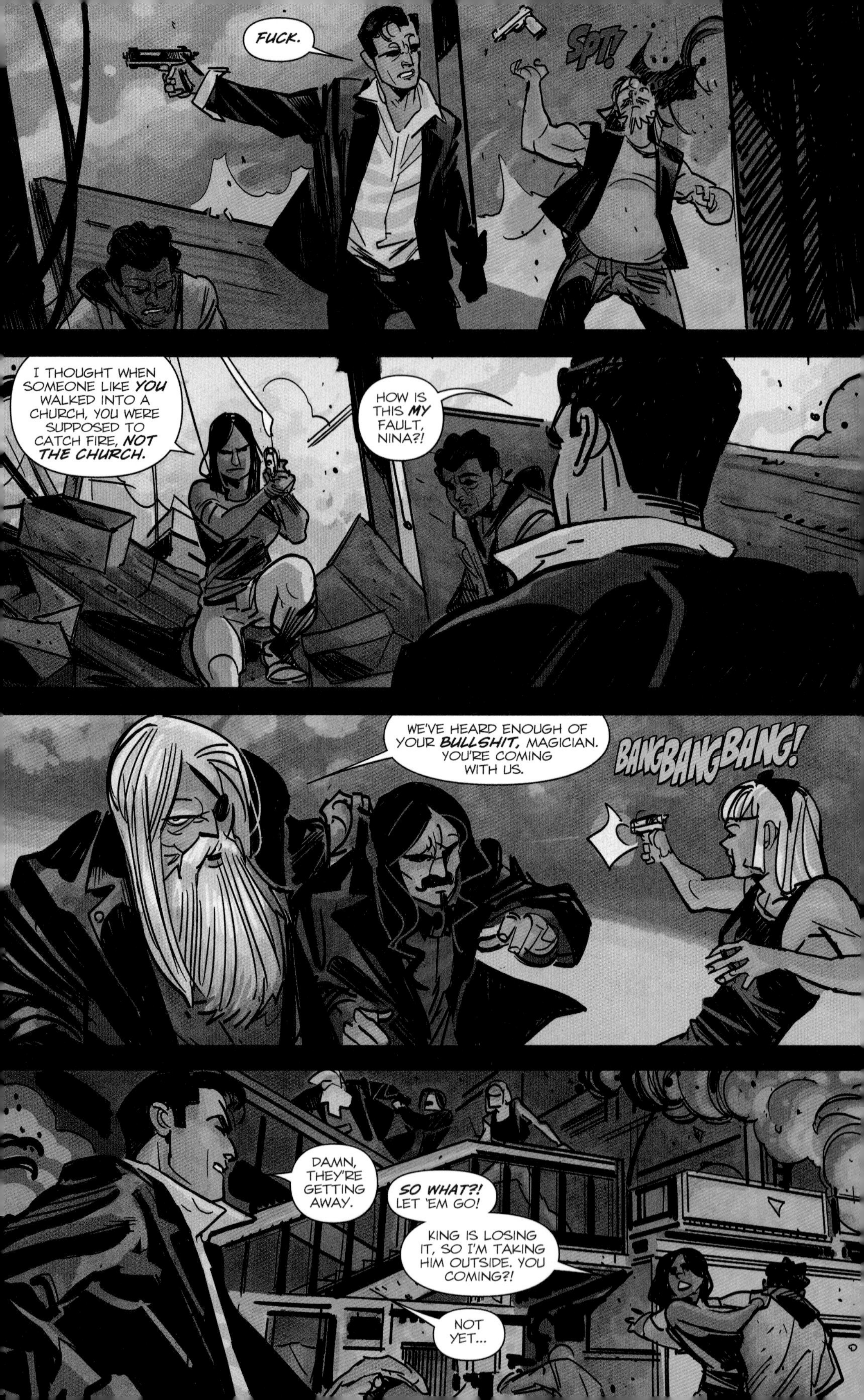
FUCK.
SPT!
I THOUGHT WHEN SOMEONE LIKE YOU WALKED INTO A CHURCH, YOU WERE SUPPOSED TO CATCH FIRE, NOT THE CHURCH.
HOW IS THIS MY FAULT, NINA?!
WE'VE HEARD ENOUGH OF YOUR BULLSHIT, MAGICIAN. YOU'RE COMING WITH US.
BANGBANGBANG!
DAMN, THEY'RE GETTING AWAY.
SO WHAT?! LET 'EM GO!
KING IS LOSING IT, SO I'M TAKING HIM OUTSIDE. YOU COMING?!
NOT YET...

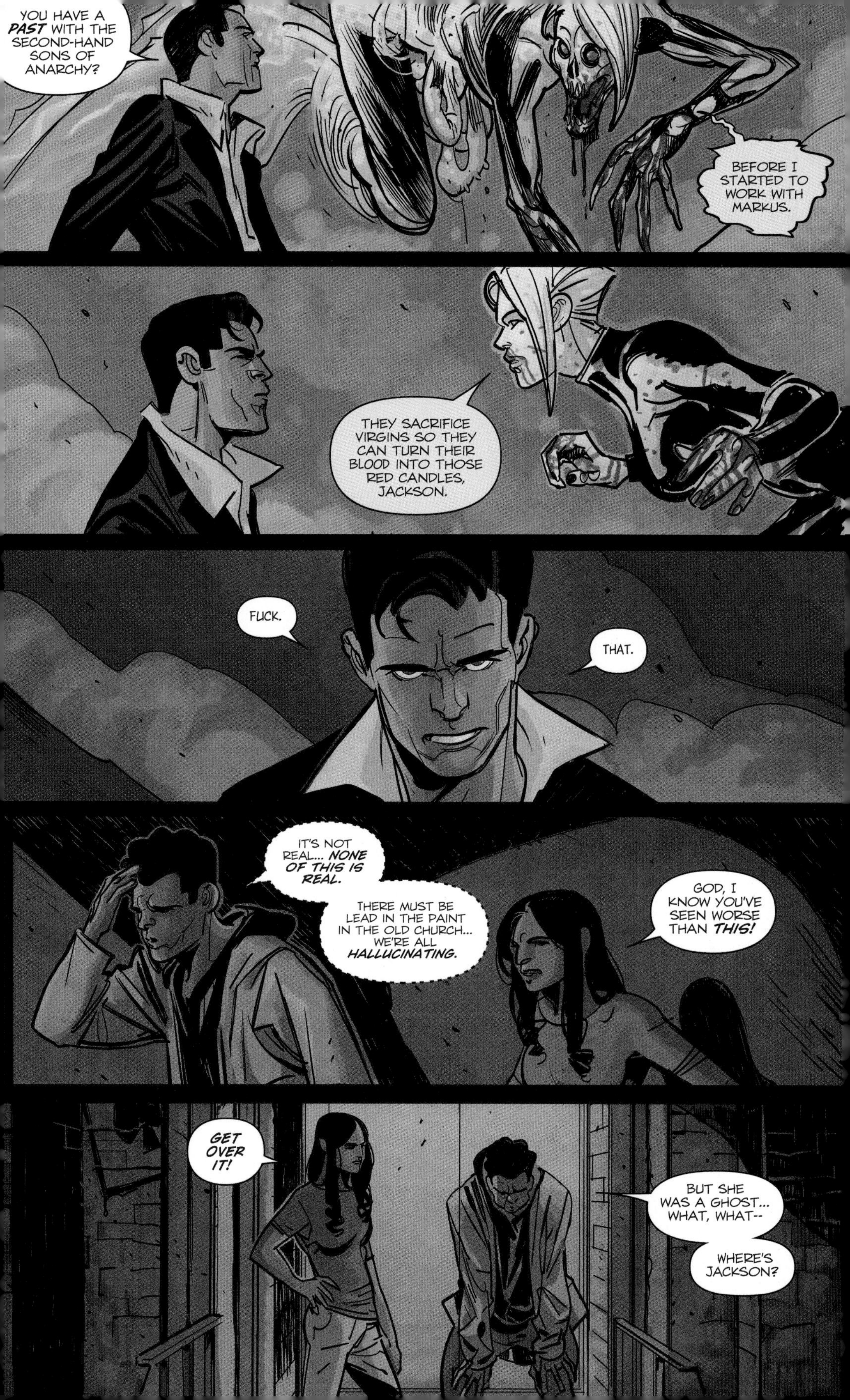
YOU HAVE A PAST WITH THE SECOND-HAND SONS OF ANARCHY?
BEFORE I STARTED TO WORK WITH MARKUS.
THEY SACRIFICE VIRGINS SO THEY CAN TURN THEIR BLOOD INTO THOSE RED CANDLES, JACKSON.
FUCK.
THAT.
IT'S NOT REAL... NONE OF THIS IS REAL.
THERE MUST BE LEAD IN THE PAINT IN THE OLD CHURCH... WE'RE ALL HALLUCINATING.
GOD, I KNOW YOU'VE SEEN WORSE THAN THIS!
GET OVER IT!
BUT SHE WAS A GHOST... WHAT, WHAT--
WHERE'S JACKSON?

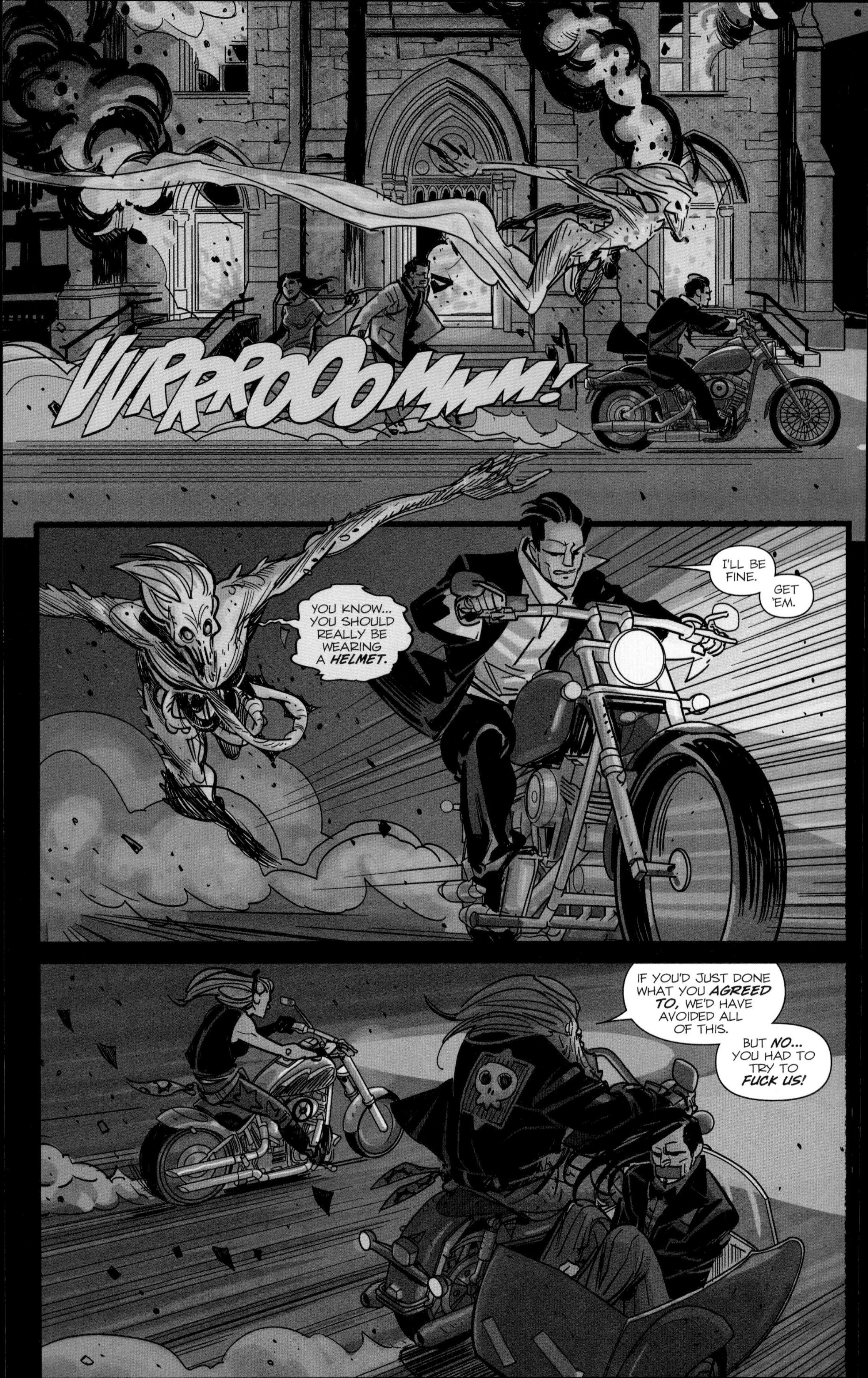
VVRRROOOOMMM!
YOU KNOW... YOU SHOULD REALLY BE WEARING A HELMET.
I'LL BE FINE.
GET 'EM.
IF YOU'D JUST DONE WHAT YOU AGREED TO, WE'D HAVE AVOIDED ALL OF THIS.
BUT NO... YOU HAD TO TRY TO FUCK US!

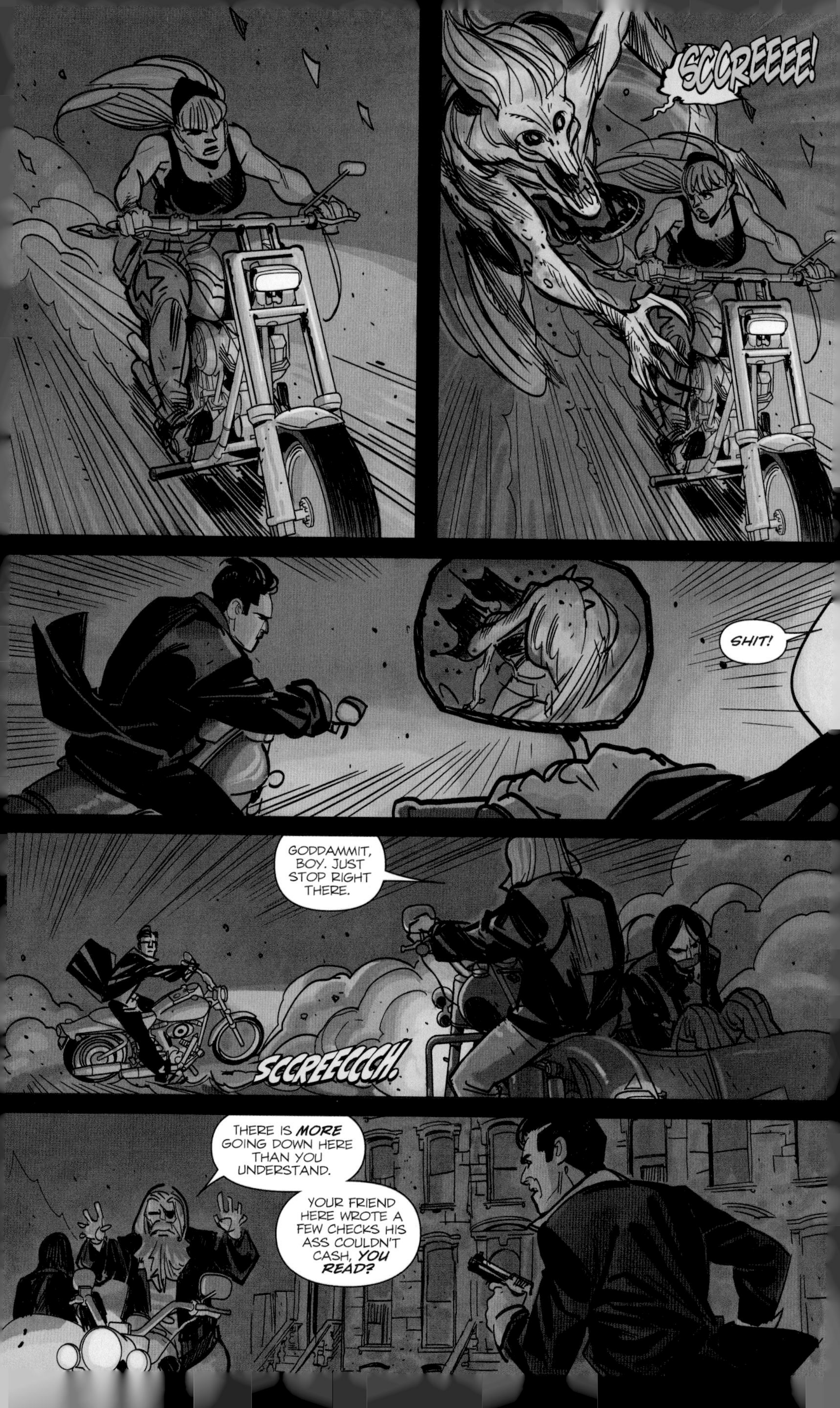
SCCREEEE!
SHIT!
GODDAMMIT, BOY. JUST STOP RIGHT THERE.
SCCREECCCH.
THERE IS MORE GOING DOWN HERE THAN YOU UNDERSTAND.
YOUR FRIEND HERE WROTE A FEW CHECKS HIS ASS COULDN'T CASH, YOU READ?

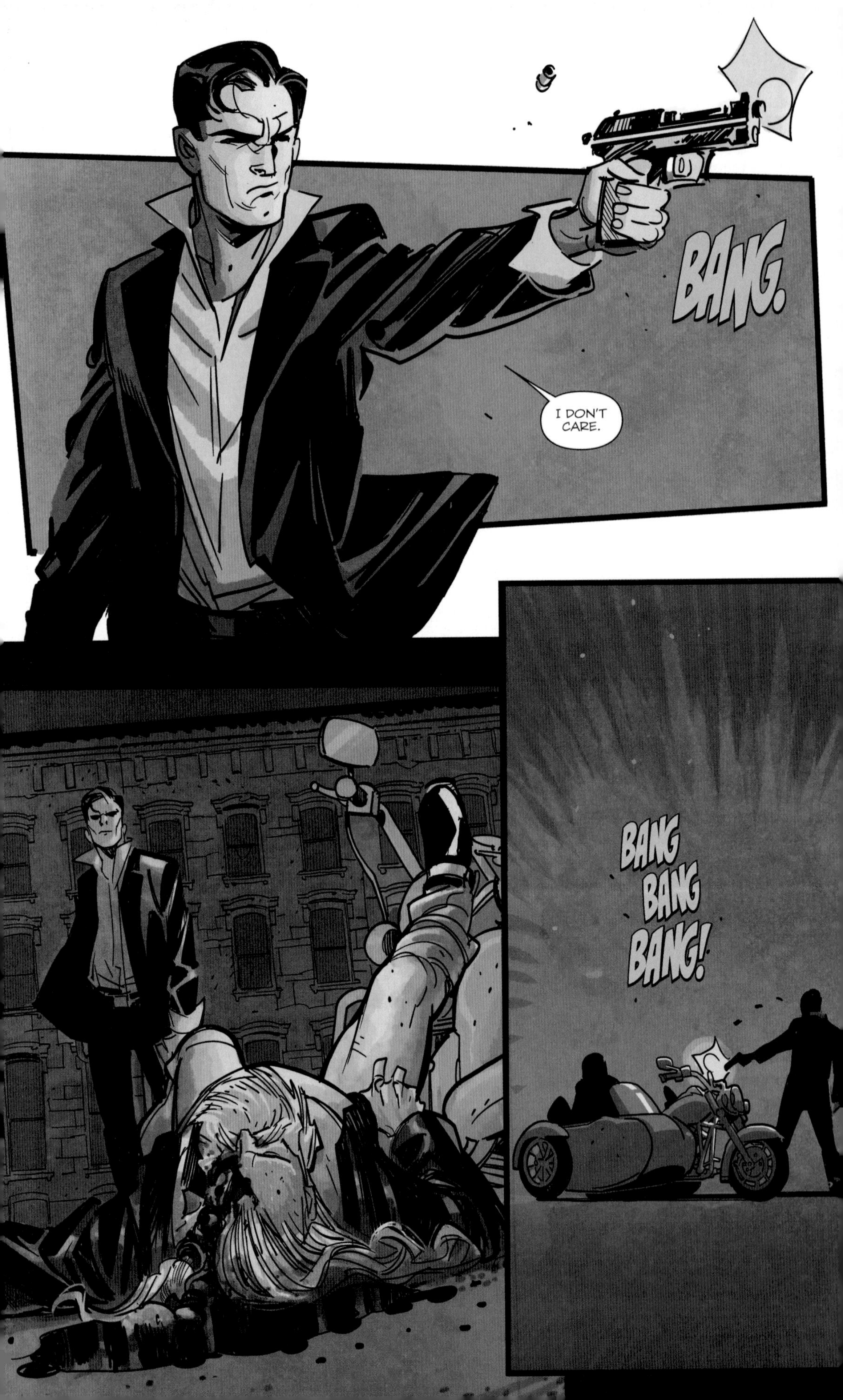
BANG.
I DON'T CARE.
BANG
BANG
BANG!

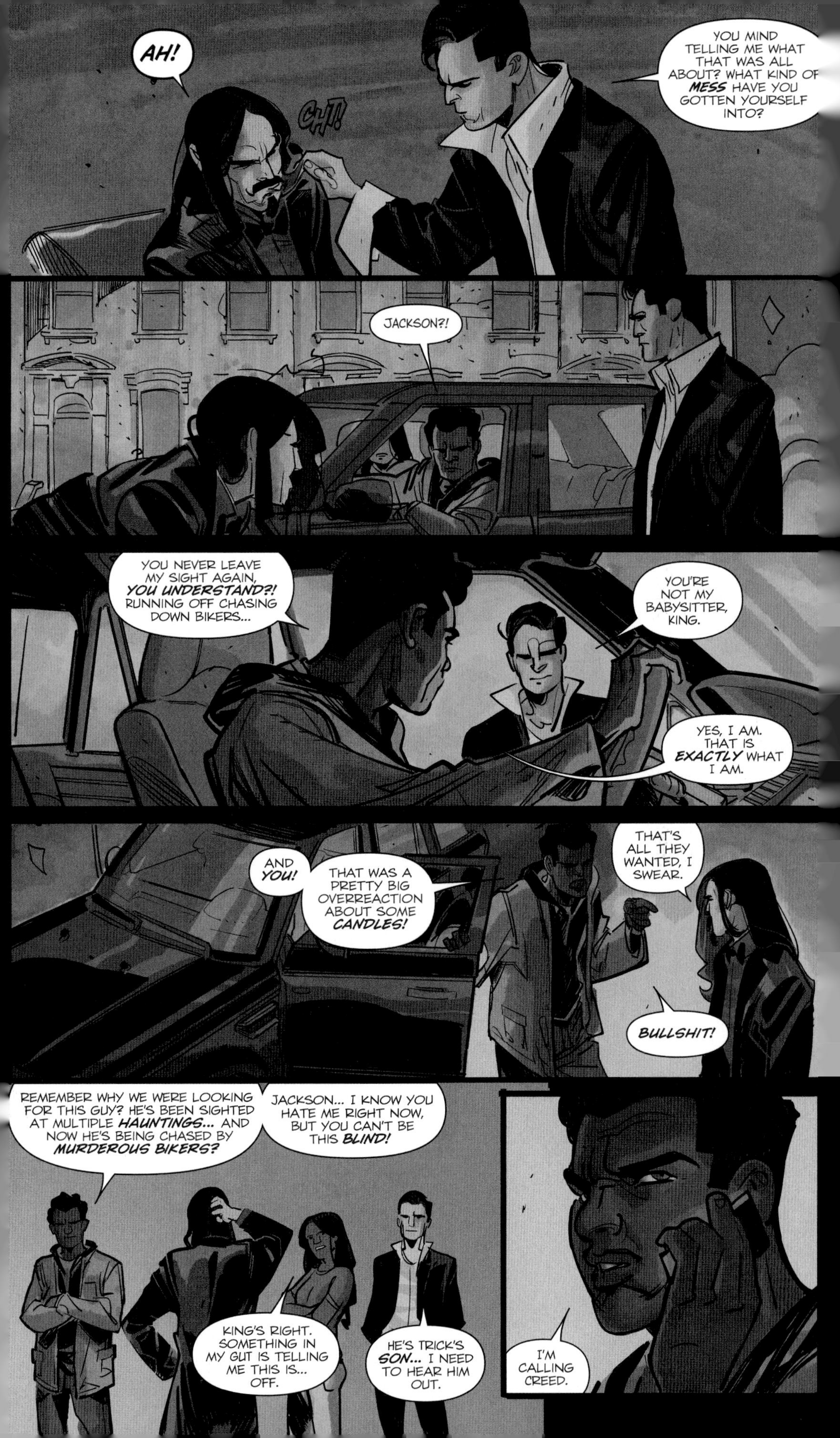
AH!
CHT!
YOU MIND TELLING ME WHAT THAT WAS ALL ABOUT? WHAT KIND OF MESS HAVE YOU GOTTEN YOURSELF INTO?
JACKSON?!
YOU NEVER LEAVE MY SIGHT AGAIN, YOU UNDERSTAND?! RUNNING OFF CHASING DOWN BIKERS...
YOU'RE NOT MY BABYSITTER, KING.
YES, I AM. THAT IS EXACTLY WHAT I AM.
AND YOU!
THAT WAS A PRETTY BIG OVERREACTION ABOUT SOME CANDLES!
THAT'S ALL THEY WANTED, I SWEAR.
BULLSHIT!
REMEMBER WHY WE WERE LOOKING FOR THIS GUY? HE'S BEEN SIGHTED AT MULTIPLE HAUNTINGS... AND NOW HE'S BEING CHASED BY MURDEROUS BIKERS?
JACKSON... I KNOW YOU HATE ME RIGHT NOW, BUT YOU CAN'T BE THIS BLIND!
KING'S RIGHT. SOMETHING IN MY GUT IS TELLING ME THIS IS... OFF.
HE'S TRICK'S SON... I NEED TO HEAR HIM OUT.
I'M CALLING CREED.

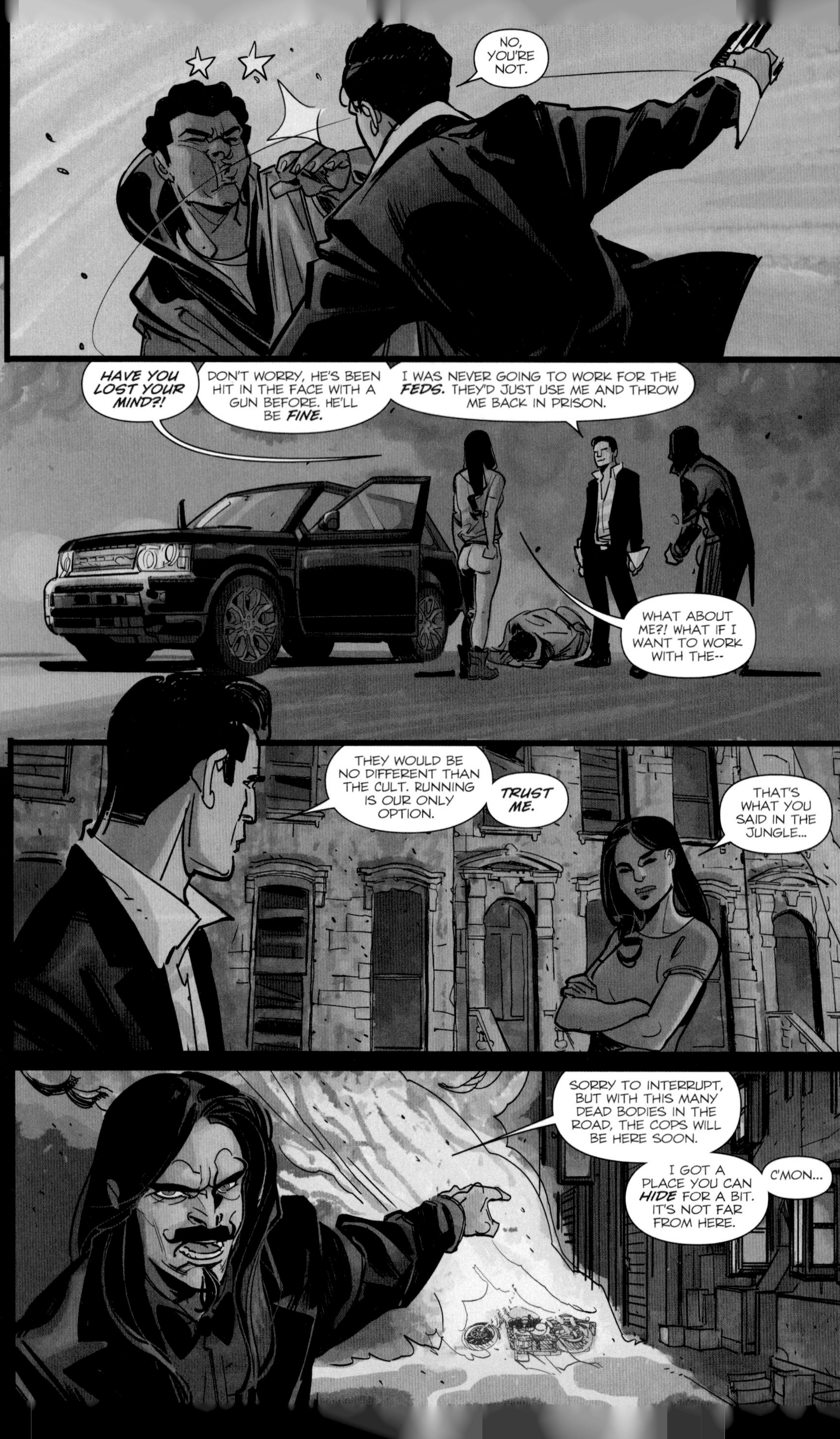

NO, YOU'RE NOT.
HAVE YOU LOST YOUR MIND?!
DON'T WORRY, HE'S BEEN HIT IN THE FACE WITH A GUN BEFORE. HE'LL BE FINE.
I WAS NEVER GOING TO WORK FOR THE FEDS. THEY'D JUST USE ME AND THROW ME BACK IN PRISON.
WHAT ABOUT ME?! WHAT IF I WANT TO WORK WITH THE--
THEY WOULD BE NO DIFFERENT THAN THE CULT. RUNNING IS OUR ONLY OPTION.
TRUST ME.
THAT'S WHAT YOU SAID IN THE JUNGLE...
SORRY TO INTERRUPT, BUT WITH THIS MANY DEAD BODIES IN THE ROAD, THE COPS WILL BE HERE SOON.
I GOT A PLACE YOU CAN HIDE FOR A BIT. IT'S NOT FAR FROM HERE.
C'MON...

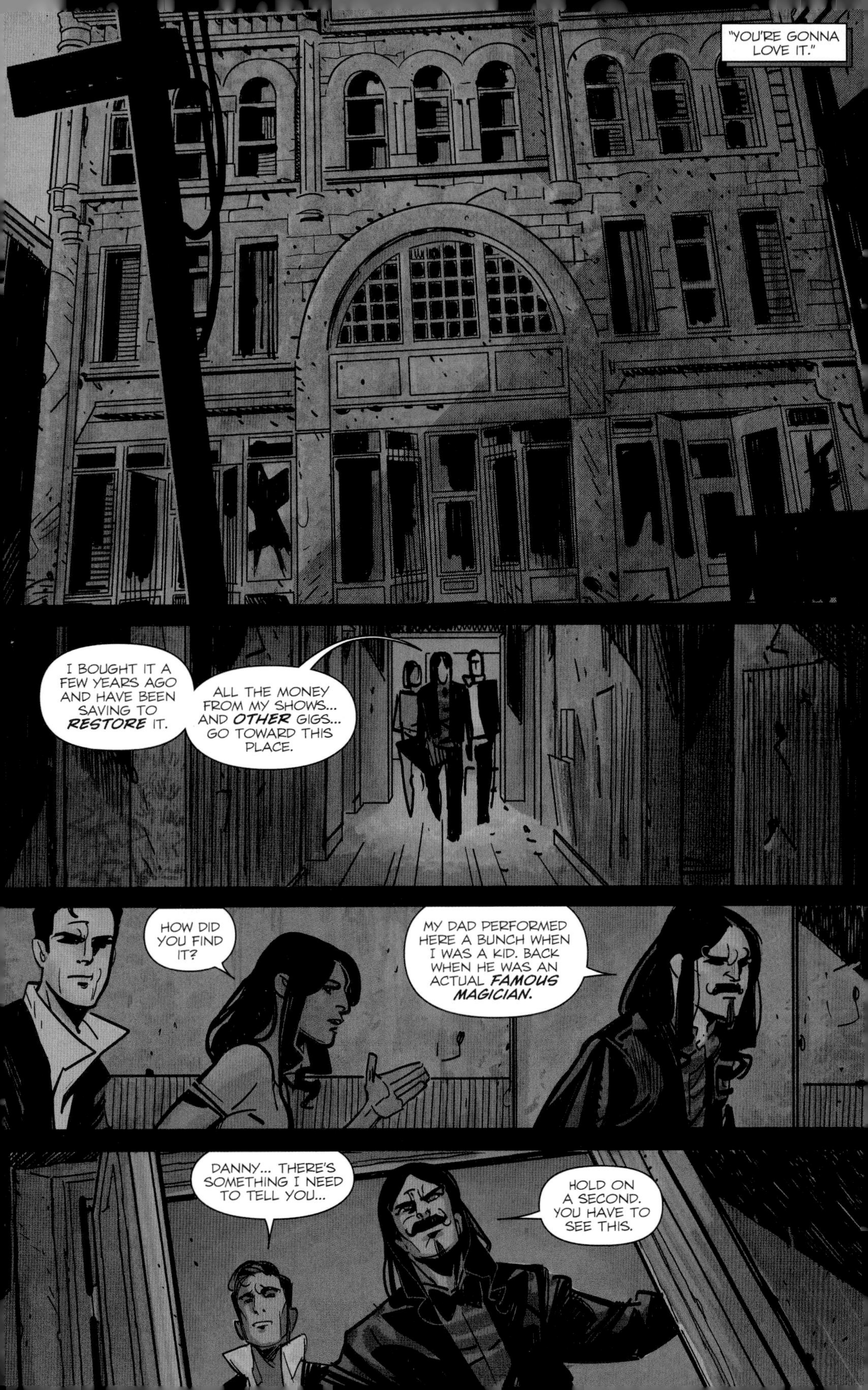
"YOU'RE GONNA LOVE IT."
I BOUGHT IT A FEW YEARS AGO AND HAVE BEEN SAVING TO RESTORE IT.
ALL THE MONEY FROM MY SHOWS... AND OTHER GIGS... GO TOWARD THIS PLACE.
HOW DID YOU FIND IT?
MY DAD PERFORMED HERE A BUNCH WHEN I WAS A KID. BACK WHEN HE WAS AN ACTUAL FAMOUS MAGICIAN.
DANNY... THERE'S SOMETHING I NEED TO TELL YOU...
HOLD ON A SECOND. YOU HAVE TO SEE THIS.

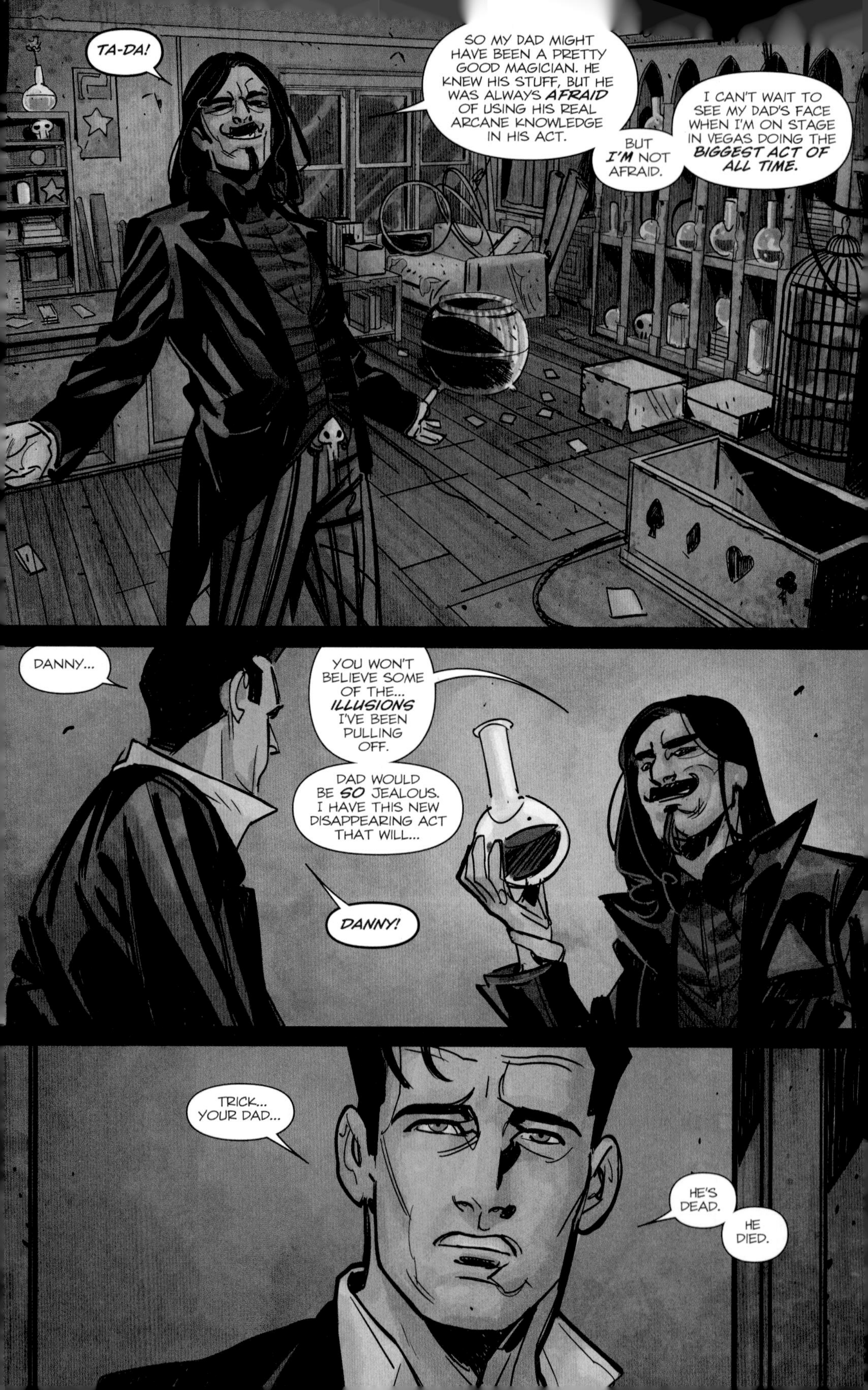
TA-DA!
SO MY DAD MIGHT HAVE BEEN A PRETTY GOOD MAGICIAN. HE KNEW HIS STUFF, BUT HE WAS ALWAYS AFRAID OF USING HIS REAL ARCANE KNOWLEDGE IN HIS ACT.
BUT I'M NOT AFRAID.
I CAN'T WAIT TO SEE MY DAD'S FACE WHEN I'M ON STAGE IN VEGAS DOING THE BIGGEST ACT OF ALL TIME.
DANNY...
YOU WON'T BELIEVE SOME OF THE... ILLUSIONS I'VE BEEN PULLING OFF.
DAD WOULD BE SO JEALOUS. I HAVE THIS NEW DISAPPEARING ACT THAT WILL...
DANNY!
TRICK... YOUR DAD...
HE'S DEAD.
HE DIED.

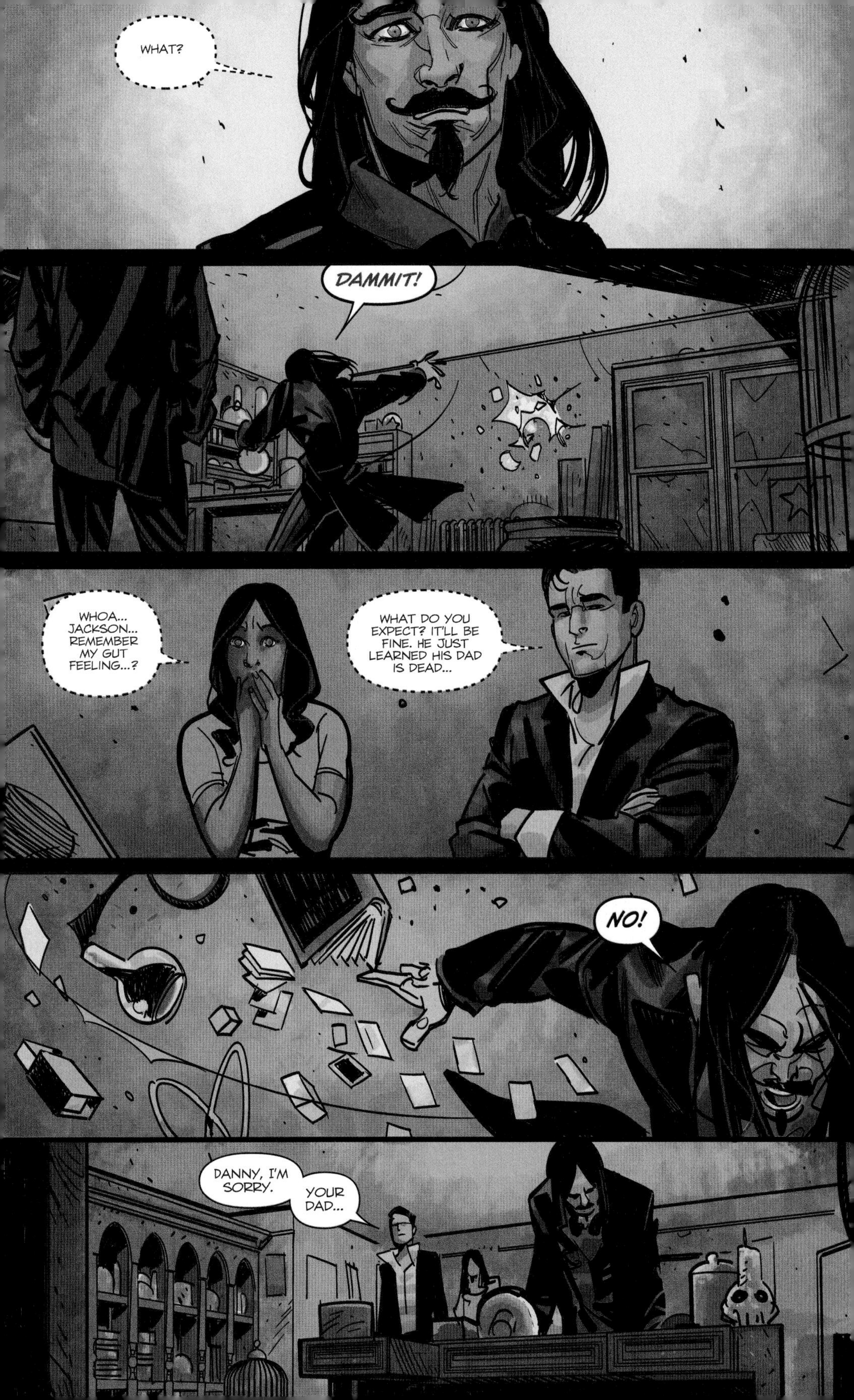
WHAT?
DAMMIT!
WHOA... JACKSON... REMEMBER MY GUT FEELING...?
WHAT DO YOU EXPECT? IT'LL BE FINE. HE JUST LEARNED HIS DAD IS DEAD...
NO!
DANNY, I'M SORRY.
YOUR DAD...

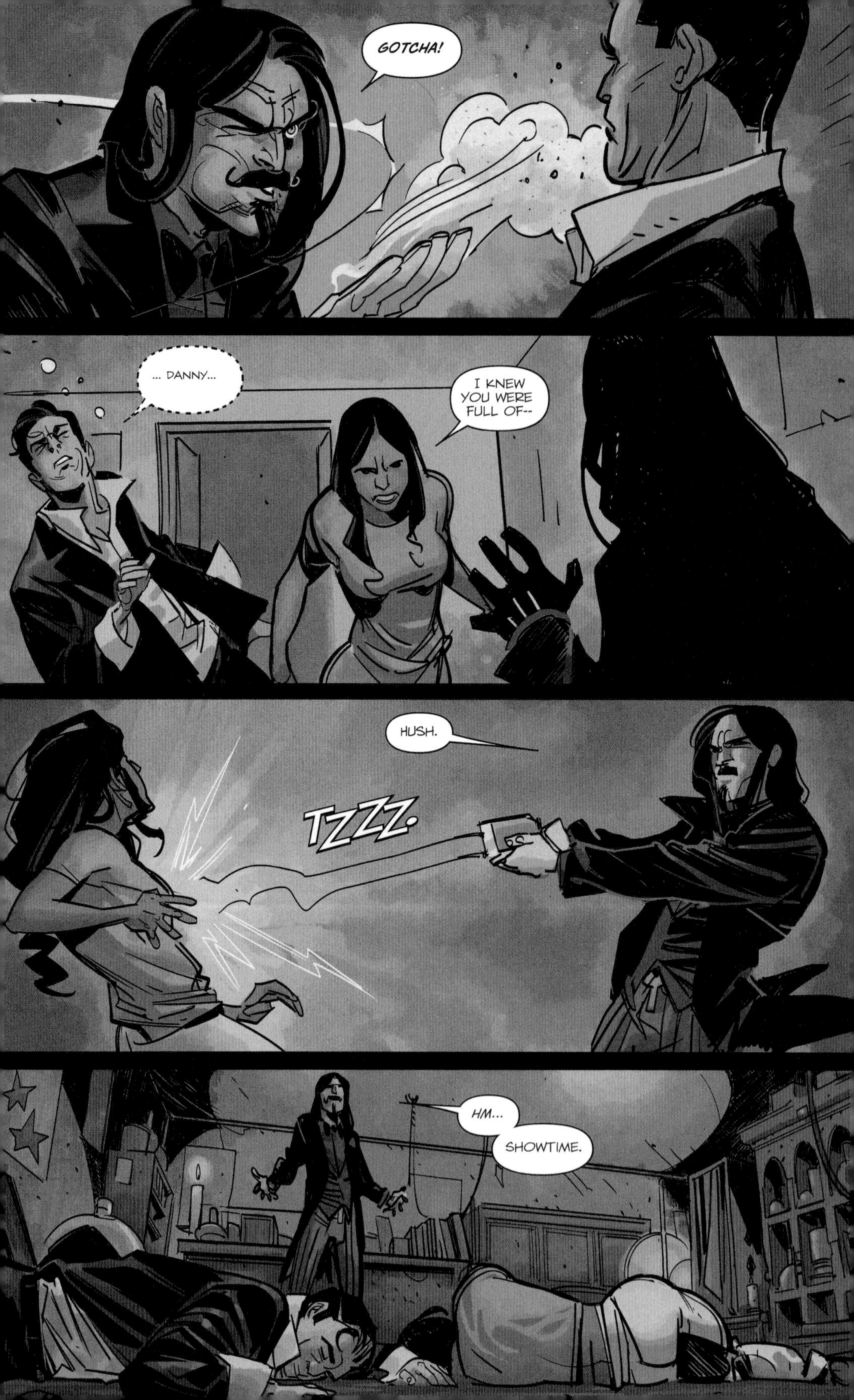
GOTCHA!
... DANNY...
I KNEW YOU WERE FULL OF--
HUSH.
TZZZ.
HM...
SHOWTIME.

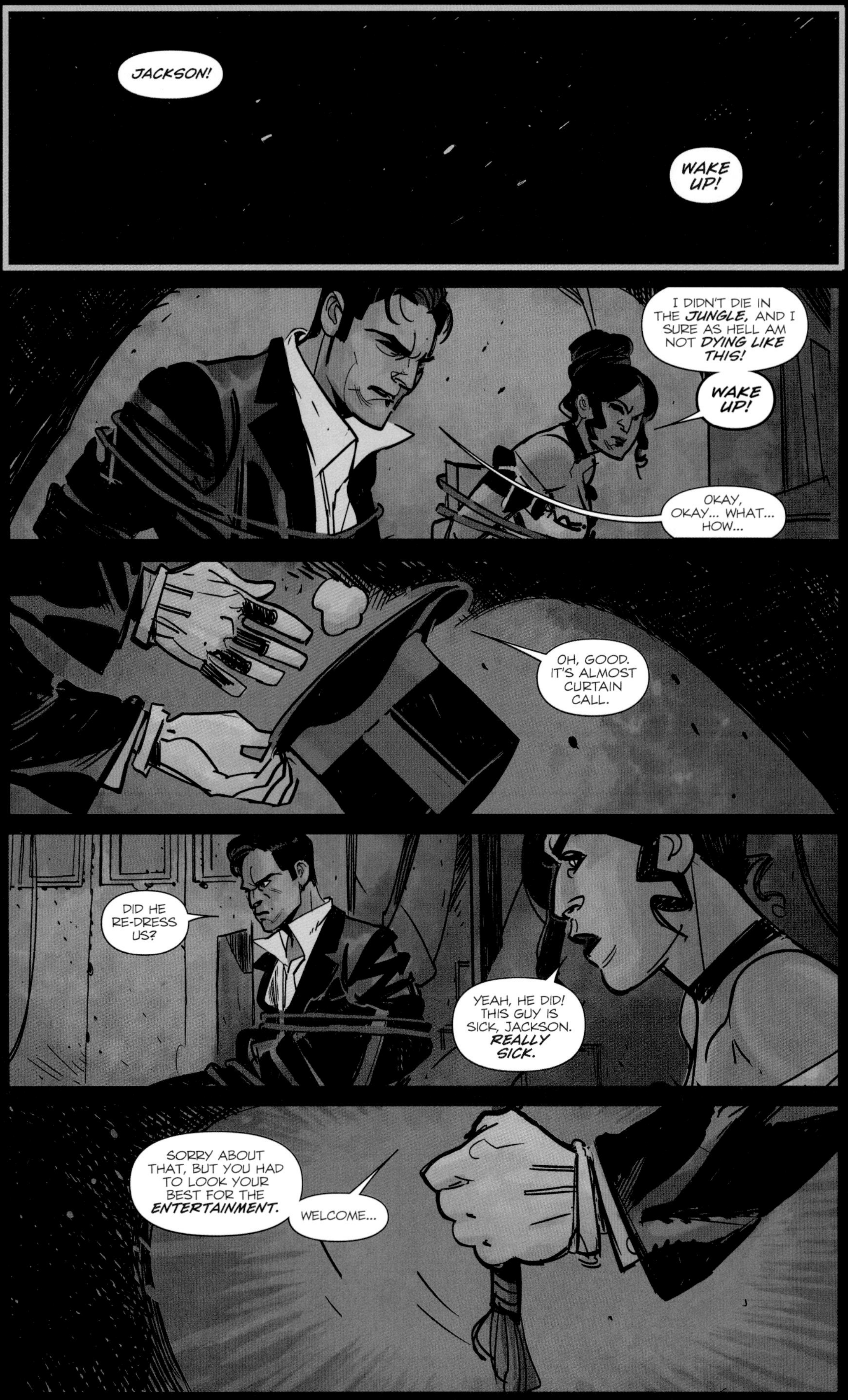
JACKSON!
WAKE UP!
I DIDN'T DIE IN THE JUNGLE, AND I SURE AS HELL AM NOT DYING LIKE THIS!
WAKE UP!
OKAY, OKAY... WHAT... HOW...
OH, GOOD. IT'S ALMOST CURTAIN CALL.
DID HE RE-DRESS US?
YEAH, HE DID! THIS GUY IS SICK, JACKSON. REALLY SICK.
SORRY ABOUT THAT, BUT YOU HAD TO LOOK YOUR BEST FOR THE ENTERTAINMENT.
WELCOME...

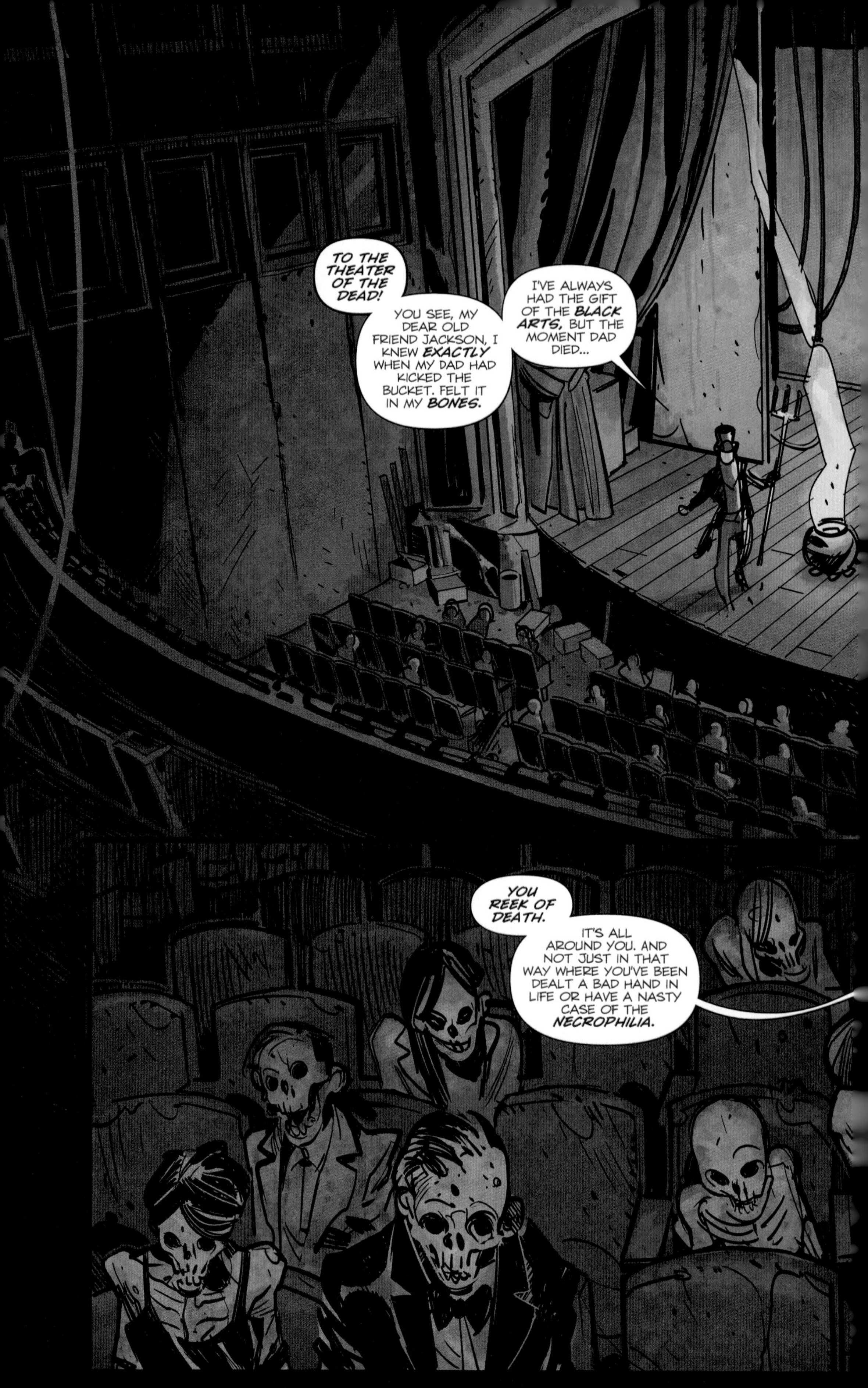
TO THE THEATER OF THE DEAD!
YOU SEE, MY DEAR OLD FRIEND JACKSON, I KNEW EXACTLY WHEN MY DAD HAD KICKED THE BUCKET. FELT IT IN MY BONES.
I'VE ALWAYS HAD THE GIFT OF THE BLACK ARTS, BUT THE MOMENT DAD DIED...
YOU REEK OF DEATH.
IT'S ALL AROUND YOU. AND NOT JUST IN THAT WAY WHERE YOU'VE BEEN DEALT A BAD HAND IN LIFE OR HAVE A NASTY CASE OF THE NECROPHILIA.

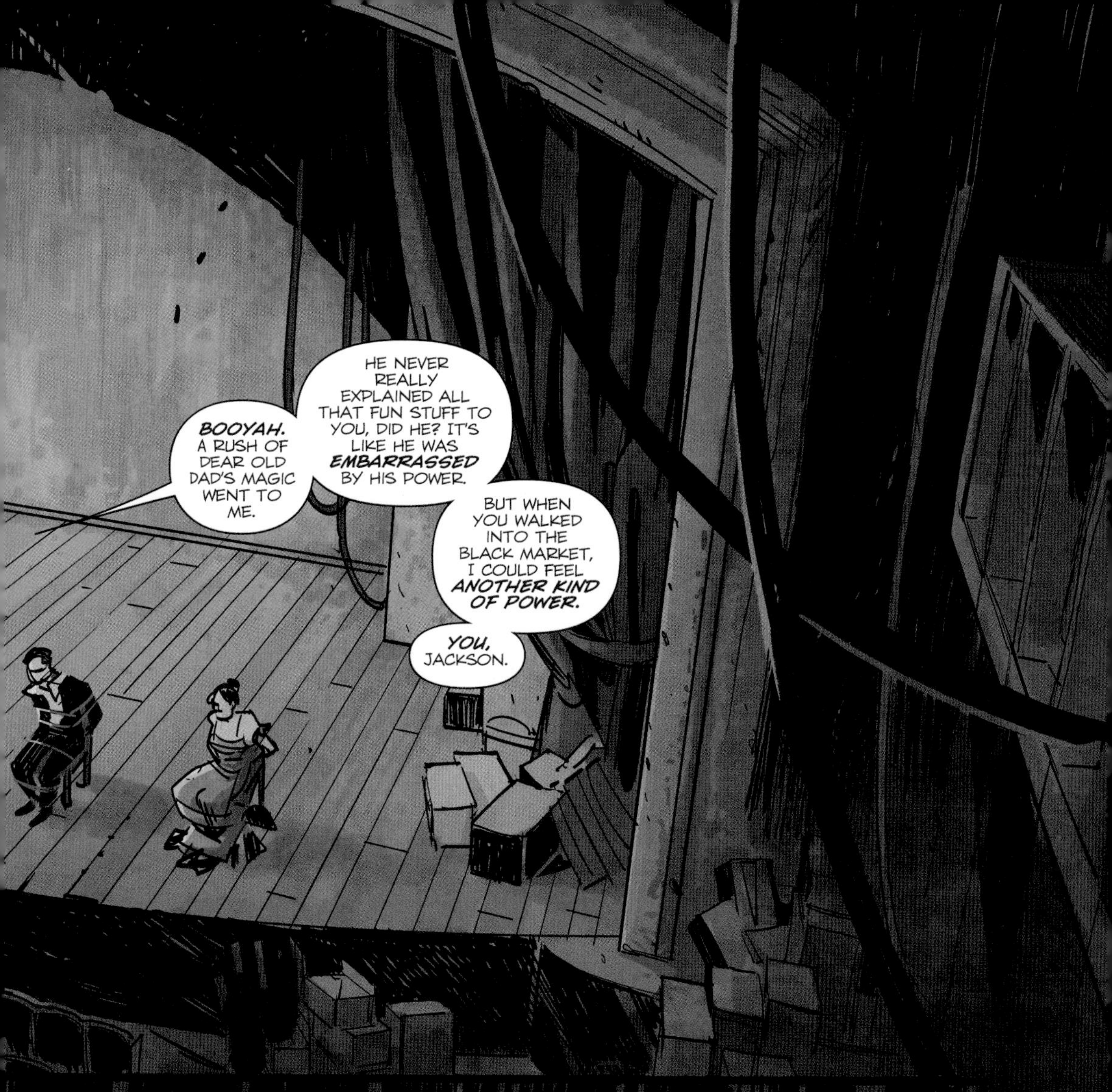
BOOYAH. A RUSH OF DEAR OLD DAD'S MAGIC WENT TO ME.
HE NEVER REALLY EXPLAINED ALL THAT FUN STUFF TO YOU, DID HE? IT'S LIKE HE WAS EMBARRASSED BY HIS POWER.
BUT WHEN YOU WALKED INTO THE BLACK MARKET, I COULD FEEL ANOTHER KIND OF POWER.
YOU, JACKSON.
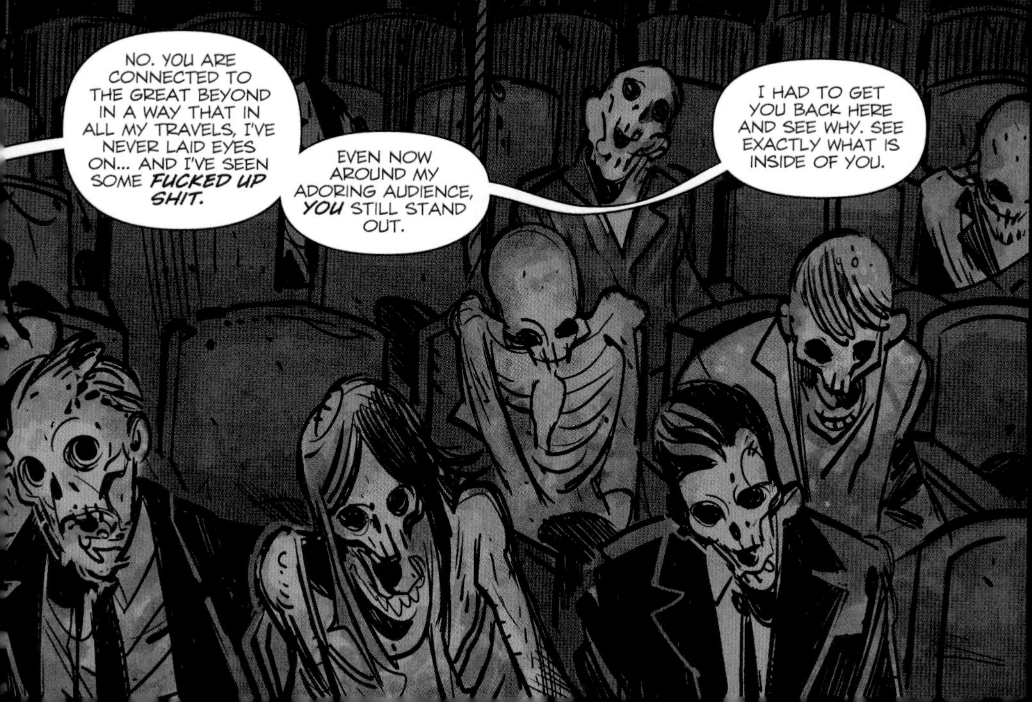
NO. YOU ARE CONNECTED TO THE GREAT BEYOND IN A WAY THAT IN ALL MY TRAVELS, I'VE NEVER LAID EYES ON... AND I'VE SEEN SOME FUCKED UP SHIT.
EVEN NOW AROUND MY ADORING AUDIENCE, YOU STILL STAND OUT.
I HAD TO GET YOU BACK HERE AND SEE WHY. SEE EXACTLY WHAT IS INSIDE OF YOU.

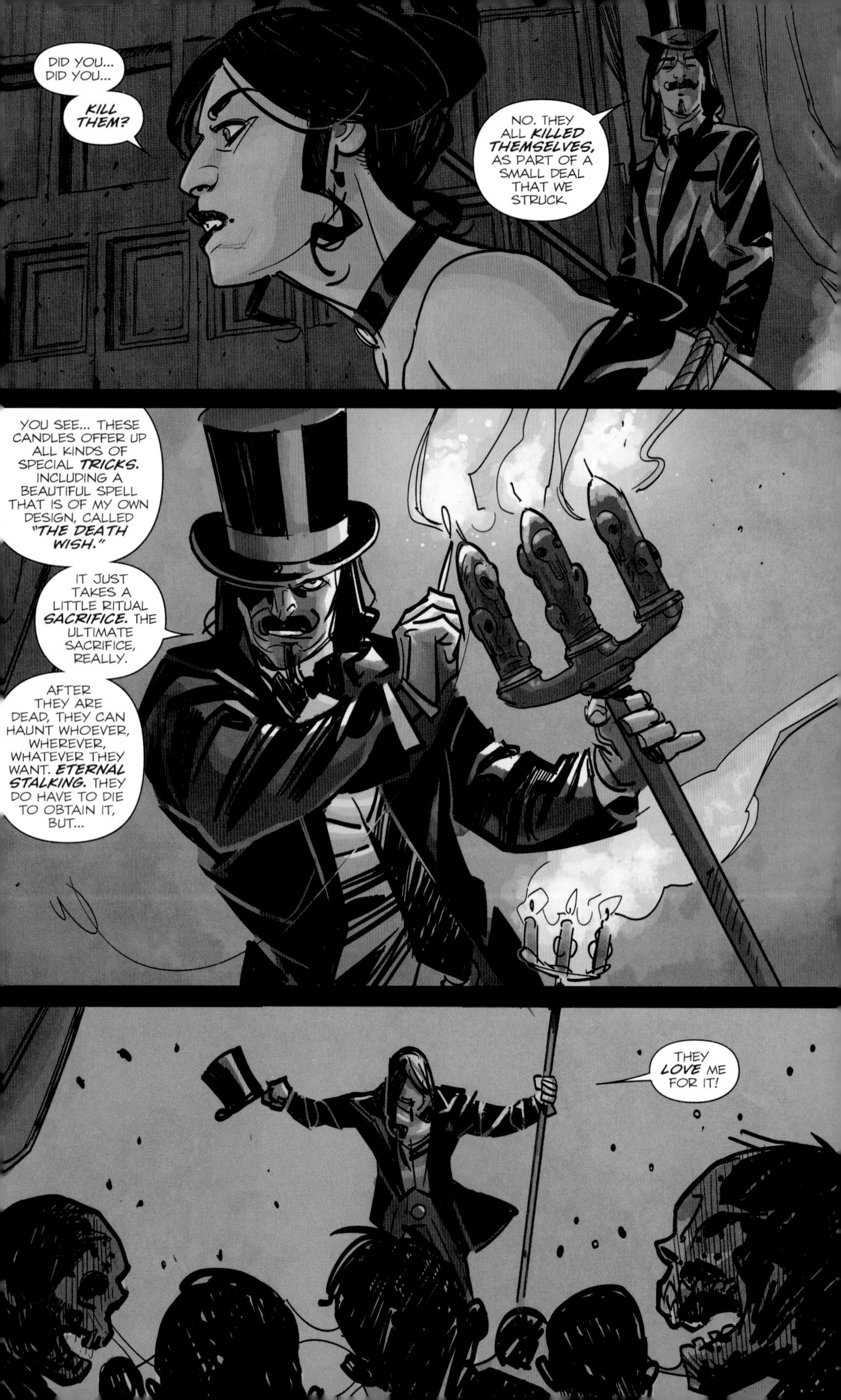
DID YOU... DID YOU... KILL THEM?
NO. THEY ALL KILLED THEMSELVES, AS PART OF A SMALL DEAL THAT WE STRUCK.
YOU SEE... THESE CANDLES OFFER UP ALL KINDS OF SPECIAL TRICKS. INCLUDING A BEAUTIFUL SPELL THAT IS OF MY OWN DESIGN, CALLED "THE DEATH WISH."
IT JUST TAKES A LITTLE RITUAL SACRIFICE. THE ULTIMATE SACRIFICE, REALLY.
AFTER THEY ARE DEAD, THEY CAN HAUNT WHOEVER, WHEREVER, WHATEVER THEY WANT. ETERNAL STALKING. THEY DO HAVE TO DIE TO OBTAIN IT, BUT...
THEY LOVE ME FOR IT!

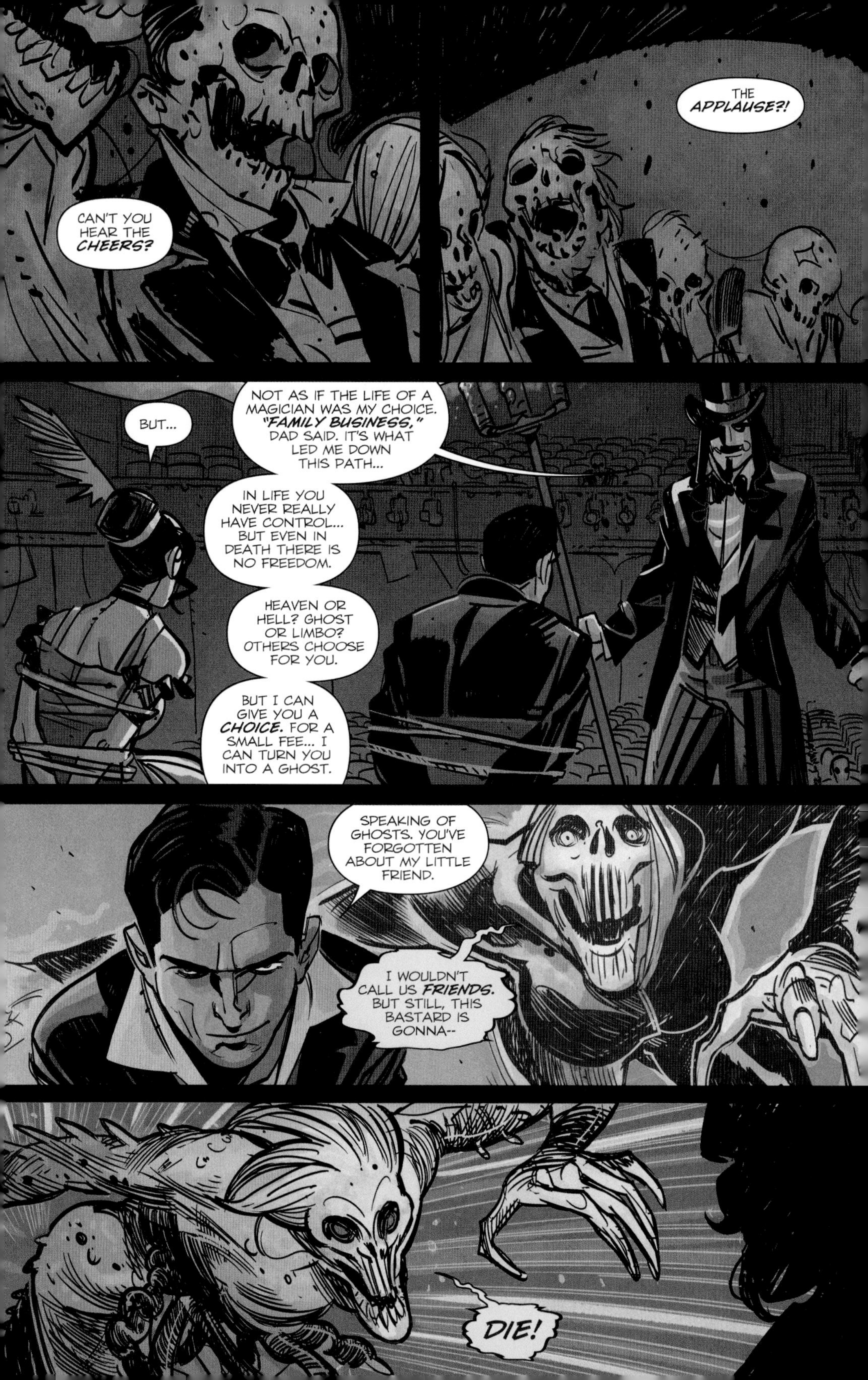
CAN'T YOU HEAR THE CHEERS?
THE APPLAUSE?!
BUT...
NOT AS IF THE LIFE OF A MAGICIAN WAS MY CHOICE. "FAMILY BUSINESS," DAD SAID. IT'S WHAT LED ME DOWN THIS PATH...
IN LIFE YOU NEVER REALLY HAVE CONTROL... BUT EVEN IN DEATH THERE IS NO FREEDOM.
HEAVEN OR HELL? GHOST OR LIMBO? OTHERS CHOOSE FOR YOU.
BUT I CAN GIVE YOU A CHOICE. FOR A SMALL FEE... I CAN TURN YOU INTO A GHOST.
SPEAKING OF GHOSTS. YOU'VE FORGOTTEN ABOUT MY LITTLE FRIEND.
I WOULDN'T CALL US FRIENDS. BUT STILL, THIS BASTARD IS GONNA--
DIE!

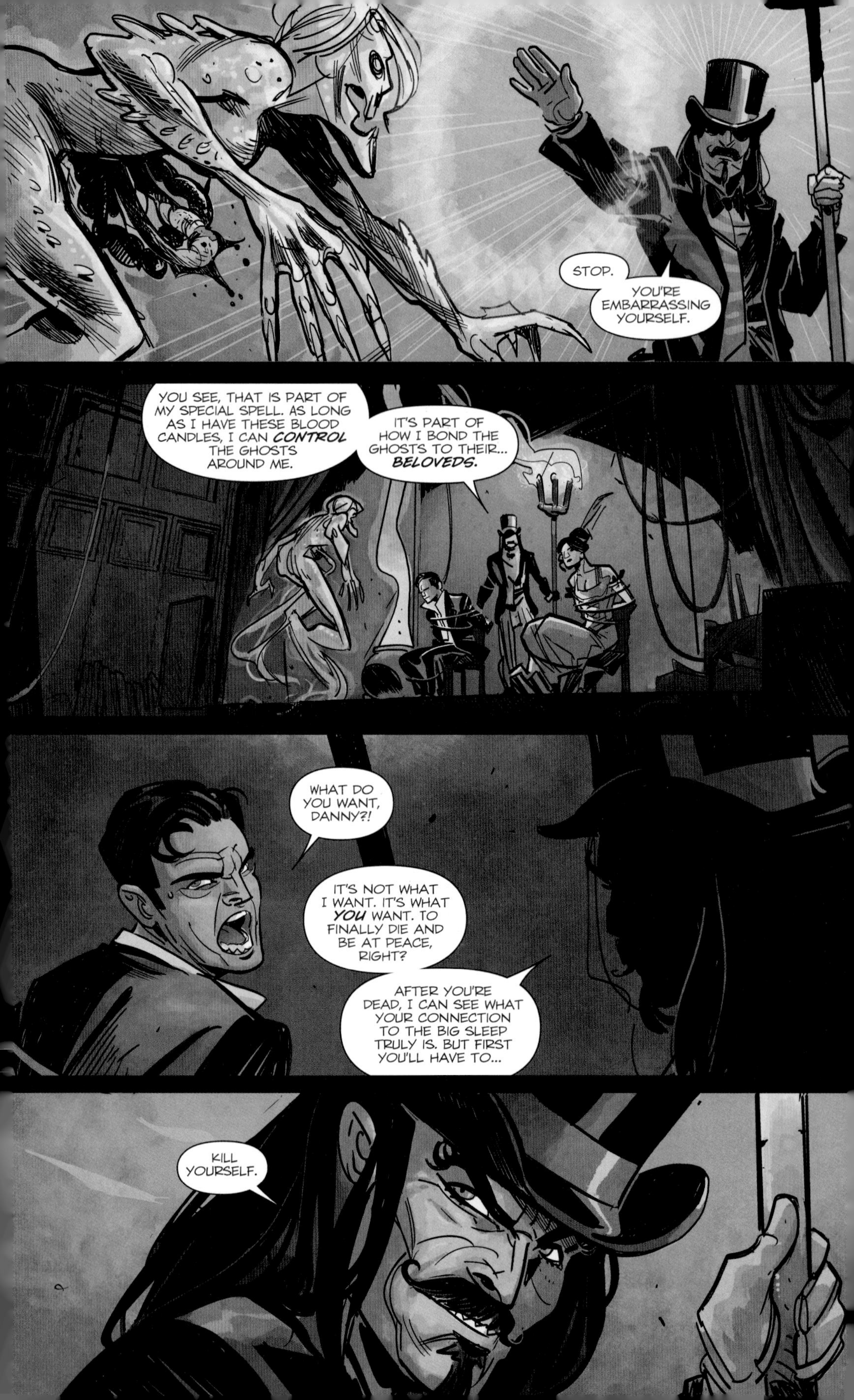
STOP.
YOU'RE EMBARRASSING YOURSELF.
YOU SEE, THAT IS PART OF MY SPECIAL SPELL. AS LONG AS I HAVE THESE BLOOD CANDLES, I CAN CONTROL THE GHOSTS AROUND ME.
IT'S PART OF HOW I BOND THE GHOSTS TO THEIR... BELOVEDS.
WHAT DO YOU WANT, DANNY?!
IT'S NOT WHAT I WANT. IT'S WHAT YOU WANT. TO FINALLY DIE AND BE AT PEACE, RIGHT?
AFTER YOU'RE DEAD, I CAN SEE WHAT YOUR CONNECTION TO THE BIG SLEEP TRULY IS. BUT FIRST YOU'LL HAVE TO...
KILL YOURSELF.

CHAPTER FIVE

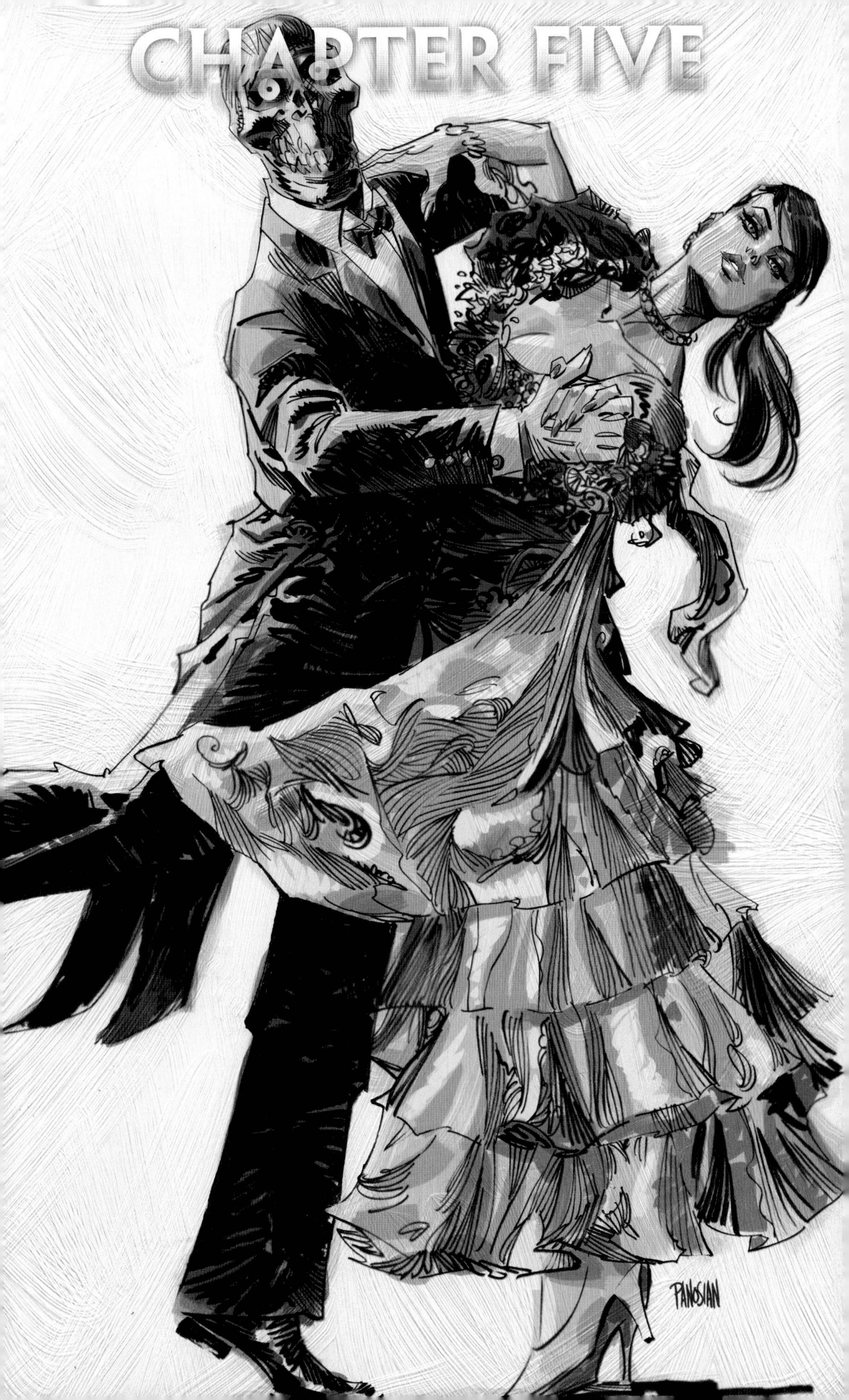
PANOSIAN

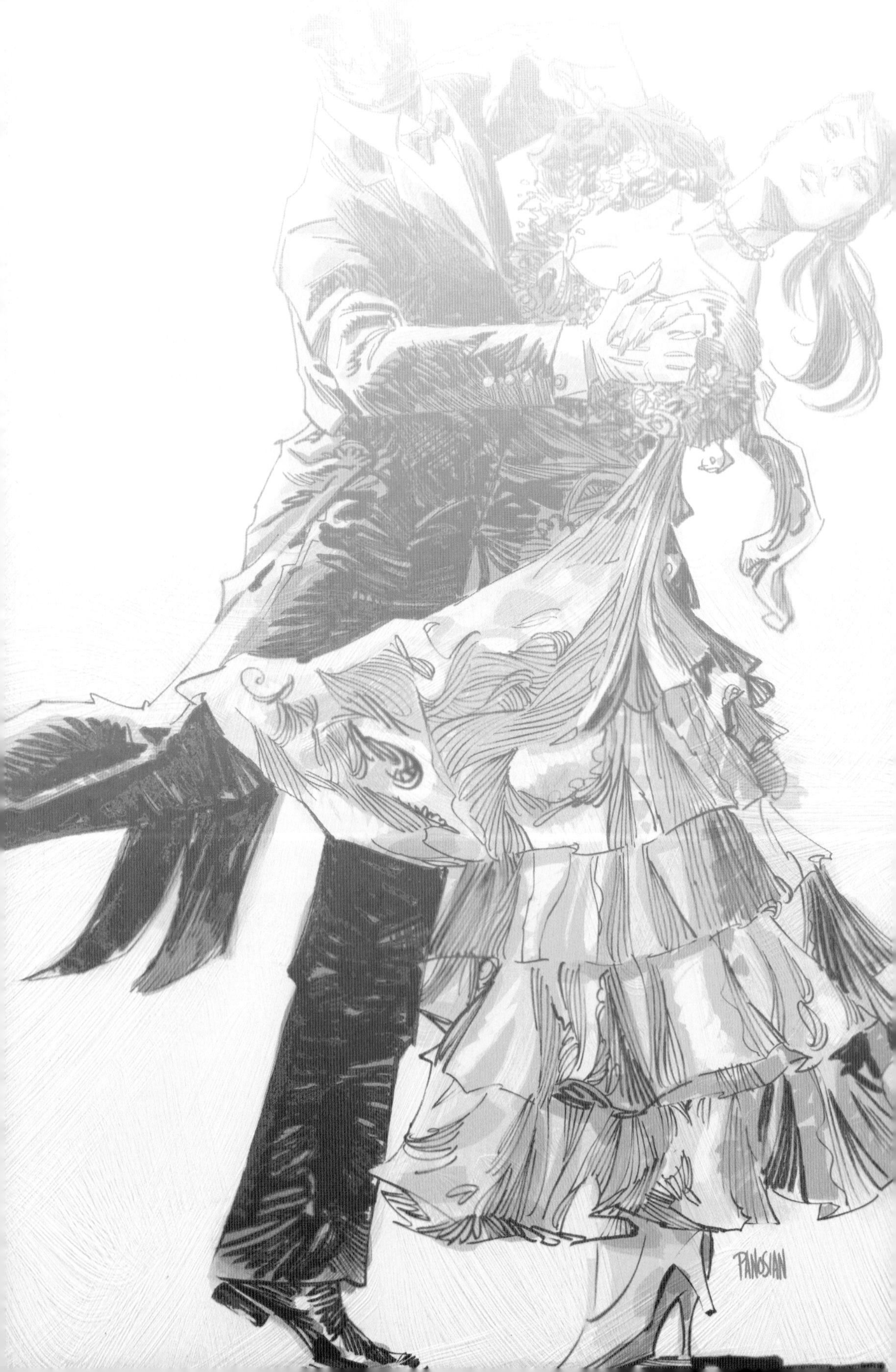
PANOSIAN

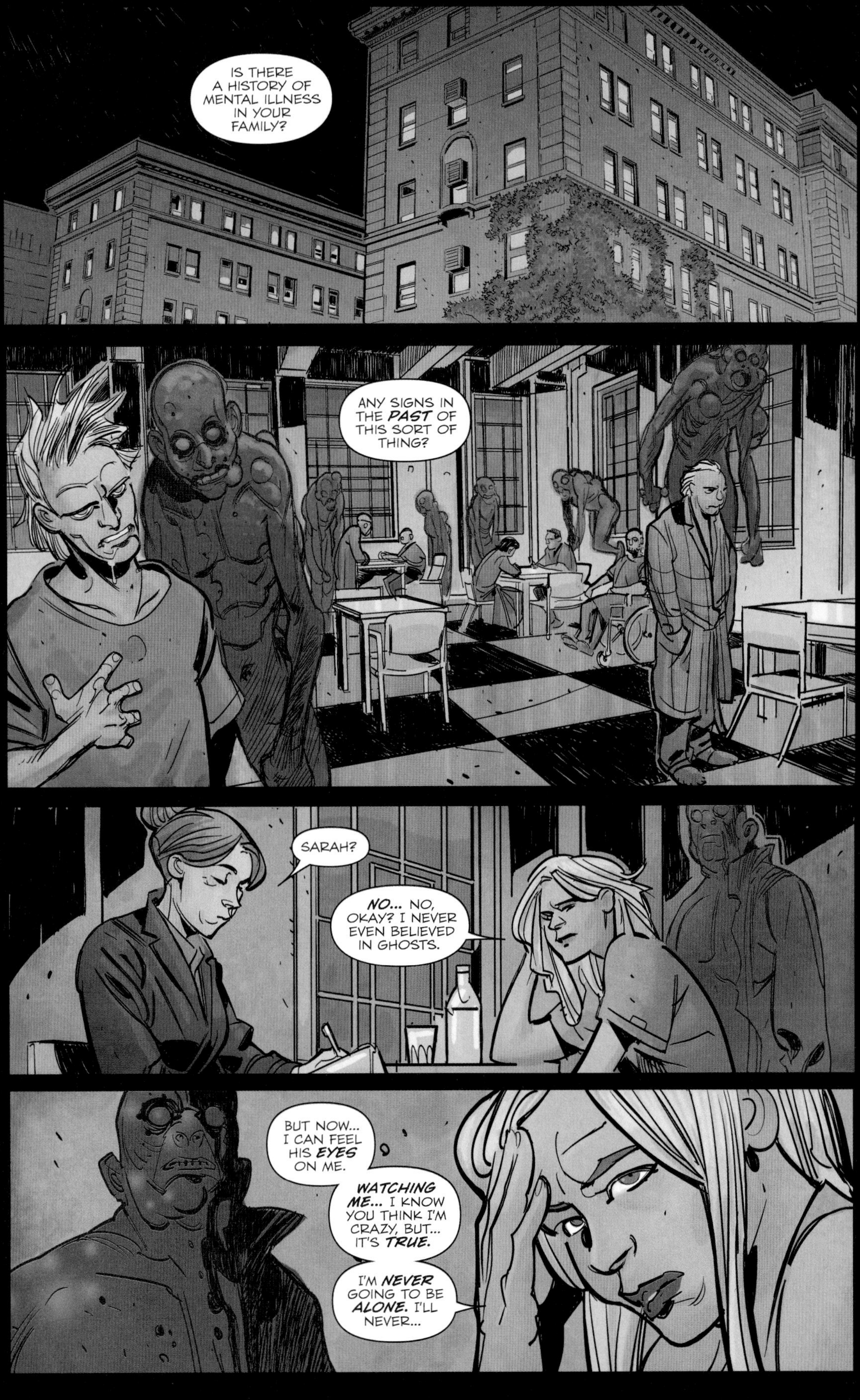
IS THERE A HISTORY OF MENTAL ILLNESS IN YOUR FAMILY?
ANY SIGNS IN THE PAST OF THIS SORT OF THING?
SARAH?
NO... NO, OKAY? I NEVER EVEN BELIEVED IN GHOSTS.
BUT NOW... I CAN FEEL HIS EYES ON ME.
WATCHING ME... I KNOW YOU THINK I'M CRAZY, BUT... IT'S TRUE.
I'M NEVER GOING TO BE ALONE. I'LL NEVER...

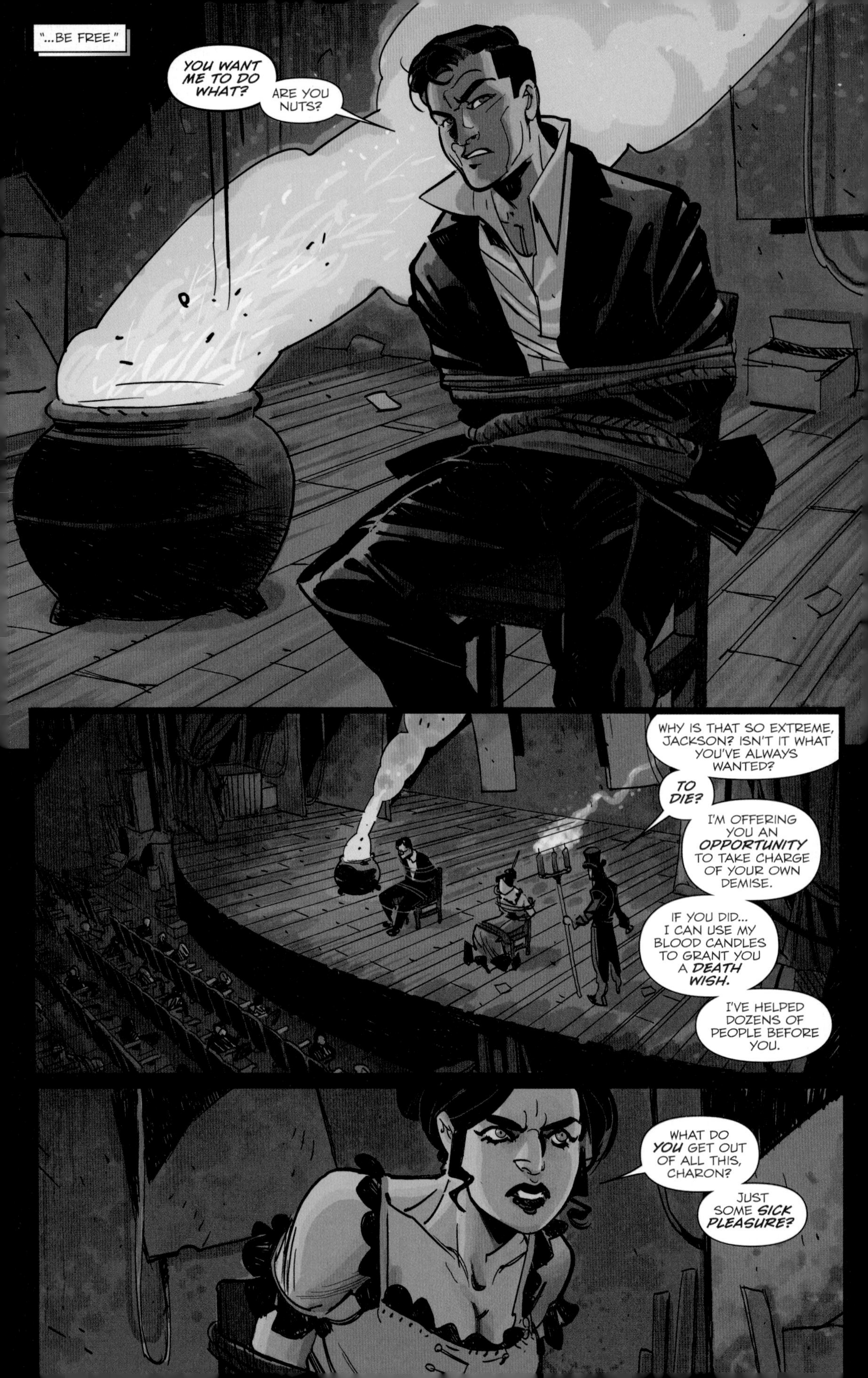
"...BE FREE."
YOU WANT ME TO DO WHAT?
ARE YOU NUTS?
WHY IS THAT SO EXTREME, JACKSON? ISN'T IT WHAT YOU'VE ALWAYS WANTED?
TO DIE?
I'M OFFERING YOU AN OPPORTUNITY TO TAKE CHARGE OF YOUR OWN DEMISE.
IF YOU DID... I CAN USE MY BLOOD CANDLES TO GRANT YOU A DEATH WISH.
I'VE HELPED DOZENS OF PEOPLE BEFORE YOU.
WHAT DO YOU GET OUT OF ALL THIS, CHARON?
JUST SOME SICK PLEASURE?

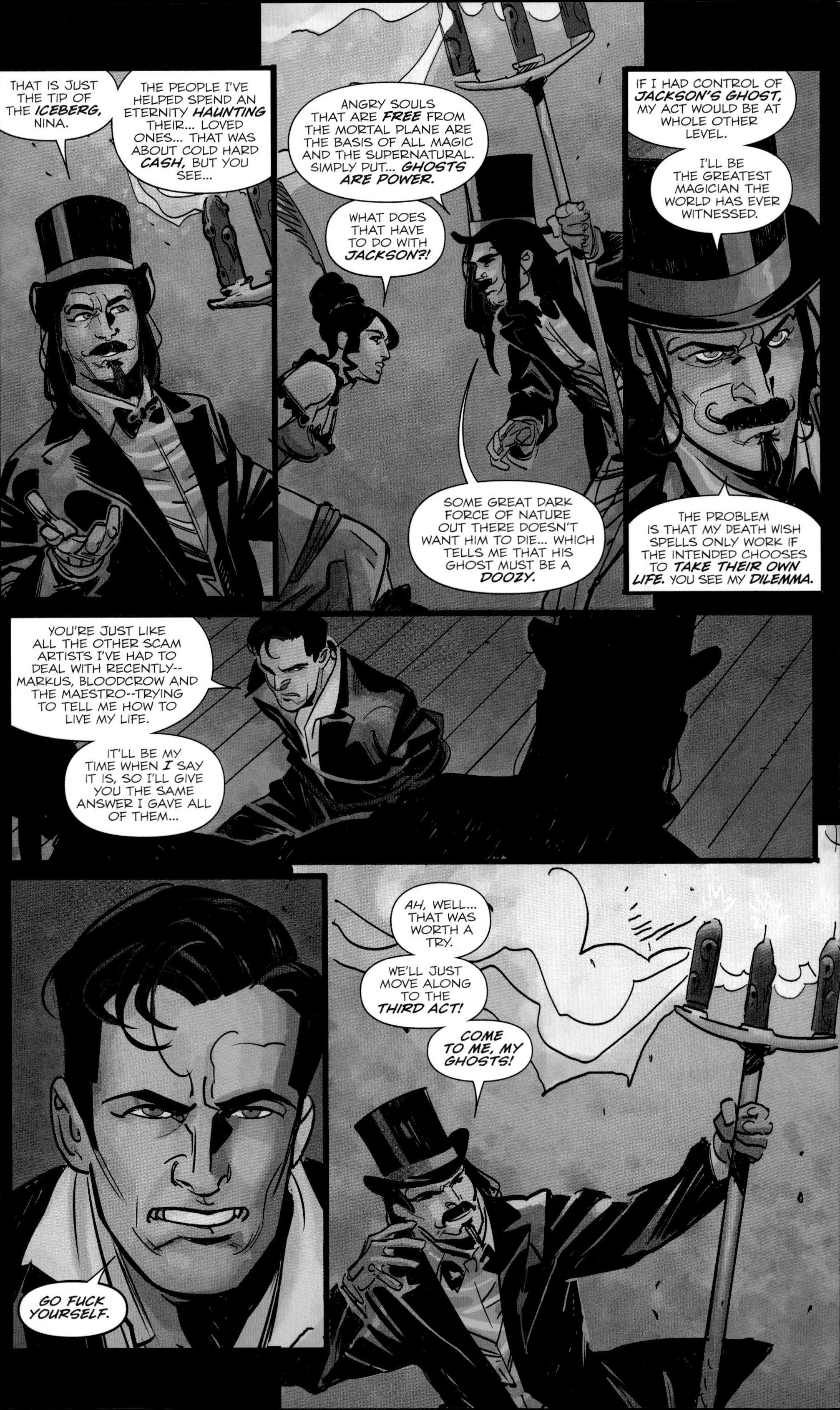

THAT IS JUST THE TIP OF THE ICEBERG, NINA.
THE PEOPLE I'VE HELPED SPEND AN ETERNITY HAUNTING THEIR... LOVED ONES... THAT WAS ABOUT COLD HARD CASH, BUT YOU SEE...
ANGRY SOULS THAT ARE FREE FROM THE MORTAL PLANE ARE THE BASIS OF ALL MAGIC AND THE SUPERNATURAL. SIMPLY PUT... GHOSTS ARE POWER.
WHAT DOES THAT HAVE TO DO WITH JACKSON?!
SOME GREAT DARK FORCE OF NATURE OUT THERE DOESN'T WANT HIM TO DIE... WHICH TELLS ME THAT HIS GHOST MUST BE A DOOZY.
IF I HAD CONTROL OF JACKSON'S GHOST, MY ACT WOULD BE AT WHOLE OTHER LEVEL.
I'LL BE THE GREATEST MAGICIAN THE WORLD HAS EVER WITNESSED.
THE PROBLEM IS THAT MY DEATH WISH SPELLS ONLY WORK IF THE INTENDED CHOOSES TO TAKE THEIR OWN LIFE. YOU SEE MY DILEMMA.
YOU'RE JUST LIKE ALL THE OTHER SCAM ARTISTS I'VE HAD TO DEAL WITH RECENTLY-- MARKUS, BLOODCROW AND THE MAESTRO--TRYING TO TELL ME HOW TO LIVE MY LIFE.
IT'LL BE MY TIME WHEN I SAY IT IS, SO I'LL GIVE YOU THE SAME ANSWER I GAVE ALL OF THEM...
GO FUCK YOURSELF.
AH, WELL... THAT WAS WORTH A TRY.
WE'LL JUST MOVE ALONG TO THE THIRD ACT!
COME TO ME, MY GHOSTS!

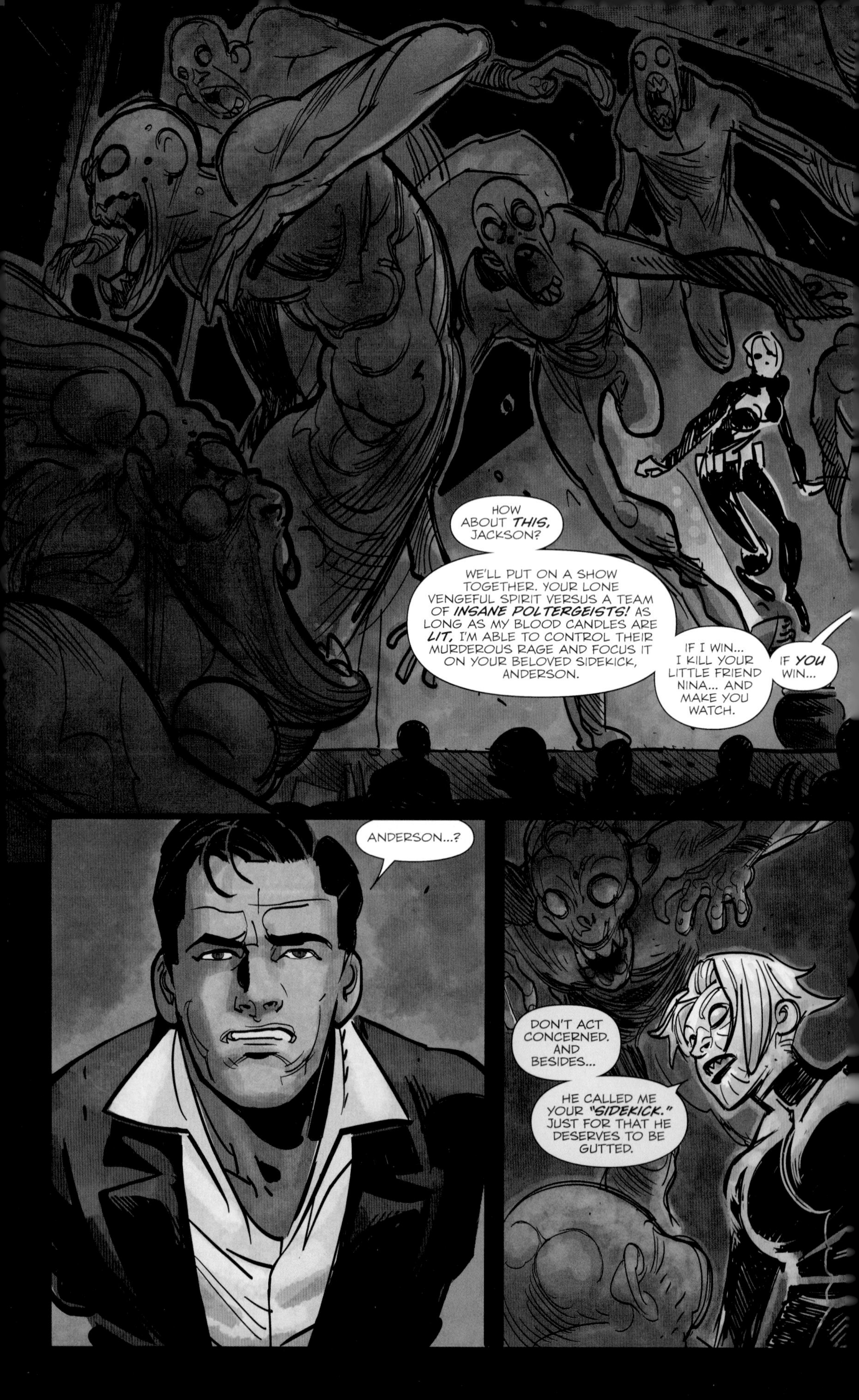
HOW ABOUT THIS, JACKSON?
WE'LL PUT ON A SHOW TOGETHER. YOUR LONE VENGEFUL SPIRIT VERSUS A TEAM OF INSANE POLTERGEISTS! AS LONG AS MY BLOOD CANDLES ARE LIT, I'M ABLE TO CONTROL THEIR MURDEROUS RAGE AND FOCUS IT ON YOUR BELOVED SIDEKICK, ANDERSON.
IF YOU WIN...
IF I WIN... I KILL YOUR LITTLE FRIEND NINA... AND MAKE YOU WATCH.
ANDERSON...?
DON'T ACT CONCERNED. AND BESIDES...
HE CALLED ME YOUR "SIDEKICK." JUST FOR THAT HE DESERVES TO BE GUTTED.

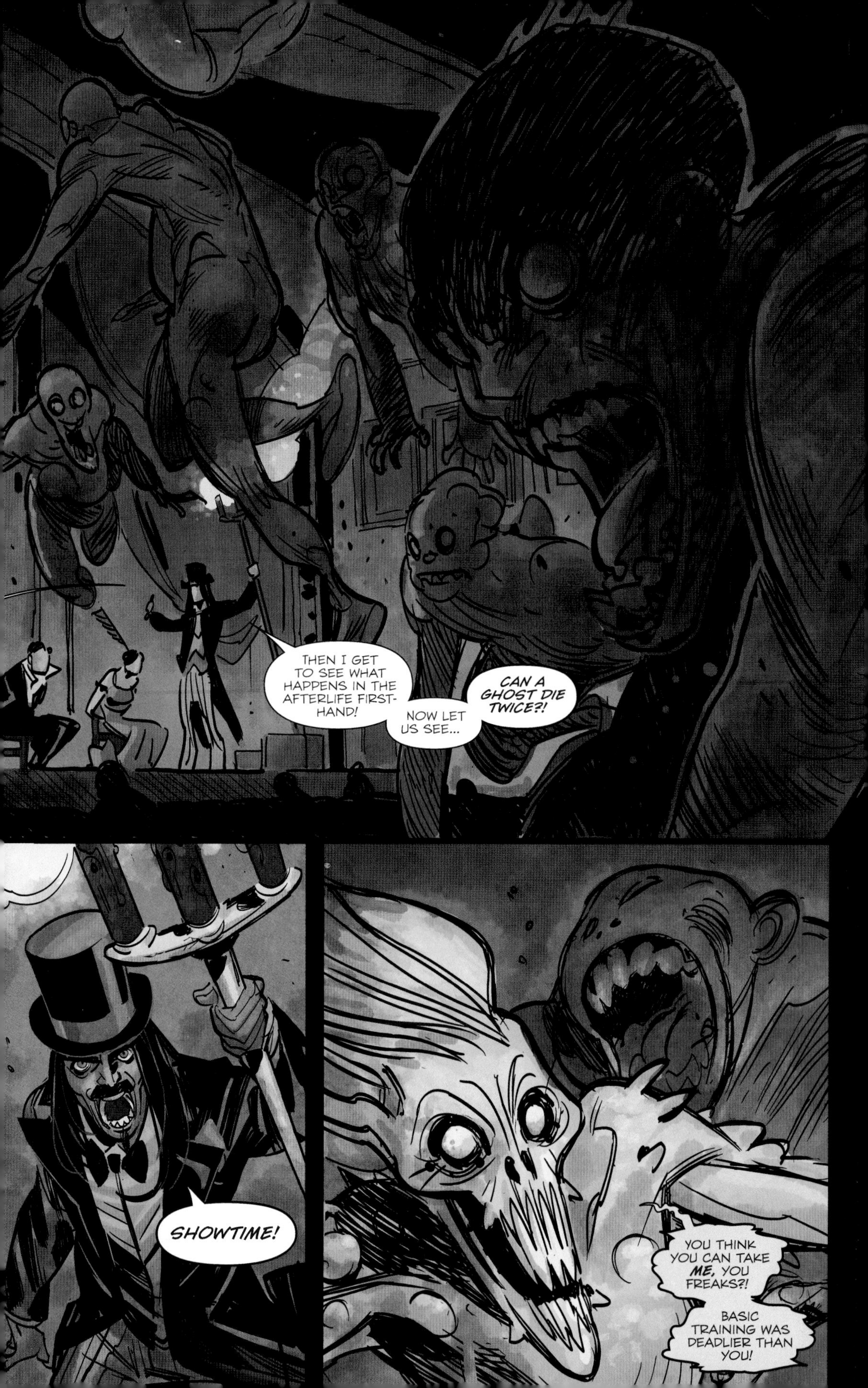
THEN I GET TO SEE WHAT HAPPENS IN THE AFTERLIFE FIRST-HAND!
NOW LET US SEE...
CAN A GHOST DIE TWICE?!
SHOWTIME!
YOU THINK YOU CAN TAKE ME, YOU FREAKS?!
BASIC TRAINING WAS DEADLIER THAN YOU!

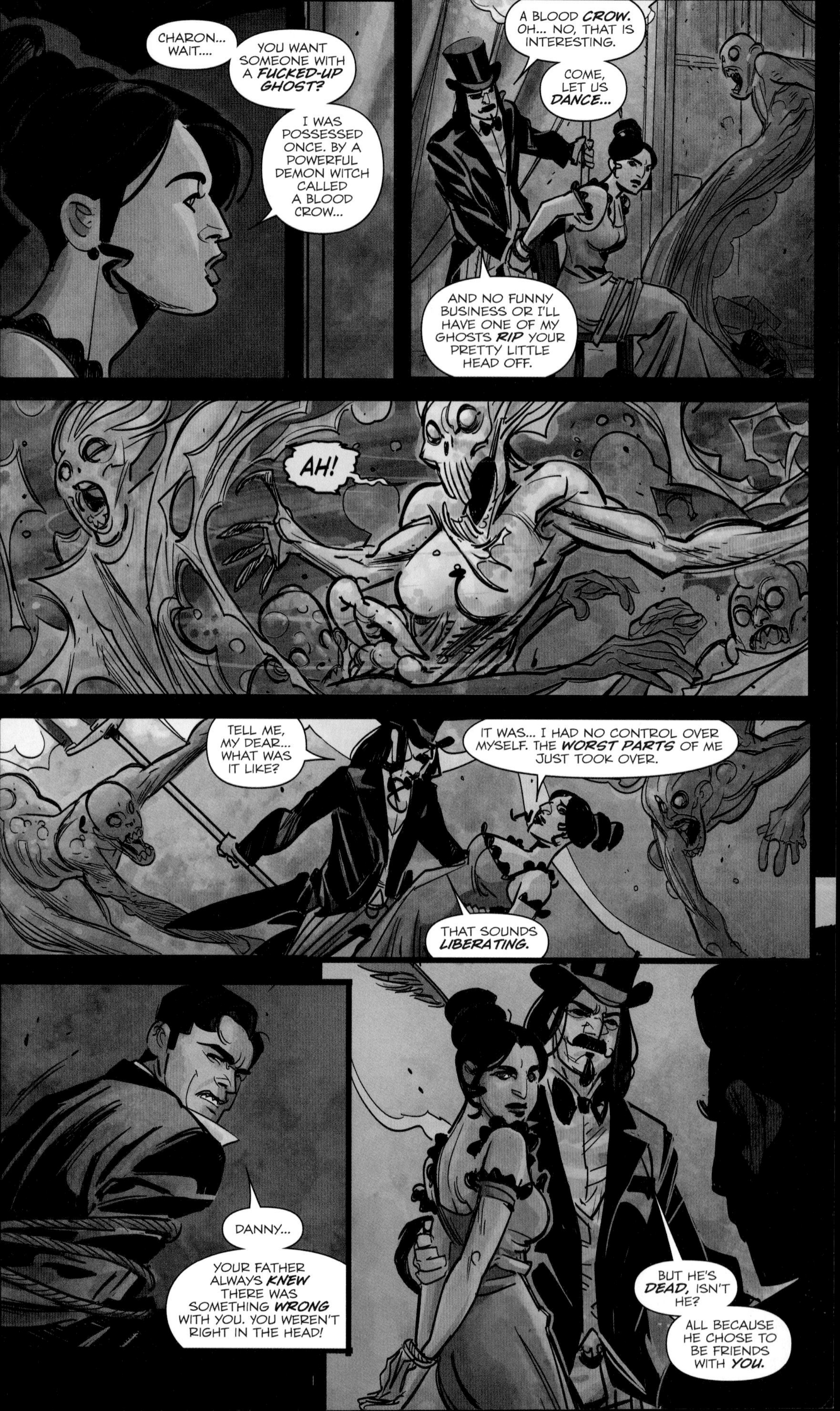
CHARON... WAIT....
YOU WANT SOMEONE WITH A FUCKED-UP GHOST?
I WAS POSSESSED ONCE. BY A POWERFUL DEMON WITCH CALLED A BLOOD CROW...
A BLOOD CROW. OH... NO, THAT IS INTERESTING.
COME, LET US DANCE...
AND NO FUNNY BUSINESS OR I'LL HAVE ONE OF MY GHOSTS RIP YOUR PRETTY LITTLE HEAD OFF.
AH!
TELL ME, MY DEAR... WHAT WAS IT LIKE?
IT WAS... I HAD NO CONTROL OVER MYSELF. THE WORST PARTS OF ME JUST TOOK OVER.
THAT SOUNDS LIBERATING.
DANNY...
YOUR FATHER ALWAYS KNEW THERE WAS SOMETHING WRONG WITH YOU. YOU WEREN'T RIGHT IN THE HEAD!
BUT HE'S DEAD, ISN'T HE?
ALL BECAUSE HE CHOSE TO BE FRIENDS WITH YOU.

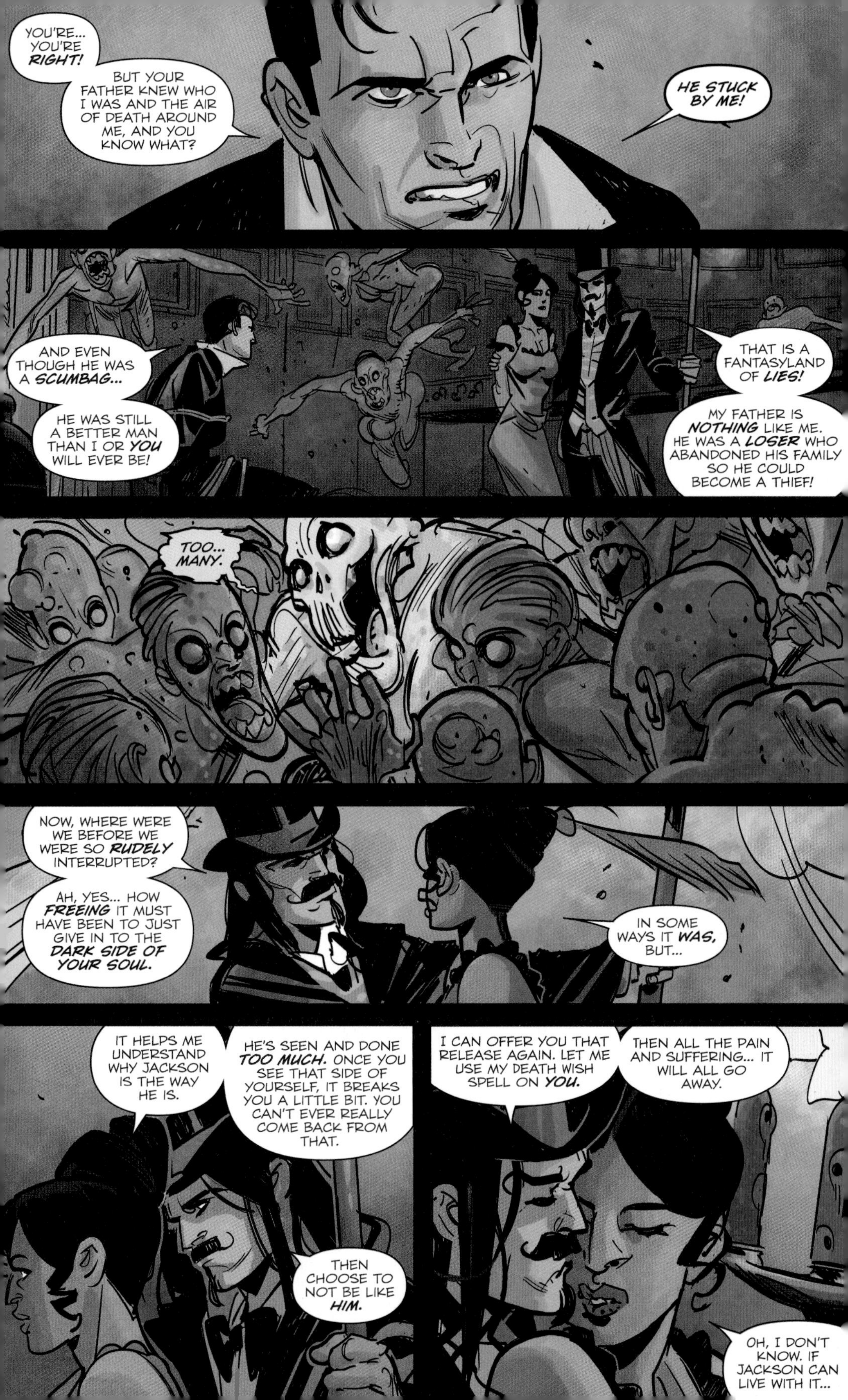
YOU'RE... YOU'RE RIGHT!
BUT YOUR FATHER KNEW WHO I WAS AND THE AIR OF DEATH AROUND ME, AND YOU KNOW WHAT?
HE STUCK BY ME!
AND EVEN THOUGH HE WAS A SCUMBAG...
HE WAS STILL A BETTER MAN THAN I OR YOU WILL EVER BE!
THAT IS A FANTASYLAND OF LIES!
MY FATHER IS NOTHING LIKE ME. HE WAS A LOSER WHO ABANDONED HIS FAMILY SO HE COULD BECOME A THIEF!
TOO... MANY.
NOW, WHERE WERE WE BEFORE WE WERE SO RUDELY INTERRUPTED?
AH, YES... HOW FREEING IT MUST HAVE BEEN TO JUST GIVE IN TO THE DARK SIDE OF YOUR SOUL.
IN SOME WAYS IT WAS, BUT...
IT HELPS ME UNDERSTAND WHY JACKSON IS THE WAY HE IS.
HE'S SEEN AND DONE TOO MUCH. ONCE YOU SEE THAT SIDE OF YOURSELF, IT BREAKS YOU A LITTLE BIT. YOU CAN'T EVER REALLY COME BACK FROM THAT.
THEN CHOOSE TO NOT BE LIKE HIM.
I CAN OFFER YOU THAT RELEASE AGAIN. LET ME USE MY DEATH WISH SPELL ON YOU.
THEN ALL THE PAIN AND SUFFERING... IT WILL ALL GO AWAY.
OH, I DON'T KNOW. IF JACKSON CAN LIVE WITH IT...

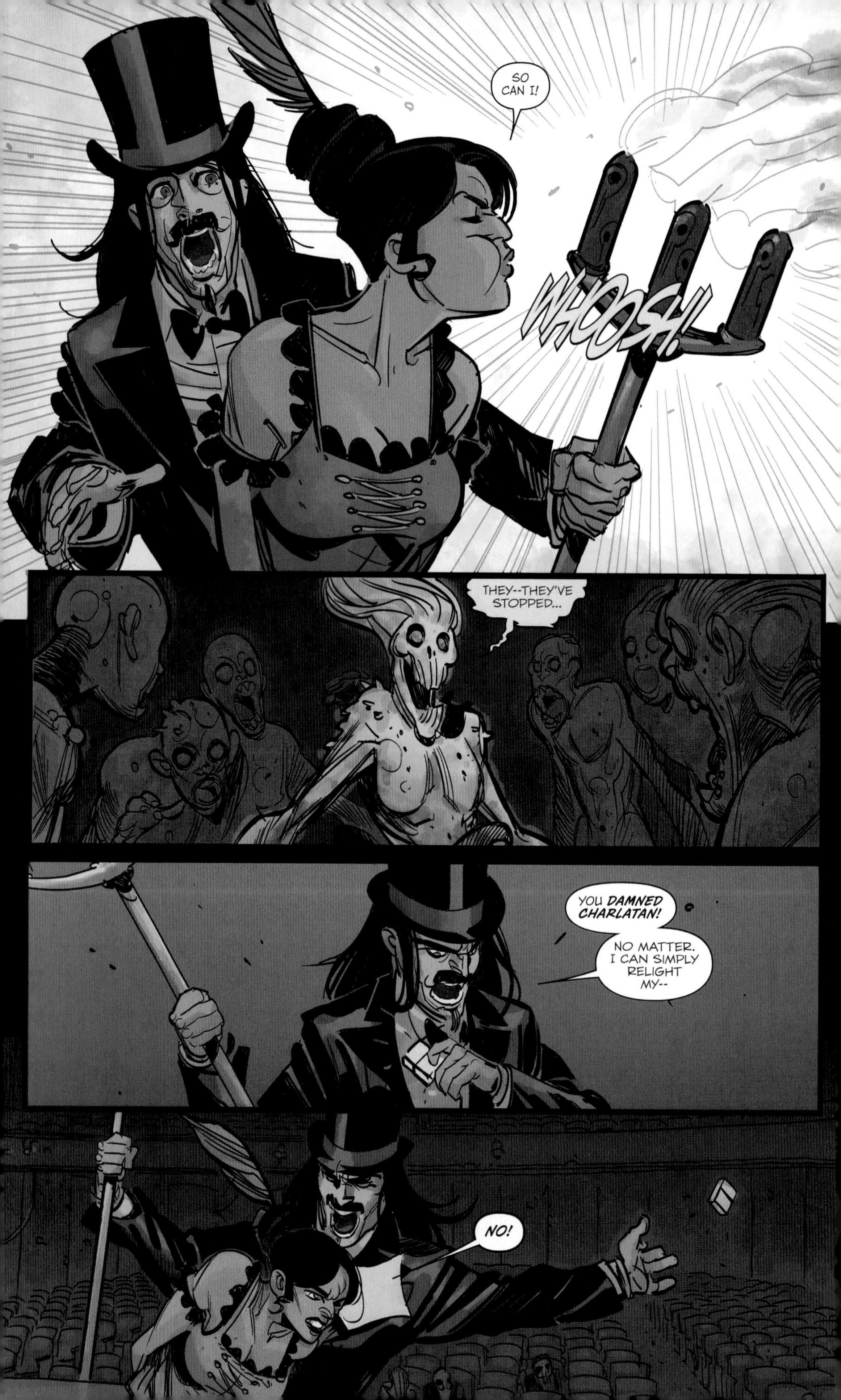
SO CAN I!
WHOOSH!
THEY--THEY'VE STOPPED...
YOU DAMNED CHARLATAN!
NO MATTER. I CAN SIMPLY RELIGHT MY--
NO!

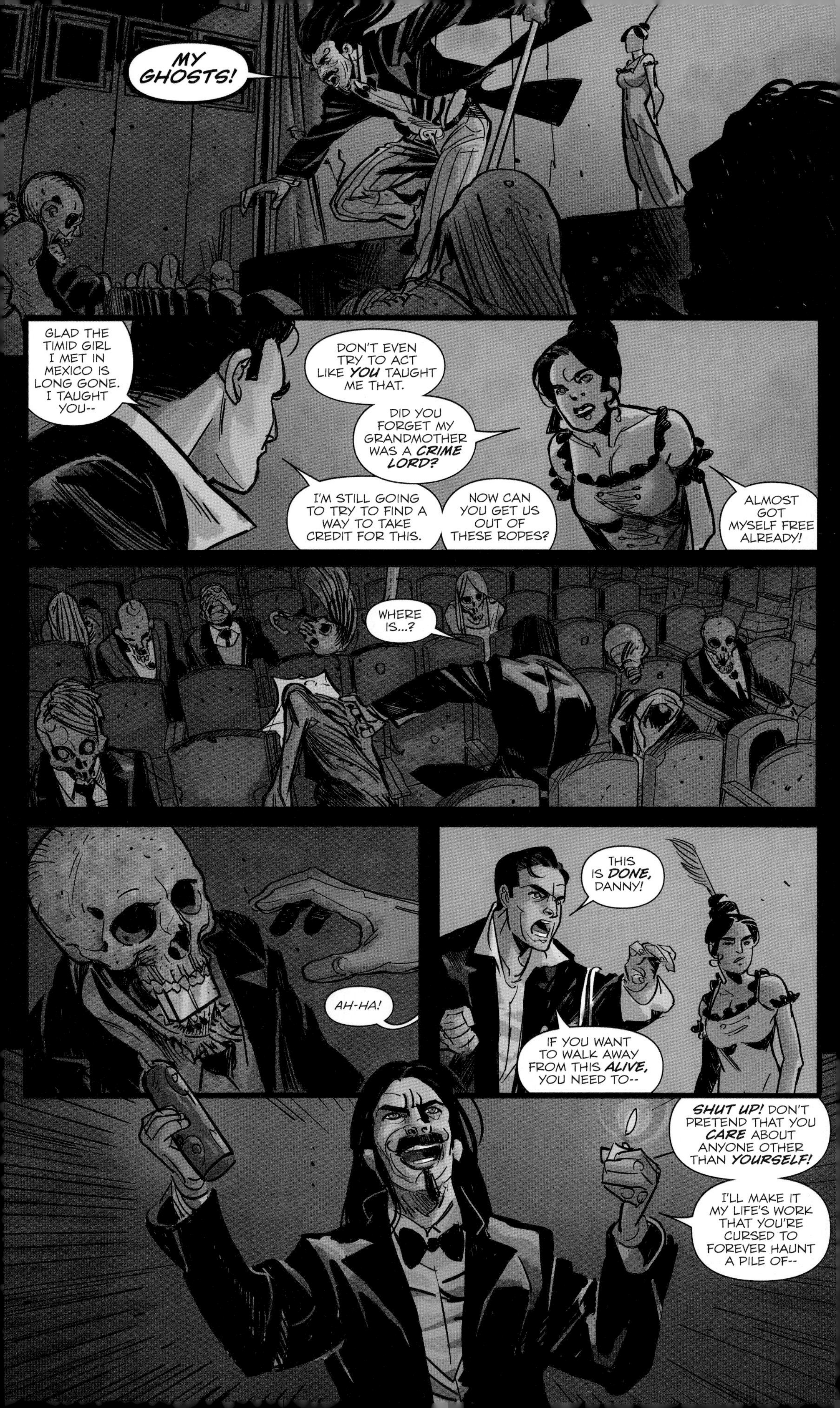
MY GHOSTS!
GLAD THE TIMID GIRL I MET IN MEXICO IS LONG GONE. I TAUGHT YOU--
DON'T EVEN TRY TO ACT LIKE YOU TAUGHT ME THAT.
DID YOU FORGET MY GRANDMOTHER WAS A CRIME LORD?
I'M STILL GOING TO TRY TO FIND A WAY TO TAKE CREDIT FOR THIS.
NOW CAN YOU GET US OUT OF THESE ROPES?
ALMOST GOT MYSELF FREE ALREADY!
WHERE IS...?
AH-HA!
THIS IS DONE, DANNY!
IF YOU WANT TO WALK AWAY FROM THIS ALIVE, YOU NEED TO--
SHUT UP! DON'T PRETEND THAT YOU CARE ABOUT ANYONE OTHER THAN YOURSELF!
I'LL MAKE IT MY LIFE'S WORK THAT YOU'RE CURSED TO FOREVER HAUNT A PILE OF--

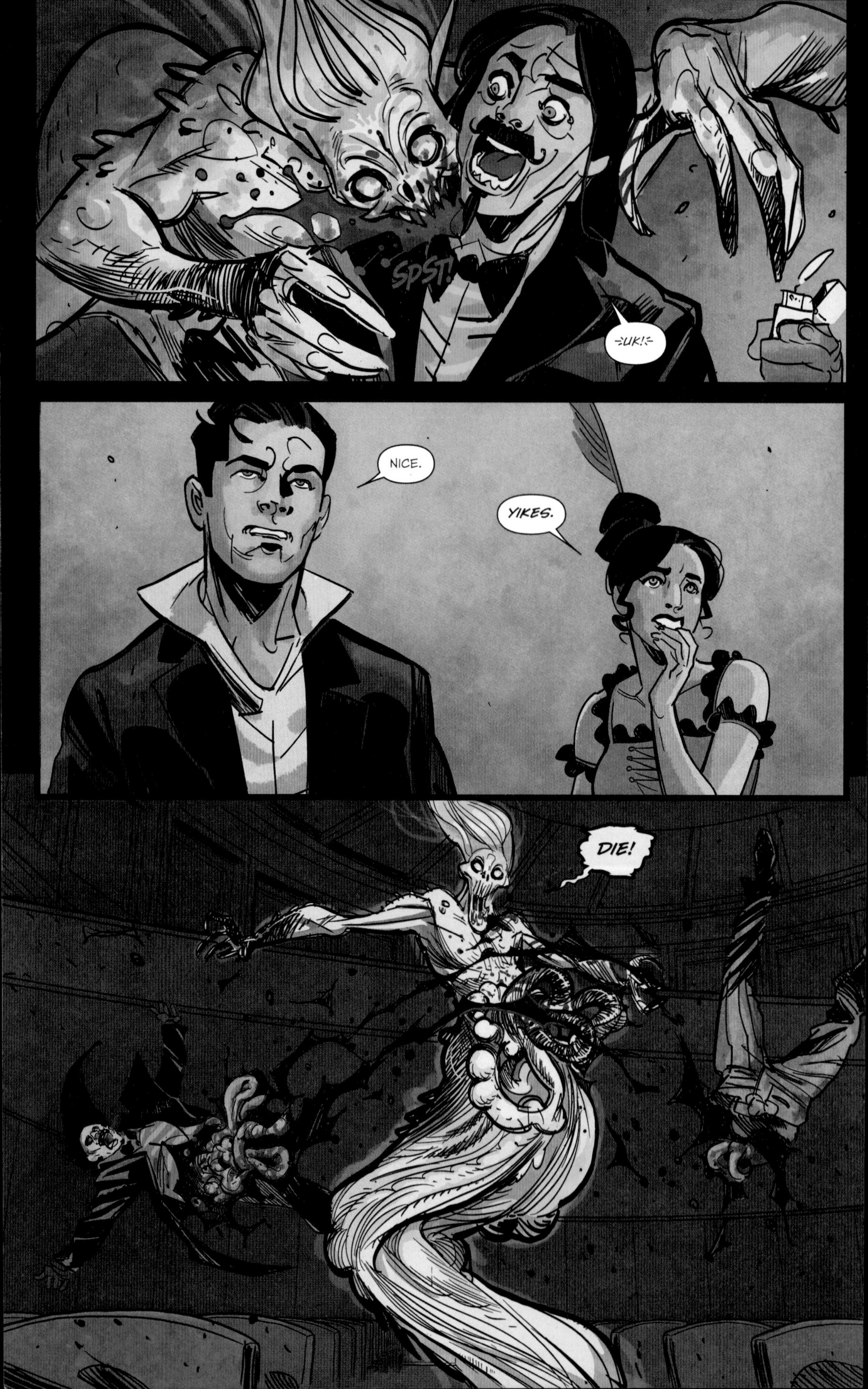
SPST!
UK!
NICE.
YIKES.
DIE!

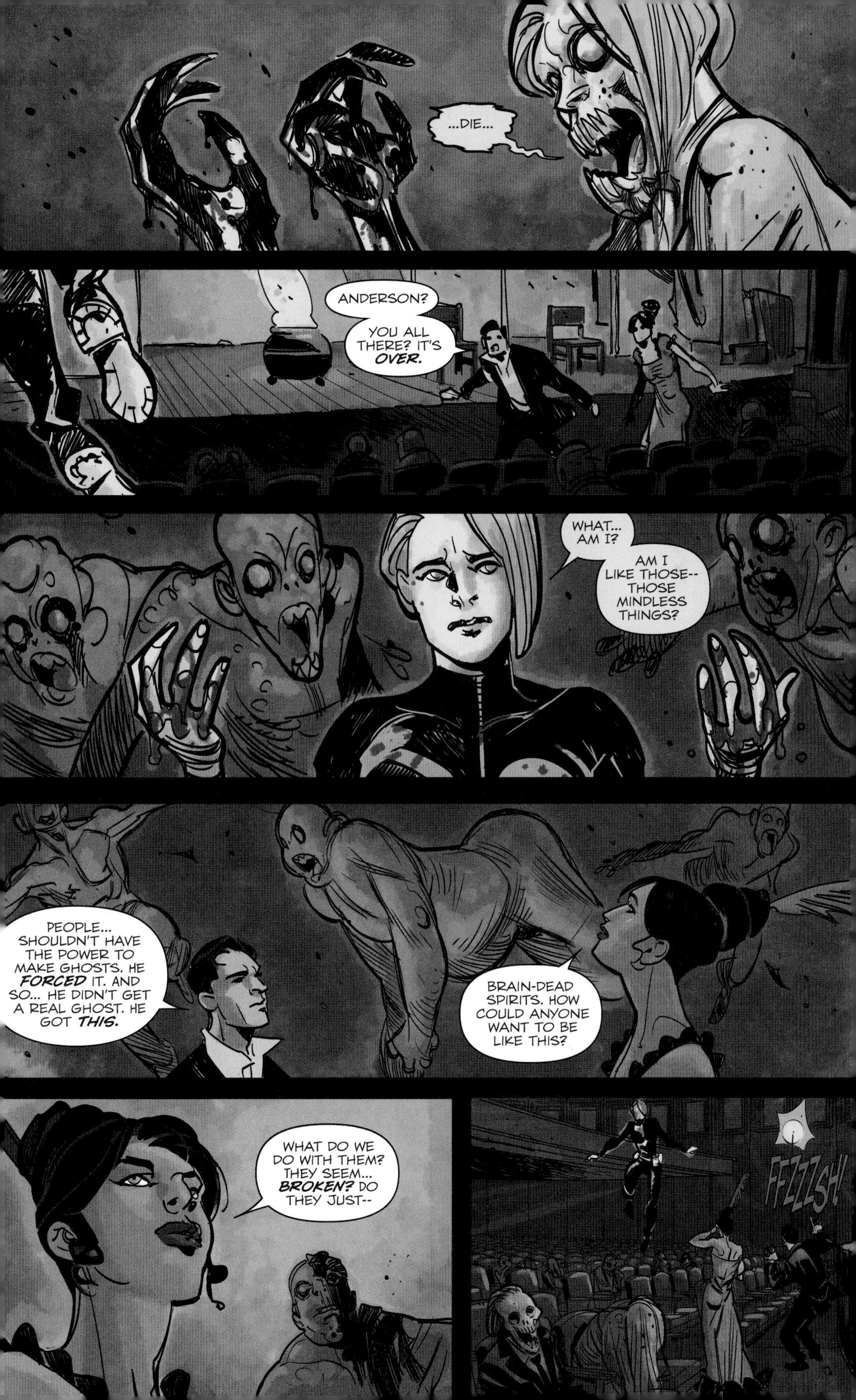
...DIE...
ANDERSON?
YOU ALL THERE? IT'S ***OVER.***
WHAT... AM I?
AM I LIKE THOSE-- THOSE MINDLESS THINGS?
PEOPLE... SHOULDN'T HAVE THE POWER TO MAKE GHOSTS. HE ***FORCED*** IT. AND SO... HE DIDN'T GET A REAL GHOST. HE GOT ***THIS.***
BRAIN-DEAD SPIRITS. HOW COULD ANYONE WANT TO BE LIKE THIS?
WHAT DO WE DO WITH THEM? THEY SEEM... ***BROKEN?*** DO THEY JUST--
FFZZZSH!

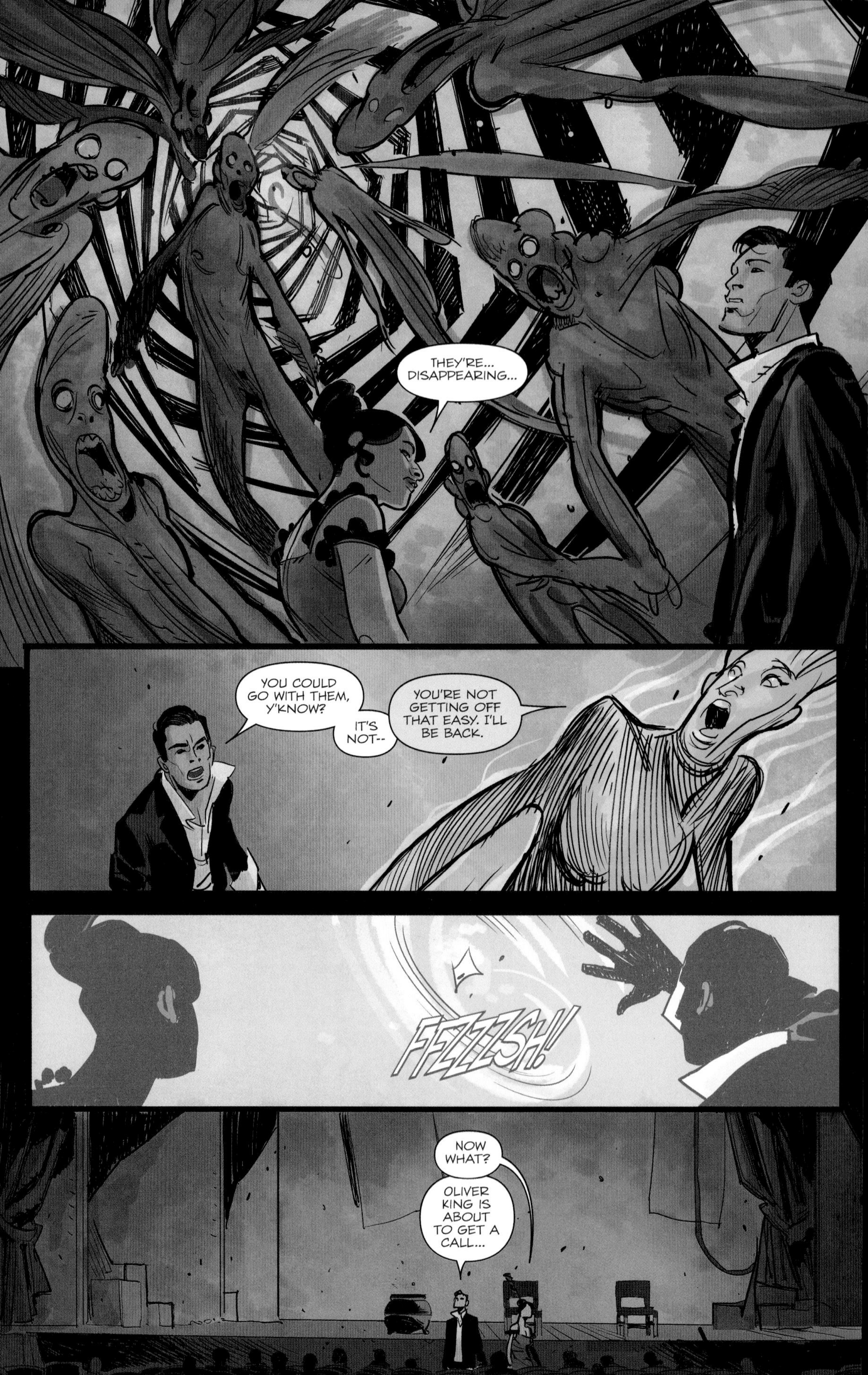
THEY'RE... DISAPPEARING...
YOU COULD GO WITH THEM, Y'KNOW?
IT'S NOT--
YOU'RE NOT GETTING OFF THAT EASY. I'LL BE BACK.
FFZZZSH!
NOW WHAT?
OLIVER KING IS ABOUT TO GET A CALL...

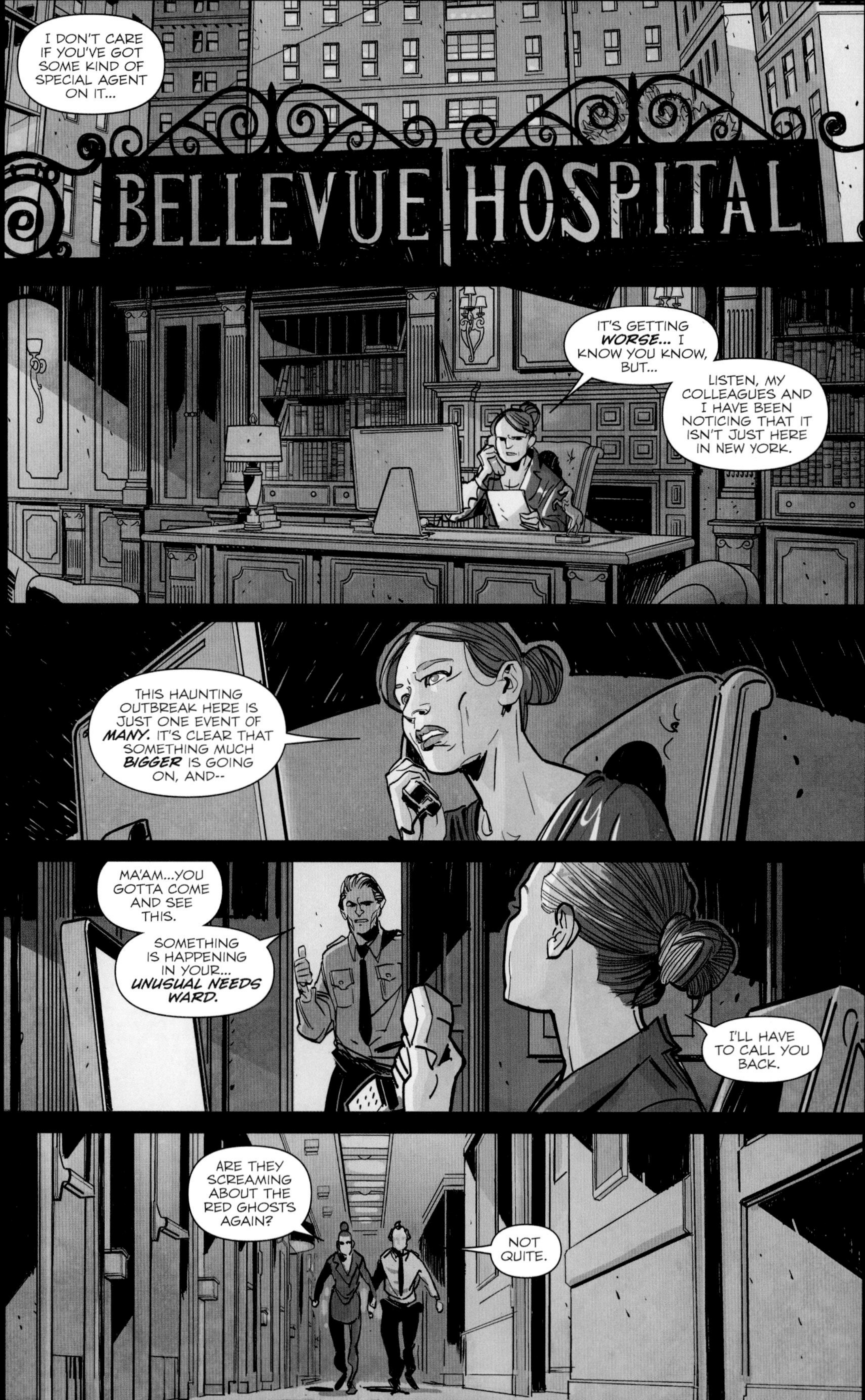
I DON'T CARE IF YOU'VE GOT SOME KIND OF SPECIAL AGENT ON IT...
BELLEVUE HOSPITAL
IT'S GETTING *WORSE...* I KNOW YOU KNOW, BUT...
LISTEN, MY COLLEAGUES AND I HAVE BEEN NOTICING THAT IT ISN'T JUST HERE IN NEW YORK.
THIS HAUNTING OUTBREAK HERE IS JUST ONE EVENT OF *MANY.* IT'S CLEAR THAT SOMETHING MUCH *BIGGER* IS GOING ON, AND--
MA'AM...YOU GOTTA COME AND SEE THIS.
SOMETHING IS HAPPENING IN YOUR... *UNUSUAL NEEDS WARD.*
I'LL HAVE TO CALL YOU BACK.
ARE THEY SCREAMING ABOUT THE RED GHOSTS AGAIN?
NOT QUITE.

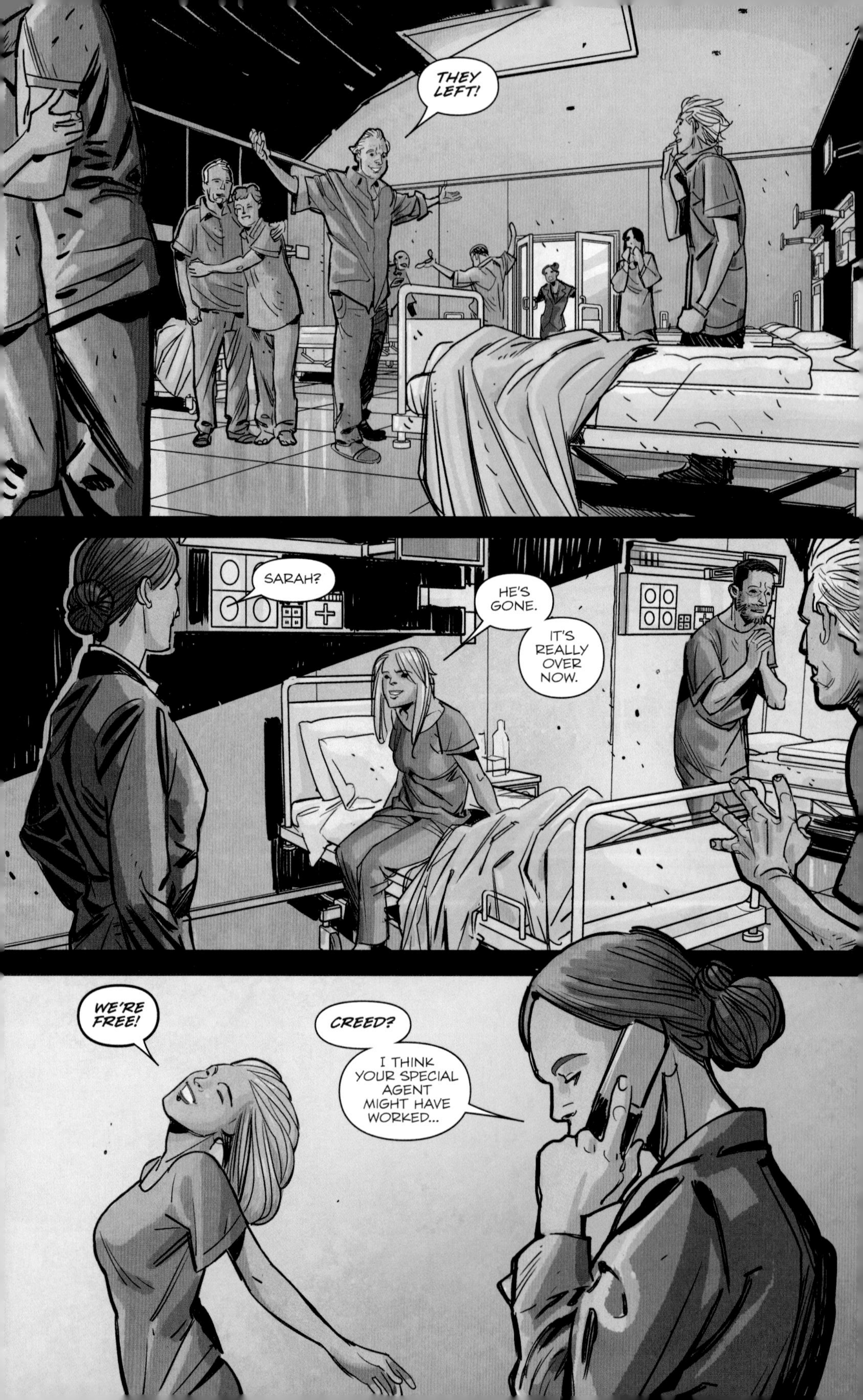
THEY LEFT!
SARAH?
HE'S GONE.
IT'S REALLY OVER NOW.
WE'RE FREE!
CREED?
I THINK YOUR SPECIAL AGENT MIGHT HAVE WORKED...

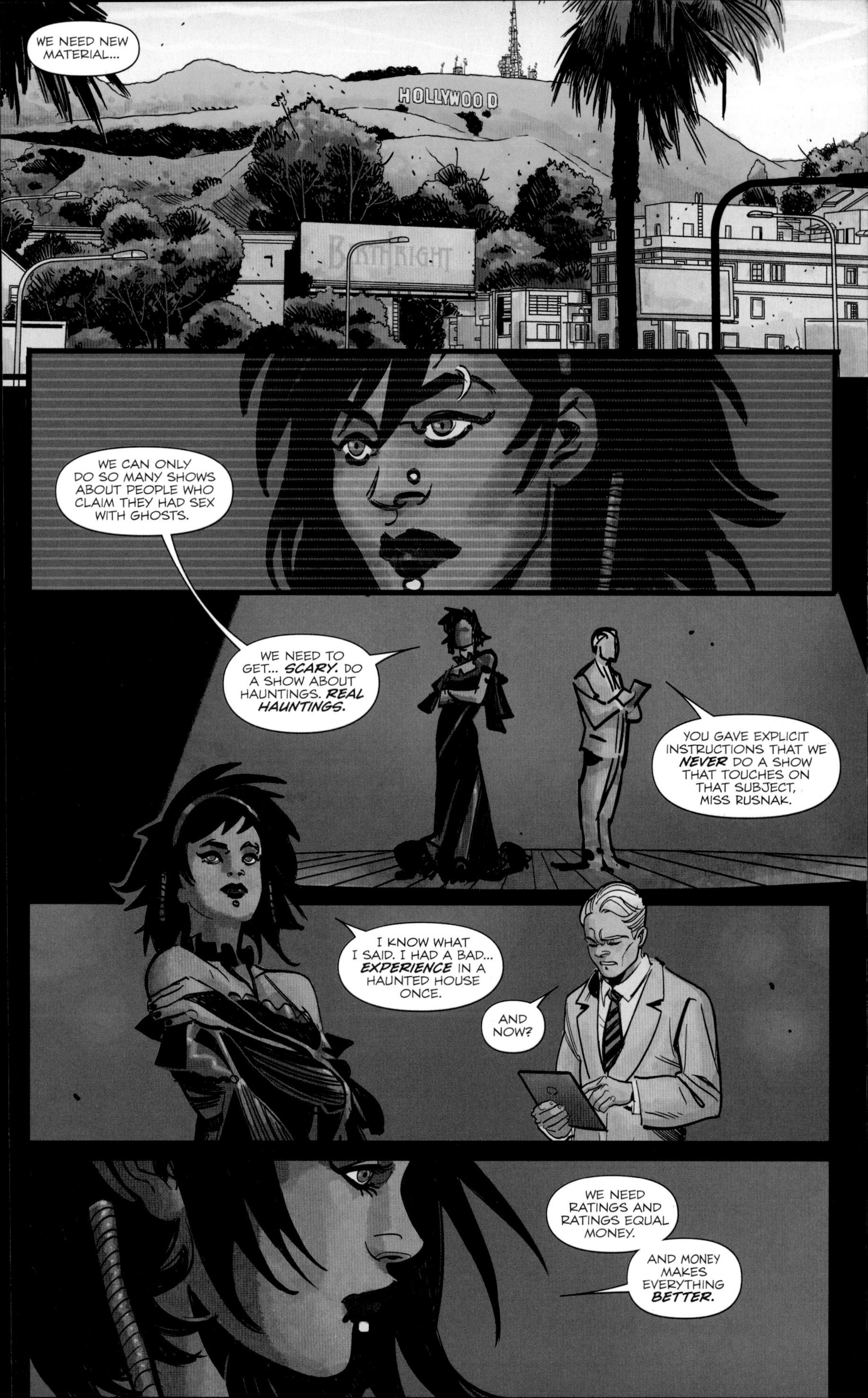
WE NEED NEW MATERIAL...
HOLLYWOOD
BIRTHRIGHT
WE CAN ONLY DO SO MANY SHOWS ABOUT PEOPLE WHO CLAIM THEY HAD SEX WITH GHOSTS.
WE NEED TO GET... **SCARY.** DO A SHOW ABOUT HAUNTINGS. ***REAL HAUNTINGS.***
YOU GAVE EXPLICIT INSTRUCTIONS THAT WE ***NEVER*** DO A SHOW THAT TOUCHES ON THAT SUBJECT, MISS RUSNAK.
I KNOW WHAT I SAID. I HAD A BAD... ***EXPERIENCE*** IN A HAUNTED HOUSE ONCE.
AND NOW?
WE NEED RATINGS AND RATINGS EQUAL MONEY.
AND MONEY MAKES EVERYTHING ***BETTER.***

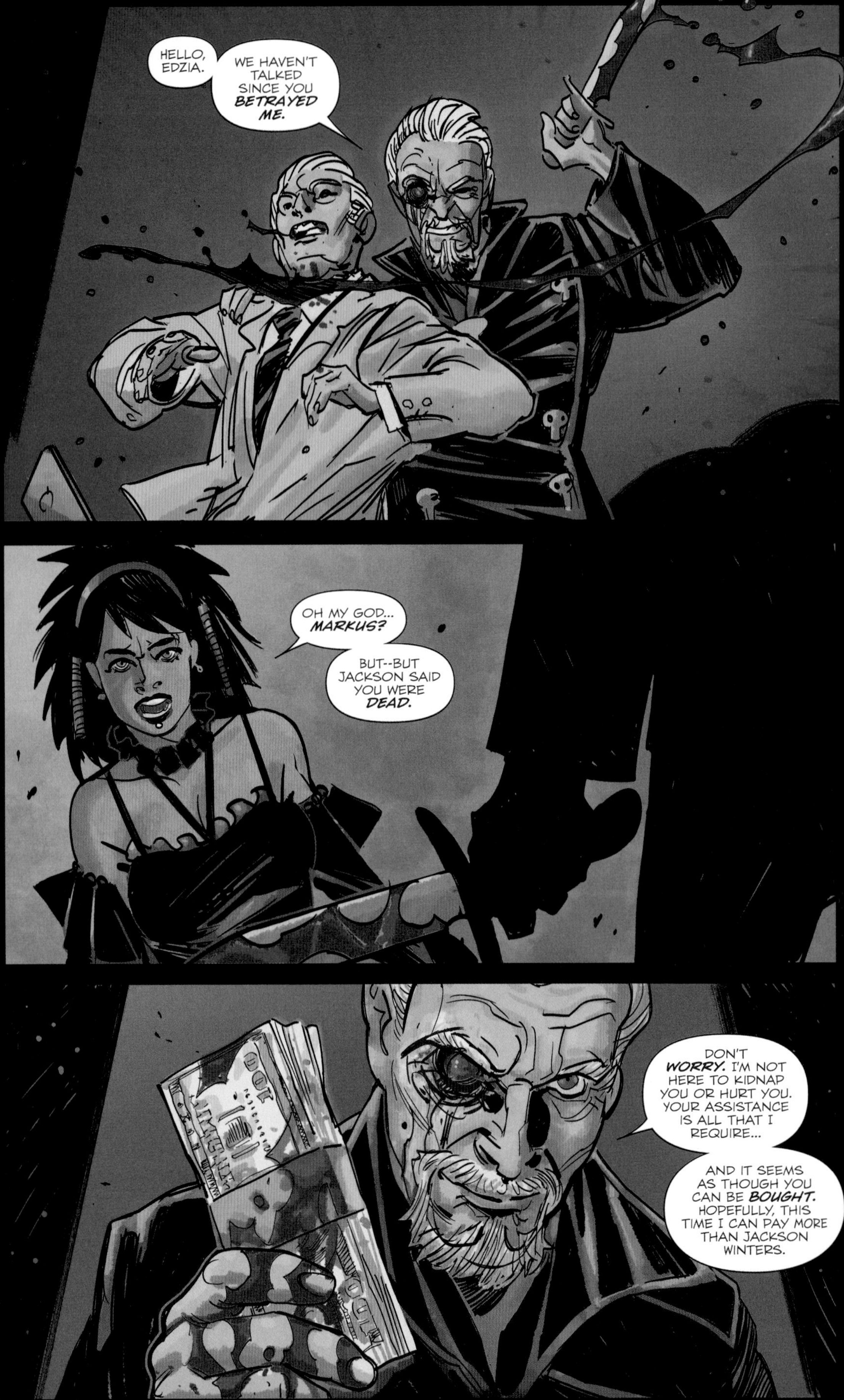
HELLO, EDZIA.
WE HAVEN'T TALKED SINCE YOU **BETRAYED ME.**
OH MY GOD... **MARKUS?**
BUT--BUT JACKSON SAID YOU WERE **DEAD.**
DON'T **WORRY.** I'M NOT HERE TO KIDNAP YOU OR HURT YOU. YOUR ASSISTANCE IS ALL THAT I REQUIRE...
AND IT SEEMS AS THOUGH YOU CAN BE **BOUGHT.** HOPEFULLY, THIS TIME I CAN PAY MORE THAN JACKSON WINTERS.

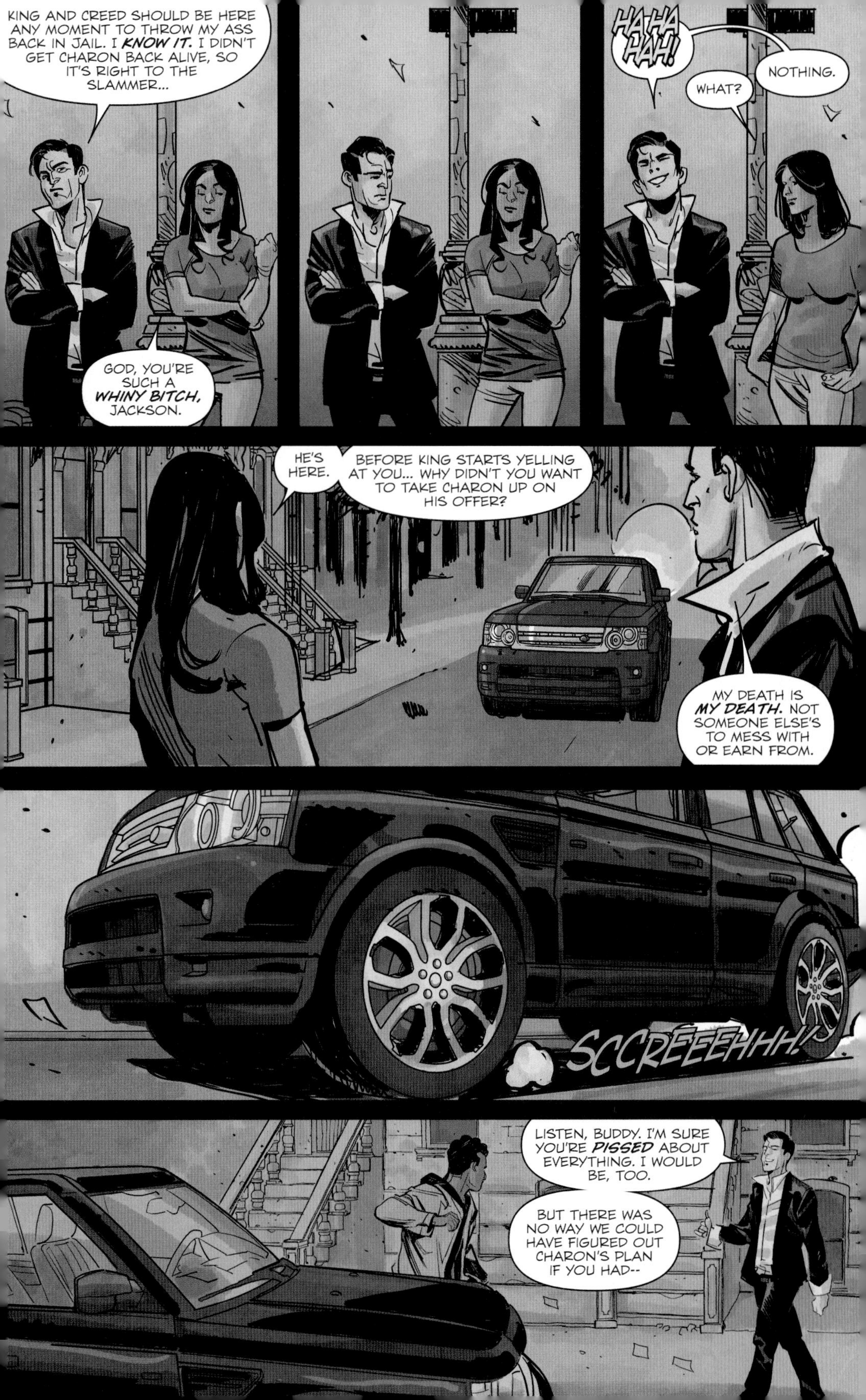

KING AND CREED SHOULD BE HERE ANY MOMENT TO THROW MY ASS BACK IN JAIL. I **KNOW IT.** I DIDN'T GET CHARON BACK ALIVE, SO IT'S RIGHT TO THE SLAMMER...
GOD, YOU'RE SUCH A **WHINY BITCH,** JACKSON.
HAHA HAH!
WHAT?
NOTHING.
HE'S HERE.
BEFORE KING STARTS YELLING AT YOU... WHY DIDN'T YOU WANT TO TAKE CHARON UP ON HIS OFFER?
MY DEATH IS **MY DEATH.** NOT SOMEONE ELSE'S TO MESS WITH OR EARN FROM.
SCCREEEEHHH!
LISTEN, BUDDY. I'M SURE YOU'RE **PISSED** ABOUT EVERYTHING. I WOULD BE, TOO.
BUT THERE WAS NO WAY WE COULD HAVE FIGURED OUT CHARON'S PLAN IF YOU HAD--

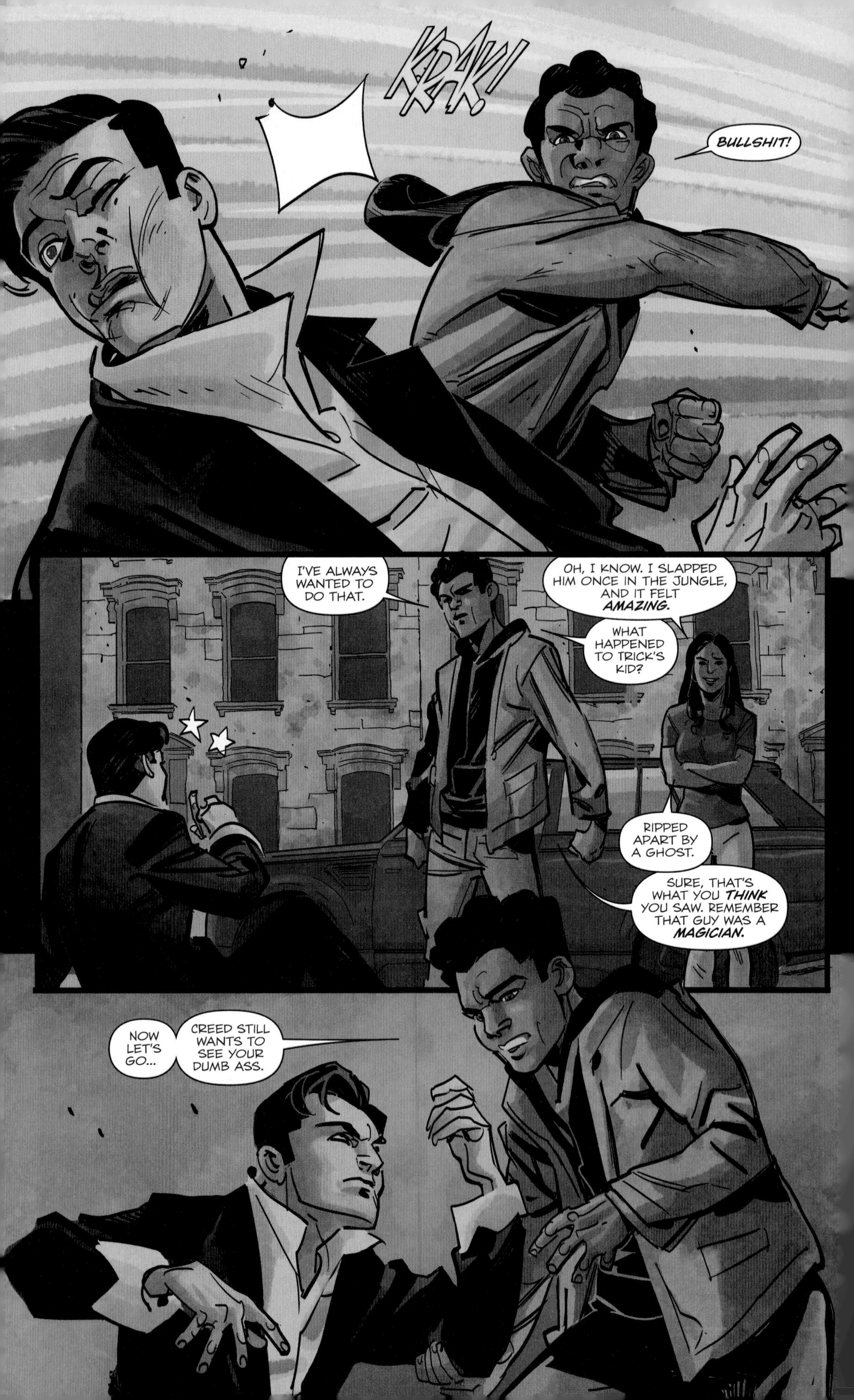
KRAK!
BULLSHIT!
I'VE ALWAYS WANTED TO DO THAT.
OH, I KNOW. I SLAPPED HIM ONCE IN THE JUNGLE, AND IT FELT ***AMAZING.***
WHAT HAPPENED TO TRICK'S KID?
RIPPED APART BY A GHOST.
SURE, THAT'S WHAT YOU ***THINK*** YOU SAW. REMEMBER THAT GUY WAS A ***MAGICIAN.***
NOW LET'S GO...
CREED STILL WANTS TO SEE YOUR DUMB ASS.

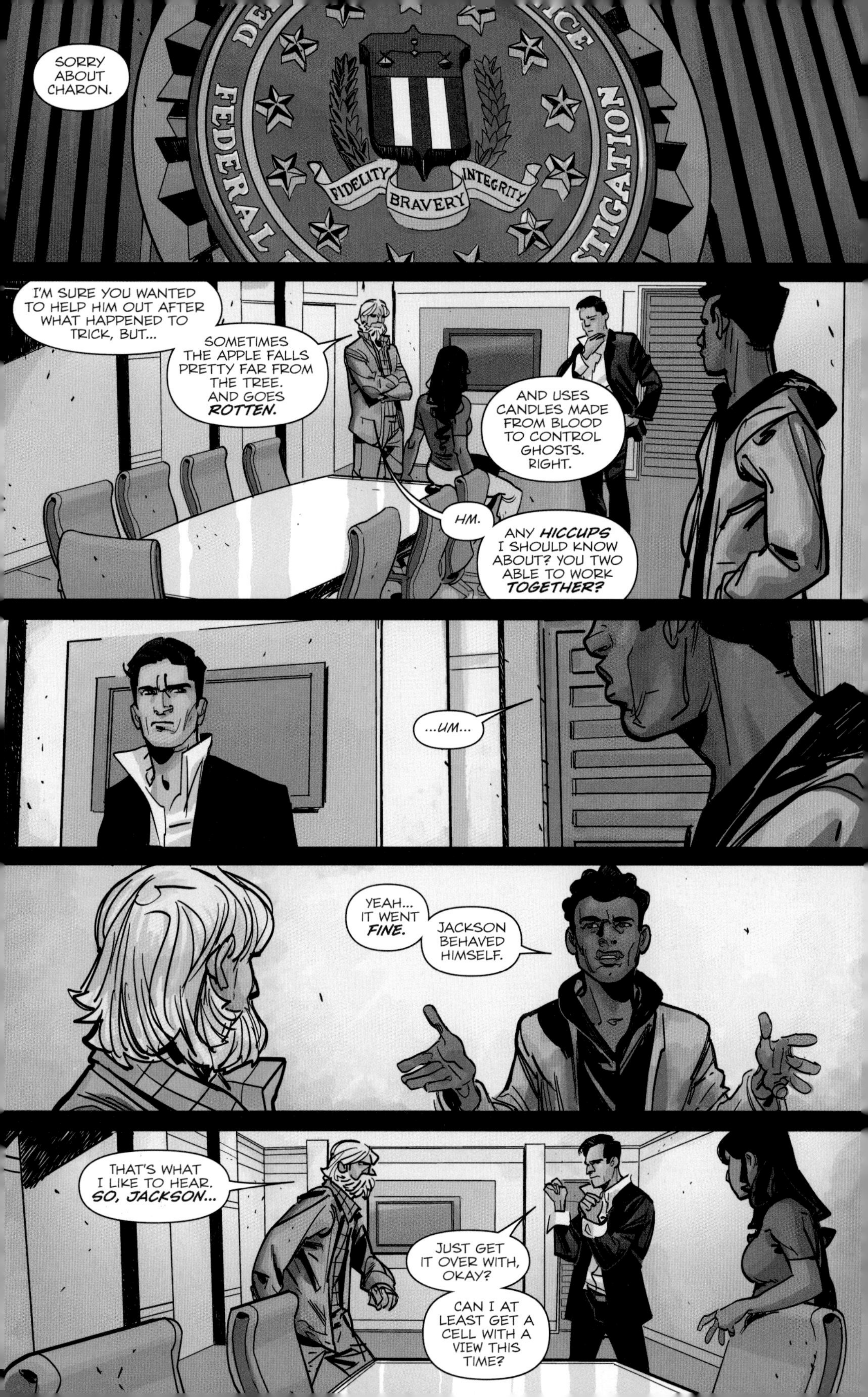

SORRY ABOUT CHARON.
FEDERAL
FIDELITY
BRAVERY
INTEGRITY
I'M SURE YOU WANTED TO HELP HIM OUT AFTER WHAT HAPPENED TO TRICK, BUT...
SOMETIMES THE APPLE FALLS PRETTY FAR FROM THE TREE. AND GOES **ROTTEN.**
AND USES CANDLES MADE FROM BLOOD TO CONTROL GHOSTS. RIGHT.
HM.
ANY **HICCUPS** I SHOULD KNOW ABOUT? YOU TWO ABLE TO WORK **TOGETHER?**
...UM...
YEAH... IT WENT **FINE.**
JACKSON BEHAVED HIMSELF.
THAT'S WHAT I LIKE TO HEAR. **SO, JACKSON...**
JUST GET IT OVER WITH, OKAY?
CAN I AT LEAST GET A CELL WITH A VIEW THIS TIME?

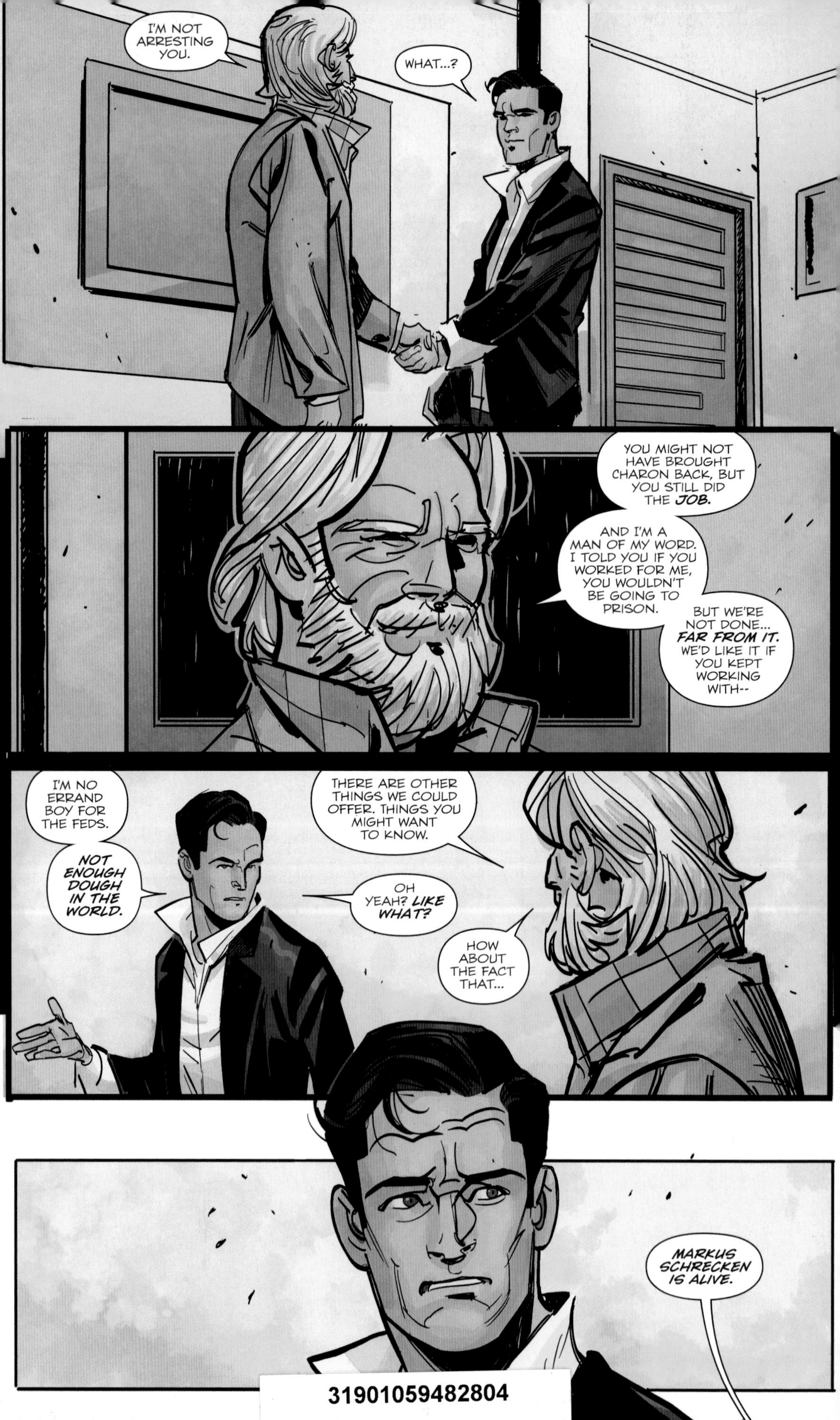
I'M NOT ARRESTING YOU.
WHAT...?
YOU MIGHT NOT HAVE BROUGHT CHARON BACK, BUT YOU STILL DID THE ***JOB.***
AND I'M A MAN OF MY WORD. I TOLD YOU IF YOU WORKED FOR ME, YOU WOULDN'T BE GOING TO PRISON.
BUT WE'RE NOT DONE... ***FAR FROM IT.*** WE'D LIKE IT IF YOU KEPT WORKING WITH--
I'M NO ERRAND BOY FOR THE FEDS.
NOT ENOUGH DOUGH IN THE WORLD.
THERE ARE OTHER THINGS WE COULD OFFER. THINGS YOU MIGHT WANT TO KNOW.
OH YEAH? ***LIKE WHAT?***
HOW ABOUT THE FACT THAT...
MARKUS SCHRECKEN IS ALIVE.